Gospel themes for Advent reflecting John the Baptist's preparation of the way and Mary's maternity.

Advent

Blessed are you among women

When Joseph awoke he did as the angel directed

And blessed is the fruit of your womb

Reform your lives! The reign of God is at hand.

Prepare the way for the Lord

Men will see the son of man coming on a cloud with great power

Blessed are you among women

When Joseph awoke
he did as
the angel directed

And blessed is the fruit
of your womb

Gospel themes for Advent reflecting John the Baptist's preparation of the way and Mary's maternity.

Reform your lives!
The reign of God
is at hand.

Prepare
the way
for the
Lord

Men will see the son
of man coming on a
cloud with great
power

First Sunday of Advent

Second Sunday of Advent

Third Sunday of Advent

Fourth Sunday of Advent

Christmas Vigil

The Advent wreath dates back to ancient celebrations of the winter solstice—that time in the year when the sun reaches its southern-most point in the heavens and the days are the darkest and most gloomy. Because they longed for the return of the sun's light and life, the ancients stopped all usual activity, sacrificed the use of their wagon wheels and hung them up, festooned with lights and greens in their celebration halls. There they awaited the return of their sun-god, thinking of the warmth and life he brought. Celebrations culminated in the "nativity" of the sun – the turning point of the year.

As Christians, we use the same meaning-ful custom to anticipate the feast of light and life; the nativity of the Savior. We add one light on the wreath for each Sunday in Advent. We think of the dark-ness after Adam's sin and watch the growing hope and light as the prophets and the Virgin help us prepare for His saving birth.

2

The Advent wreath dates back to ancient celebrations of the winter solstice—that time in the year when the sun reaches its southern-most point in the heavens and the days are the darkest and most gloomy. Because they longed for the return of the sun's light and life, the ancients stopped all usual activity, sacrificed the use of their wagon wheels and hung them up, festooned with lights and greens in their celebration halls.

There they awaited the return of their sun-god, thinking of the warmth and life he brought. Celebrations culminated in the "nativity" of the sun – the turning point of the year.

As Christians, we use the same meaningful custom to anticipate the feast of light and life; the nativity of the Savior. We add one light on the wreath for each Sunday in Advent. We think of the darkness after Adam's sin and watch the growing hope and light as the prophets and the Virgin help us prepare for His saving birth.

First Sunday of Advent

Second Sunday of Advent

Third Sunday of Advent

Fourth Sunday of Advent

Christmas Vigil

First Sunday of Advent

Second Sunday of Advent

Third Sunday of Advent

Fourth Sunday of Advent

Christmas Vigil

Oh that you would rend the heavens and come down

Men will see the son of man coming on a cloud with great power

The night is far spent the day draws nigh

3

Oh that you would rend the heavens and come down

Men will see the son of man coming on a cloud with great power

The night is far spent the day draws nigh

Christmas

And so Joseph went from the town of Nazareth to David's town of Bethlehem

There was no room for them in the place where travelers lodged

Glory to God in the highest

I come to proclaim good news to you

Your God is King 4

And so Joseph went from the town of Nazareth to David's town of Bethlehem

There was no room for them in the place where travelers lodged

Glory to God in the highest

I come to proclaim good news to you

Your God is King

Christmas and other major feasts are times to richly illustrate printed materials.

Let us go to Bethlehem and see this event which the Lord has made known to us

Let this be a sign to you: in a manger you will find an infant wrapped in swaddling clothes

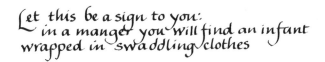

A light will shine on us this day: The Lord is born for us

Let us go to Bethlehem
and see this event
which the Lord has made
known to us

A light will shine on
us this day:
The Lord is born for us

Let this be a sign to you:
in a manger you will find an infant
wrapped in swaddling clothes

Cover and card art for Christmas
and Epiphany are here and on the next page.

6

Epiphany

Try a star or a crown or a gift container in the small blank areas on your bulletin.

Where is the newborn king of the Jews?
We observed his star at its rising

They received a message in a dream
not to return to Herod

Epiphany

They received a message in a dream
not to return to Herod

Holy Family + Solemnity of Mary

These feasts are particularly well suited to illustrate. Variety in your layout from week to week will gain your reader's attention.

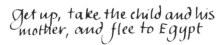

Get up, take the child and his mother, and flee to Egypt

Out of Egypt I have called my son

Now, Master, you can dismiss your servant in peace

Why did you search for me? Did you not know I had to be in my father's house?

Get up, take the child and his
mother, and flee to Egypt

Holy family + Solemnity of Mary

Out of Egypt I have called my son

Now, Master, you can
dismiss your servant in peace

Why did you search for me?
Did you not know I had
to be in my father's house?

Baptism of the Lord

Jesus coming from Galillee appeared before John at the Jordan to be baptised by him

The voice of the Lord is over the waters. The voice of the Lord is mighty; the voice of the Lord is majestic

The voice of the Lord is over the waters. The voice of the Lord is mighty; the voice of the Lord is majestic

Jesus coming from Galilee appeared before John at the Jordan to be baptised by him

Baptism of the Lord

The voice of the Lord is over the waters. The voice of the Lord is mighty; the voice of the Lord is majestic

Headlines for Lent with seasonal illustrations and texts for cards, notes or bulletin use:

Lent means Spring

Remember man that you are dust and into dust you shall return.

First Sunday of Lent

Second Sunday of Lent

Third Sunday of Lent

Fourth Sunday of Lent

Fifth Sunday of Lent

 prayer for the good of your soul

 fasting for the good of your body

 almsgiving for the good of your neighbor

10

Lent means Spring

Lent means Spring

First Sunday of Lent
Second Sunday of Lent
Third Sunday of Lent
Fourth Sunday of Lent
Fifth Sunday of Lent

Remember man that you are dust and into dust you shall return.

Remember man that you are dust and into dust you shall return.

 almsgiving for the good of your neighbor

First Sunday of Lent
Second Sunday of Lent
Third Sunday of Lent
Fourth Sunday of Lent
Fifth Sunday of Lent

 prayer for the good of your soul

 fasting for the good of your body

Lent

Ash Wednesday

Imposition of ashes

Turn away from sin and be faithful to the Gospel.

Keep your deeds of mercy secret

1st Sunday, cycle A

Away with you Satan!

3rd Sunday, cycle A

Whoever drinks the water I give him will never be thirsty

4th Sunday, cycle A

3rd Sunday, cycle B

Stop turning my Father's house into a market place

3rd Sunday, cycle C

A man had a fig tree growing in his vineyard

2nd Sunday, cycles A, B, C

He was transfigured before their eyes

4th Sunday, cycle A

So the man went off and washed and came back able to see

11

Lent

Keep your deeds of
mercy secret

Turn away from
sin and
be faithful
to the Gospel.

Away with you Satan!

Lent

Whoever drinks the water
I give him will never
be thirsty

Stop turning my Father's
house into a market place

A man had a fig tree growing in
his vineyard

He was transfigured
before their eyes

So the man went off and washed
and came back able to see

1st Sunday. cycle A

The woman saw that the tree was good for food

1st Sunday. cycle B

I will recall the covenant I have made between me and you and all living beings

2nd Sunday, cycle B

Take your son Isaac, your only one. Offer him up as a holocaust

1st Sunday, cycle C

I have brought you the first fruits

3rd Sunday, cycle C

An angel of the Lord appeared to him in fire flaming out of a bush

5th Sunday, cycle B

I will place my law within them and write it upon their hearts

12

The woman saw that
the tree was good for food

I will recall the covenant I
have made between me and
you and all living beings

Take your son Isaac, your
only one. Offer him up
as a holocaust

Old Testament themes from
the first reading of the Sundays
as noted are illustrated.

I have brought you the first fruits

An angel of the Lord appeared
to him in fire flaming out
of a bush

I will place my law within them
and write it upon their hearts

I have brought you the first fruits

An angel of the Lord appeared
to him in fire flaming out
of a bush

I will place my law within them
and write it upon their hearts

A continuation of the themes for the Sundays of Lent.

4th Sunday, cycle A

5th Sunday, cycle A

Lazarus, come out

5th Sunday, cycle C

Nor do I condemn you

4th Sunday, cycle C

Father, I have sinned against God and against you

4th Sunday, cycle A

I have chosen my king from among his sons

5th Sunday, cycle C

The Lord who opens a way in the sea

Lazarus, come out

Nor do I condemn you

A continuation of the themes for the Sundays of Lent.

Father, I have sinned against God and against you

I have chosen my king from among his sons

The Lord who opens a way in the sea

Passion Sunday

Hosannah! Blessed is He who comes in the name of the Lord

Jesus Christ is Lord!

My father, if it is possible let this cup pass me by

Judas went off to the chief priests to hand Jesus over to them

14

Jesus Christ is Lord!

Jesus Christ is Lord!

Hosannah! Blessed is He who comes in the name of the Lord

Passion Sunday

My father, if it is possible let this cup pass me by

Judas went off to the chief priests to hand Jesus over to them

Holy Thursday

I give you a new commandment: love one another as I loved you

If I do not wash you
you can have no share
in my heritage

Love one another as I have loved you

Behold the Lamb of God

Holy Thursday

I give you a new commandment: love one another as I loved you

Holy Thursday

If I do not wash you
you can have no share
in my heritage

Love one another as I have loved you

Behold the Lamb of God

good Friday

School projects will use these passion symbols. The crucifixion drawings are useful throughout the year.

Christ became obedient for us even to death

16

good Friday

good Friday

Christ became
obedient for us
even to death

Easter Vigil

Easter Vigil, baptism, first communion and confirmation rites are here.

This is a night in which heavenly things are united to those of earth and things divine to those which are human.

Alleluia · Alleluia · Alleluia

Alleluia Alleluia

17

This is a night in which
heavenly things are
united to those of earth
and things divine to
those which are human.

Alleluia · Alleluia · Alleluia

Alleluia Alleluia

Easter Vigil

Alleluia Alleluia

Easter Sunday

The Resurrection of the Lord

For use on Easter Sunday or for combined illustration of Christ's Passion, death and resurrection.

He has risen · alleluia

He has risen · alleluia

For use on Easter Sunday or
for combined illustration of
Christ's passion, death and
resurrection.

Easter Sunday

The Resurrection
of the Lord

He has risen · alleluia

Christ our light

Titles for the Easter season with drawings for the second and Third Sundays.

Second Sunday of Easter

Third Sunday of Easter

Fourth Sunday of Easter

Fifth Sunday of Easter

Sixth Sunday of Easter

Seventh Sunday of Easter

3rd Sunday, cycle B

They knew him in the breaking of the bread

2nd Sunday, cycles A·B·C

Peace be to you!

19

Christ our light

Second Sunday of Easter

Third Sunday of Easter

Fourth Sunday of Easter

Fifth Sunday of Easter

Sixth Sunday of Easter

Seventh Sunday of Easter

They knew him in the breaking
of the bread

Peace be to you!

Second Sunday of Easter

Third Sunday of Easter

Fourth Sunday of Easter

Fifth Sunday of Easter

Sixth Sunday of Easter

Seventh Sunday of Easter

Continuing the Easter Season with specific illustrations that will also be popular at other times in the year.

4th Sunday, cycles A·B·C

4th Sunday, cycle C

6th Sunday, cycles A·B·C

3rd Sunday, cycle C

Lord, let your face shine on us

3rd Sunday, cycle C

Cast your net off to the starboard and you will find something

I am the Way the truth and the Life

5th Sunday, cycle A

I am the vine you are the branches

5th Sunday, cycle B

20

I
am the
Way
the truth
and
the life

Lord, let your face shine on us

Cast your net off to the
starboard and you
will find something

I am the vine
you are the branches

This larger illustration should fit
most church printed material.

Pentecost

Pentecost

Solemnities of the Lord

Trinity Sunday

Glory to
the Father
the Son and the Holy Spirit

Sacred Heart

Corpus Christi

Jesus said: The man
who feeds in my
flesh and drinks
my blood remains
in me, and I in him

Christ the King

The Lord will reign forever and
will give his people the gift
of peace

Triumph of the Holy Cross

So must the Son
of Man be lifted up
that all who believe
may have eternal
life in Him

Ascension

God mounts his throne
amid shouts of joy;
the Lord amid trumpet
blasts

Corpus Christi

Jesus said: The man
who feeds in my
flesh and drinks
my blood remains
in me, and I in him

Sacred Heart

Trinity Sunday

Glory to
the Father
the Son and the Holy Spirit

Solemnities of the Lord

Triumph of the Holy Cross

Ascension

Christ the King

The Lord will reign forever and
will give his people the gift
of peace

Triumph of the Holy Cross

So must the Son
of Man be lifted up
that all who believe
may have eternal
life in Him

Ascension

God mounts his throne
amid shouts of joy;
the Lord amid trumpet
blasts

Feasts of Mary

Mary · Mother of God

Annunciation

Visitation

Assumption

Immaculate Conception

Feasts of Mary

Mary Mother of God
Annunciation
Visitation
Assumption
Immaculate Conception

Parables of Christ

The Parables, Miracles and Public life scenes are a resource for Ordinary Time and general Student publications.

They were spellbound by his teaching, for his words had authority.

Let everyone heed what he hears

I will hoe around it and manure it, then perhaps it will bear fruit.

Let the man with two coats give to him who has none

Sir, did you not sow good seed in your field?

They were spellbound by his teaching, for his words had authority.

Let everyone heed what he hears

I will hoe around it and manure it, then perhaps it will bear fruit.

Parables of Christ

Let the man with two coats give to him who has none.

Sir, did you not sow good seed in your field?

And was moved to pity at the sight.
He approached him and dressed his wounds

Go into my vineyard

Lazarus longed to eat
the scraps that fell
from the rich man's
table

The good shepherd drawings are also on pages 11, 13, 20 and 26.

This son of mine was dead
and has come back to
life. He was lost and is
found

The
wise man
builds
his house
on
rock

Rejoice with me because
I have found my
lost sheep

And was moved to pity at the sight.
He approached him and dressed his wounds

Go into my vineyard

Lazarus longed to eat
the scraps that fell
from the rich man's
table

This son of mine was dead
and has come back to
life. He was lost and is
found

The
wise man
builds
his house
on
rock

Rejoice with me because
I have found my
lost sheep

Foxes have lairs and birds of the sky have nests, but the son of man has nowhere to lay his head

A tree planted near running water, that yields its fruit in due season, and whose leaves never fade

Many of these scenes are appropriate for a number of different gospel texts.

The reign of God is like a buried treasure which a man found in a field

Two men went up to the temple to pray

The harvest is good but laborers are scarce

The Lord is my shepherd, there is nothing I shall want

Foxes have lairs and birds of the sky have nests but the son of man has nowhere to lay his head

A tree planted near running water, that yields its fruit in due season, and whose leaves never fade

The reign of God is like a buried treasure which a man found in a field

Two men went up to the temple to pray

The harvest is good but laborers are scarce

The Lord is my shepherd, there is nothing I shall want

Miracles of Christ

Your faith has cured you.
Go in peace

He rebuked the winds and said
to the sea: Quiet! Be Still!

There is a lad here
who has five barley
loaves and a couple
of dried fish

Put out into the deep water
and lower your nets for a catch

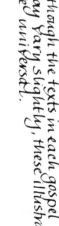

Although the texts in each gospel
may vary slightly, these illustrations
are universal.

Fill those jars with water

27

*Your faith has cured you.
Go in peace*

*He rebuked the winds and said
to the sea: Quiet! Be Still!*

*Put out into the deep water
and lower your nets for a catch*

*There is a lad here
who has five barley
loaves and a couple
of dried fish*

Fill those jars with water

The child is not dead. She is asleep

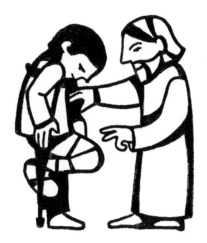

The blind and the lame came to him and he healed them

These drawings of healing may be used with different texts or together for ritual programs.

If you will to do so you can cure me

Rabboni, I want to see

The dead man came out

My son, your sins are forgiven

28

The child is not dead. She is asleep

The blind
and the lame
came to him
and he
healed them

If you will to do so you
can cure me

Miracles of Christ

Rabboni, I want to see

The dead man came out

My son, your sins are forgiven

Christ's Public Life

Some of these figures are easily separated. They may be used also refused during Ordinary Time—

It is to just such as these that the kingdom of God belongs

 you will draw water joyfully from the springs of salvation

Go first and be reconciled with your brother

Blessed are the peace makers, for they shall be called sons of God

29

It is to just such as these that
the kingdom of god belongs

you will
draw
water
joyfully
from
the
springs
of
salvation

go first and be
reconciled
with your brother

Blessed are the peace makers,
for they shall be called sons of god

The reign of God is like a mustard seed

Unless the grain of wheat dies it remains just a grain of wheat

Her many sins are forgiven because of her great love

From now on you shall be catching men

Stay with us. It is nearly evening, the day is practically over

The last page for Ordinary Time. For more abstract texts a selection may be made from the next two pages.

They saw him walking on the water

30

The reign of God is like a mustard seed

Unless the grain of wheat dies
it remains just a grain of wheat

Her many sins are
forgiven because of
her great love.

From now on you shall be catching men

Stay with us. It is nearly evening,
the day is practically over

They saw him walking
on the water

The need exists for special illustrations and spot art especially when texts vary in length.

The earth has yielded its fruits
God our God
has blessed us

The need exists for special
illustrations and spot art
especially when texts vary
in length.

The earth has yielded
its fruits
God our God
has blessed us

Contemporary figures will enhance current announcements, bulletins, liturgical programs.

32

The Sacraments

Christian Initiation of Adults

Baptism of Children

34

The Sacraments

Christian Initiation of Adults

Baptism of Children

Christian Initiation of Adults

Baptism of Children

Confirmation

Eucharist

Penance

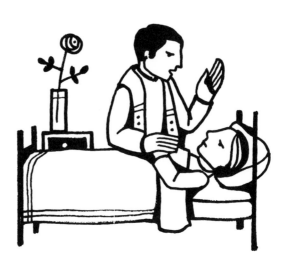

Anointing of the sick

Marriage

Ordination

35

Confirmation

Eucharist

Penance

Confirmation

Eucharist

Penance

Anointing of the sick

Marriage

Ordination

Anointing of the sick

Marriage

Ordination

Baptism

Confirmation

Reconciliation

Penance

Eucharist

Anointing the sick

Holy Orders

Marriage

36

Baptism

Confirmation

 Penance

 Reconciliation

Eucharist

 Eucharist

 Reconciliation

Baptism

Confirmation

Penance

Anointing the sick

Marriage

Holy Orders

 Anointing the sick

 Marriage

 Holy Orders

Christian Initiation of Adults

So shall your descendants be. To your descendants I give this land.

Naam went down and washed himself seven times in the river Jordan and became CLEAN

There is WATER. What prevents me from being baptised?

Jesus was baptized by John in the Jordan.

He who believes and is BAPTISED will be saved.

So shall your descendants be.
To your descendants I give this
Land.

Naam went down
and washed him-
self seven times in
the river Jordan and
became CLEAN

There is
WATER.
What prevents me
from being baptised?

Jesus was
baptized
by John
in the
Jordan.

He who believes
and is BAPTISED
will be saved.

Baptism for Children

You must strike the Rock and WATER will flow from it for the people to drink.

You are a chosen race, a royal priesthood, a holy people. Praise God who called you out of darkness and into his marvelous light.

For more Baptism illustrations see p. 9

Anyone who does not welcome the kingdom of God like a little child will never enter it.

Confirmation

The Lord God has anointed me and has sent me to bring Good News to the poor to give them the oil of gladness.

see p. 21 for another illustration for Confirmation.

Baptism for Children

 You must strike the Rock and WATER will flow from it for the people to drink.

 Anyone who does not welcome the kingdom of God like a little child will never enter it.

Baptism for Children

You are a chosen race, a royal priesthood, a holy people. Praise God who called you out of darkness and into his marvelous light.

Confirmation

The Lord God has anointed me and has sent me to bring Good News to the poor to give them the oil of gladness.

Forgive your neighbor when he hurts you, and then your sins will be forgiven when you pray.

Penance

The Lord said: I will not destroy the city for the sake of ten good men.

Cain set on his brother and killed him.

His father saw him and was moved with mercy.

Peter went outside and wept.

Forgive your neighbor
when he hurts you,
and then your
sins will be
forgiven when
you pray.

The Lord said: I will
not destroy the city
for the sake of ten
good men.

Peter went outside and wept.

Cain set on his brother
and killed him.

His father saw him
and was moved with
mercy.

Eucharist

Get up and eat or the journey will be too long for you.

see page 15 for more illustrations on the Eucharist.

I will rain bread from heaven upon you.

When the Lord sees the blood on the door, he will pass over your home.

All the people ate and were satisfied.

Melchisedech brought bread + wine

40

Get up and eat or the journey will be too long for you.

I will rain bread from heaven upon you.

When the Lord sees the blood on the door, he will pass over your home.

All the people ate and were satisfied.

Melchisedech brought bread + wine

Reception and Anointing of the Sick at Mass

In the name of Jesus arise
and walk.

We groan while we wait
for the redemption of our
bodies.

41

Reception and Anointing of the Sick at Mass

In the name of Jesus arise and walk.

We groan while we wait for the redemption of our bodies.

Come, follow me, says the Lord, and I will make you fishers of men.

Ask the Lord of the harvest to send laborers to the harvest.

The spirit of the Lord has been given to me, for he has anointed me. He has sent me to bring the good news to the poor, to proclaim liberty to captives and to the blind new sight, to set the downtrodden free, to proclaim the Lord's year of favour.

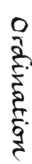

Ordination

At your word I will lower the nets.

42

Come, follow me, says the Lord, and I will make you fishers of men.

Ask the Lord of the harvest to send laborers to the harvest.

The spirit of the Lord has been given to me, for he has anointed me. He has sent me to bring the good news to the poor, to proclaim liberty to captives and to the blind new sight, to set the downtrodden free, to proclaim the Lord's year of favour.

At your word I will lower the nets.

Male and female he created them.

A sensible man builds his house on rock.

God is Love; let us love one another as he has loved us.

Marriage

This was the first of the signs given by Jesus; it was given at Cana in Galilee.

Male and female he created them.

God is Love; let us love one another as he has loved us.

This was the first of the signs given by Jesus; it was given at Cana in Galilee.

Ministries

45

Saints

Matthew

Mark

Luke

John

Paul

Andrew

Matthew

Mark

Luke

Matthew

Mark

Luke

John

Paul

Andrew

John

Paul

Andrew

Thomas Aquinas · Albert the great

Patrick

Raphael and Tobias

Joseph the Worker

Michael

Lawrence

48

Thomas Aquinas

Albert the great

Patrick

Raphael and Tobias

Thomas Aquinas

Albert the great

Patrick

Raphael and Tobias

Joseph the Worker

Michael

Lawrence

Joseph the Worker

Michael

Lawrence

Martin of
Tours

Martin
de
Porres

Thomas More

Augustine and Monica

John of the Cross

and Teresa of Jesus

Thomas a Becket

49

Martin of Tours

Thomas More

Martin of Tours

Martin de Porres

Thomas More

Augustine and Monica

John of the Cross and Teresa of Jesus

Thomas a Becket

Augustine and Monica

John of the Cross and Teresa of Jesus

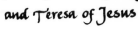

Thomas a Becket

Pope Leo

Anne

Agnes

Cecelia

Joan of Arc

Therese of Lisieux

Peter

Clare

Nicholas

50

Pope Leo

Pope Leo

Anne

Anne

Agnes

Cecelia

Agnes

Joan of Arc

Therese of Lisieux

Cecelia

Therese of Lisieux

Joan of Arc

Peter

Peter

Clare

Clare

Nicholas

Nicholas

Holy Apostles

Elizabeth of Hungary

Francis Xavier   Ignatius

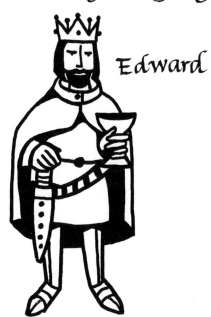

Edward

Catherine of Alexandria

Martha

Vincent de Paul 51

Holy Apostles

Elizabeth of Hungary

Holy Apostles

Francis Xavier

Elizabeth of Hungary

Ignatius

Francis Xavier

Edward

Ignatius

Catherine of Alexandria

Martha

Edward

Catherine of Alexandria

Martha

Vincent de Paul

Vincent de Paul

Catherine of Siena

Margaret of Scotland

Stephen

John Bosco

Scholastica·Benedict

Francis of Assisi

52

Catherine of Siena

Margaret of Scotland

Stephen

Catherine of Siena

Margaret of Scotland

Stephen

John Bosco

Scholastica·Benedict

Francis of Assisi

John Bosco

Scholastica·Benedict

Francis of Assisi

Feast of All Saints—

Kateri Tekakwitha

Charles Lwanga · Uganda

Isaac Jogues + John de Brebeuf + Companions

Paul Miki + Companions

Elizabeth Ann Seton

Kateri Tekakwitha

Kateri Tekakwitha

Charles Lwanga · Uganda

Isaac Jogues · John de Brebeuf + Companions

Isaac Jogues · John de Brebeuf + Companions

Paul Miki + Companions

Elizabeth Ann Seton

Paul Miki + Companions

Elizabeth Ann Seton

S0-CAA-044

Vocabulary
for Achievement

FOURTH COURSE

Margaret Ann Richek

Arlin T. McRae

Susan K. Weiler

GREAT SOURCE
WILMINGTON, MA

AUTHORS

Margaret Ann Richek
Professor of Education, Northeastern Illinois University; consultant in reading and vocabulary study; author of The World of Words *(Houghton Mifflin)*

Arlin T. McRae
Supervisor of English, Evansville-Vanderburgh School Corporation, Evansville, Indiana; Adjunct Instructor in English, University of Evansville

Susan K. Weiler
Instructor of Art History at John Carroll University in Cleveland, Ohio; former teacher of Latin, Beaumont School for Girls, Cleveland Heights, Ohio

CONSULTANT

Larry S. Krieger
Social Studies Supervisor, Montgomery Township Public Schools, New Jersey; author of World History *and* U.S. History *(D.C. Heath), co-author of* Mastering the Verbal SAT 1/PSAT *(Great Source)*

CLASSROOM CONSULTANTS

Jack Pelletier
Teacher of English, Mira Loma High School, Sacramento, California

Valerie M. Webster
Teacher of English, Walnut Hill School, Natick, Massachusetts

ACKNOWLEDGMENTS

Definitions for the three hundred words taught in this textbook are based on Houghton Mifflin dictionaries—in particular, the *Houghton Mifflin College Dictionary,* copyright © 1986—but have been abbreviated and adapted for instructional purposes. The dictionary passages in the skill lesson on pages 19–20 are from *The American Heritage Dictionary, Second College Edition,* copyright © 1985. The pronunciation key on the inside front cover is adapted from the same source and from *The American Heritage Dictionary of the English Language, Third Edition,* copyright © 1992. The reading passage on page 100 is adapted from *The Restless Universe* by Harry L. Shipman. Copyright © 1978 by Houghton Mifflin Company. Reprinted by permission of Houghton Mifflin Company.

CREDITS

Production: PC&F, Inc.

Illustrations: Anthony Accardo: pages 91, 165, 197; Alex Bloch: pages 137, 171, 177; Simon Galkin: pages 17, 25, 37; Paul Lackner: pages 11, 51; Charles Scogins: pages 85, 105

Copyright © 1998 by Great Source Education Group, a division of Houghton Mifflin Company. All rights reserved.

No part of this work may be reproduced or transmitted in any form or by any means, electronic or mechanical, including photocopying and recording, or by any information storage or retrieval system without the prior written permission of Great Source Education Group,, unless such copying is expressly permitted by federal copyright law. Address inquiries to Permissions, Great Source Education Group, 181 Ballardvale Street, Wilmington, MA 01887.

Great Source® is a registered trademark of Houghton Mifflin Company.

Printed in the United States of America

ISBN: 0-669-46480-5

9 10 HS 04

CONTENTS

COMPLETE WORD LIST

Suppose that Rip Van Winkle were to awaken today from a twenty-year sleep. How might he react to the following statement?

> The laser read the digitally encoded pattern on the compact-disc, and rock music filled the room.

Most likely, Van Winkle would neither recognize nor understand the terminology used in the sentence. Over the last several decades, thousands of new inventions and scientific advances have created the need for new words to label and describe them.

In this lesson you will be introduced to the colorful and creative aspects of language that make the generation of new words possible. These vocabulary words will help you to be aware of how our language offers extensive resources for expressing ourselves.

WORD LIST

acronym
affix
coinage
colloquial
malapropism
onomatopoeia
palindrome
portmanteau word
simile
spoonerism

DEFINITIONS

After you have studied the definitions and example for each vocabulary word, write the word on the line to the right.

1. **acronym** (ăk′rə-nĭm′) *noun*   A word formed from the initial letters of a name or by combining initial letters or parts of a series of words: *WAC* for *Women's Army Corps.*

    Example   *Acronyms* are frequently used in official and political circles to shorten long titles of organizations or systems.

1. _____
MEMORY CUE: *Acronym* comes from *acro*, meaning "tip" or "beginning," and *nym*, meaning "name."

2. **affix** (ăf′ĭks′) *noun*   **a.** A word element, such as a prefix or suffix, that is attached to a base, stem, or root.   **b.** Something that is attached, joined or added. *trans. verb* (ə-fĭks′)   **a.** To secure (an object) to another; attach: *affix a stamp to a letter.*   **b.** To place at the end: *affix a postscript.* (From the Latin *ad-*, meaning "to," and *figere*, meaning "to fasten")

    Example   The word *reappearance* has two *affixes: re-* and *-ance.*

2. _____

3. **coinage** (koi′nĭj) *noun*   **a.** The invention of new words.   **b.** An invented word or phrase.   **c.** The process of making coins: *coinage of silver.*

    Related Word   **coin** *verb*
    Example   The word *hobbit* was a *coinage* of J.R.R. Tolkien.

3. _____

4. **colloquial** (kə-lō′kwē-əl) *adjective*   **a.** Used in or suitable to spoken language or to writing that imitates speech; conversational.   **b.** Informal in style of expression. (From the Latin *com-*, meaning "together," and *loqui*, meaning "to speak")

    Related Words **colloquialism** *noun;* **colloquially** *adverb*
    Example   Connie suggested to Joe that he substitute "narrow escape" for his *colloquial* expression "a close call."

4. _____
USAGE NOTE: *Colloquial* speech is everyday conversation; *slang* is very informal language that coins new words or uses old words in new, colorful ways.

5. **malapropism** (măl'ə-prŏp-ĭz'əm) *noun*   The use of a word sounding somewhat like the one intended but humorously wrong in the context: *"polo bear" rather than "polar bear."* (From the French phrase *mal à propos,* meaning "unsuitable")

   Example   In Sheridan's eighteenth-century play, *The Rivals,* Mrs. Malaprop makes such *malapropisms* as "the very pineapple of politeness" for "the very pinnacle of politeness."

   5. _____

6. **onomatopoeia** (ŏn'ə-măt'ə-pē'ə) *noun*   The formation or use of a word that imitates or resembles what it stands for. (From the Greek words *onoma,* meaning "name," and *poiein,* meaning "to make")

   Related Word   onomatopoetic *adjective*
   Example   *Buzz* and *hiss* are examples of *onomatopoeia* that the poet used to make the meadow come alive.

   6. _____

7. **palindrome** (păl'ĭn-drōm') *noun*   A word, phrase, or sentence that reads the same backward or forward. (From the Greek words *palin,* meaning "again," and *dromos,* meaning "a running")

   Example   "A man, a plan, a canal, Panama" was the only *palindrome* that Richard could remember.

   7. _____

8. **portmanteau word** (pôrt-măn'tō, pôrt'măn-tō' wûrd) *compound noun*   A word formed by merging the sounds and meanings of two different words; blend.

   Example   Arlin didn't realize that the word *slithy* in Lewis Carroll's poem "Jabberwocky" is a *portmanteau word* formed from *slimy* and *lithe.*

   8. _____

9. **simile** (sĭm'ə-lē) *noun*   A figure of speech in which two essentially unlike things are compared, often in a phrase introduced by *like* or *as.* (From the Latin word *similis,* meaning "like")

   Example   Some *similes,* such as "hungry as a bear" and "sly like a fox," are considered to be overused.

   9. _____

   USAGE NOTE: Figures of speech with comparisons that omit "like" or "as" are called *metaphors.* Examples are "the song soared" and "The team crushed its opponent."

10. **spoonerism** (spōo'nə-rĭz'əm) *noun*   An accidental but humorous distortion of words in a phrase formed by interchanging the initial sounds: *"the tons of soil" rather than "the sons of toil."*

    Example   The word *spoonerism* comes from the name of William A. Spooner, an English clergyman who was noted for such verbal slips.

    10. _____

   © Great Source   DO NOT COPY

EXERCISE I COMPLETING DEFINITIONS

On the answer line, write the word from the vocabulary list that best completes each definition.

1. A humorous misuse of a word sounding like the one intended is a(n) _____.

2. A figure of speech in which two unlike things are compared is a(n) _____.

3. Informal speech is known as _____ language.

4. A(n) _____ is a word or sentence that reads the same backward or forward.

5. A word or name formed by combining the first letters of words in a series is a(n) _____.

6. An interchange of the initial sounds of two or more words is a(n) _____.

7. _____ is the invention of new words.

8. A word part, such as a prefix or suffix, that is attached to a base or root is a(n) _____.

9. _____ is the use of a word that imitates what it stands for.

10. A word formed by merging the sounds and meanings of two words is a(n) _____.

1. _____
2. _____
3. _____
4. _____
5. _____
6. _____
7. _____
8. _____
9. _____
10. _____

EXERCISE 2 USING WORDS CORRECTLY

Each of the following questions contains an italicized vocabulary word. Choose the correct answer to the question, and write *Yes* or *No* on the answer line.

1. If you speak too quickly, might you utter a *spoonerism*?

2. Would you use *colloquial* language in a formal essay?

3. Would you use *onomatopoeia* to express the sound of a pebble dropping into a lake?

4. If you formed a word from the first letters of words in a group, would you be adding an *affix*?

5. Is the word *splatter* a *portmanteau word* formed from the combination of *splash* and *spatter*?

6. Would you be guilty of a *malapropism* if you said that you went out with your friends for *piazza* rather than *pizza*?

7. Is the invention of new words described as the *acronym* of new words?

8. Would a word such as *claptrap* be considered a *palindrome*?

9. Is the *coinage* of a word a deliberate misuse of a word?

10. Is a *simile* the comparison of two unlike things?

1. _____
2. _____
3. _____
4. _____
5. _____
6. _____
7. _____
8. _____
9. _____
10 _____

EXERCISE 3 CHOOSING THE BEST WORD

Decide which vocabulary word or related form best completes the sentence, and write the letter of your choice on the answer line.

1. *Swish, ping,* and *zoom* are examples of _____?
   a. palindromes **b.** onomatopoeia **c.** affixes **d.** acronyms

1. _____

2. When Laurie said that the sea gulls were *consecrating*, instead of *congregating*, around the lobster boat, everyone laughed at her _____.
   a. colloquialism   **b.** acronym   **c.** malapropism   **d.** simile

2. _____

3. *ASAP* is a(n) _____ formed from the phrase *as soon as possible*.
   a. malapropism   **b.** spoonerism   **c.** palindrome   **d.** acronym

3. _____

4. *Blurt*, formed from the words *blow* and *spurt*, is a(n) _____.
   a. palindrome   **b.** acronym   **c.** affix   **d.** portmanteau word

4. _____

5. By adding a(n) _____ to the word, Jim changed its meaning.
   a. affix   **b.** acronym   **c.** simile   **d.** palindrome

5. _____

6. Danny used a(n) _____ when he described the music as being like dark velvet.
   a. acronym   **b.** simile   **c.** malapropism   **d.** palindrome

6. _____

7. Aunt Eunice used _____ when she spoke of her relatives as "kith and kin."
   a. a colloquialism   **c.** a portmanteau word
   b. a palindrome   **d.** onomatopoeia

7. _____

8. No one caught Lila's _____; she said "roaring pain" rather than "pouring rain."
   a. simile   **b.** malapropism   **c.** spoonerism   **d.** acronym

8. _____

9. The question "Did Hannah say as Hannah did?" is an example of _____.
   a. an acronym   **b.** a palindrome   **c.** onomatopoeia   **d.** coinage

9. _____

10. The _____ of the word *splashdown* seemed necessary to describe the water landing of a missile or spacecraft.
    a. acronym   **b.** colloquialism   **c.** coinage   **d.** palindrome

10. _____

EXERCISE 4 USING DIFFERENT FORMS OF WORDS

Decide which form of the vocabulary word in parentheses best completes the sentence. The form given may be correct. Write your answer on the answer line.

1. *Snafu* is an _____ for the phrase "situation normal all fouled up." (*acronym*)

1. _____

2. Rachel wrote about the _____ effects of the words *thump, crunch,* and *thud* in the description. (*onomatopoeia*)

2. _____

3. The computer industry has been responsible for _____ many new words. (*coinage*)

3. _____

4. Greg's goal was to write several original _____. (*palindrome*)

4. _____

5. Denise knew that memorizing the meanings of _____ was an excellent way to build her vocabulary. (*affix*)

5. _____

6. _____ are labeled as such in the thesaurus. (*colloquial*)

6. _____

7. Joaquin's favorite _____ is E.B. White's "Records fell like ripe apples on a windy day." (*simile*)

7. _____

8. The concert program had a _____ in it: the writer referred to the talent of the musical *progeny* rather than *prodigy*. (*malapropism*)

8. _____

9. Marty couldn't understand why the audience was giggling; he didn't realize that his _____ "well-boiled icicle" had replaced "well-oiled bicycle." (*spoonerism*)

9. _____

10. "Can anyone tell me what _____ comes from combining *chuckle* and *snort*?" asked Mrs. Davidson. (*portmanteau word*)

10. _____

© Great Source DO NOT COPY

READING COMPREHENSION

Each numbered sentence in the following passage contains an italicized vocabulary word or related form. After you read the passage, you will complete an exercise.

OUR CHANGING VOCABULARY

Few languages can rival English in the richness, flexibility, and creativity of its vocabulary. Speakers of English have a long and colorful tradition of welcoming words from other languages to express new thoughts. Because of a history of invasions by other people, trade, exploration, colonization, and immigration, foreign borrowings have greatly increased the size and versatility of the vocabulary. In addition, English is freer than most languages in its modifications to existing words and in its creation of new words. (1) From the materials in our enormous vocabulary storehouse, we can *coin* new words to suit our needs in an ever-changing world.

(2) One of the most common and frequently used methods of creating new words is by adding an *affix* to a familiar root or base word. The addition of a prefix or suffix changes both the word and its meaning. For example, the addition of the prefix *super-*, meaning "superior or excessive in size, quality, or degree" or "over or upon," has produced such words as *supermarket, superimpose,* and *superabundant*. (3) The addition of the suffix *-ly* to nouns creates adjectives that are actually *similes*. Words like *cowardly* and *saintly* are abbreviated ways of saying "like a coward" or "like a saint." The same comparative effect is achieved by adding the suffix *-like*, producing words such as *childlike* and *birdlike*.

Many of our English words have their origins in the names of real or imaginary people or places. You probably know already that the sandwich is named for the Earl of Sandwich and that pasteurized milk gets its name from Louis Pasteur, the man who invented the process. (4) In the same way, a *spoonerism* gets its name from the Reverend William Spooner, who frequently tripped over his own words. Spooner was supposed to have told a groom at the end of the wedding ceremony, "It is kisstomary to cuss the bride."

(5) Similar to the spoonerism in its humorous effect, the *malapropism* gets its name from a literary character. Mrs. Malaprop, who chose her words inappropriately, was guilty of such errors as "a progeny of learning" and "illiterate him, I say, quite from your memory."

Occasionally words are coined spontaneously out of the creative play of the imagination. (6) Lewis Carroll, author of *Alice in Wonderland*, invented the term *portmanteau word.* In his poem "Jabberwocky," he used words like *chortle (chuckle + snort), gallumph (gallop + triumph),* and *mimsy (miserable + flimsy)*. Today we commonly use such portmanteau words as *motel (motor + hotel), brunch (breakfast + lunch), transistor (transfer + resistor),* and *flurry (fluster + hurry)*.

It is interesting to note that of all Lewis Carroll's coinages, only *chortle* has become part of standard usage. Not all invented words are incorporated into formal speech and writing. (7) For example, a *chump (chunk + lump* or *stump),* meaning "a stupid person," is an example of a portmanteau word that remains a *colloquialism*. To become part of standard usage, a word must pass the tests of utility, permanence, and acceptance by large numbers of people.

Many of our word inventions represent a form of verbal shorthand. When Franklin Delano Roosevelt became president of the United States, he created many new government agencies, all with long titles. (8) To avoid saying or writing the lengthy names of these organizations, people began using *acronyms.* Whether the letters are pronounced individually (*U.N.* or *G.I.*) or combined into words (ZIP code, *laser, scuba*), acronyms are a convenient way of adding words to the language.

(9) *Onomatopoeia,* another type of verbal shorthand, is a particularly vivid and expressive method of inventing new words. For example, the word *zing* is a short way of saying "a high-pitched sound of something moving at an extremely fast speed." Words like *fling* and *flop* suggest awkward movement, while *pop, snip,* and *rap* suggest clipped sound or movement.

(10) Although *palindromes* use existing words and are not a means of adding words to the language, they do illustrate the flexibility and creativity of the language. Palindromes may be single words, such as *civic, kayak, radar,* and *deed*. Other palindromes are phrases or sentences and are often associated with famous people. When he went into exile, Napoleon was supposed to have uttered, "Able was I ere I saw Elba." Adam allegedly introduced himself to Eve by saying "Madam, I'm Adam."

English is a powerful and dynamic language that has always demonstrated a capacity to absorb the many influences that bear on it. The enormous extent and infinite variety of our vocabulary will no doubt continue as changing institutions and new discoveries expand our resources for expressing ourselves.

Each of the following statements corresponds to a numbered sentence in the passage. Each statement contains a blank and is followed by four answer choices. Decide which choice fits best in the blank. The word or phrase that you choose must express roughly the same meaning as the italicized word in the passage. Write the letter of your choice on the answer line.

1. We can _____ new words from our storehouse of vocabulary.
   a. learn   **b.** teach   **c.** promote   **d.** invent

   1. _____

2. Adding a(n) _____ to a root or base word is a common method of creating a new word.
   a. ending   **b.** prefix or suffix   **c.** hyphen   **d.** position

   2. _____

3. Adding the suffix -*ly* to nouns creates adjectives that are _____.
   a. comparisons   **b.** contrasts   **c.** imaginative   **d.** expressive

   3. _____

4. A(n) _____ gets its name from a man who frequently tripped over his own words.
   a. tongue-twister
   b. accidental interchange of the initial sounds of words
   c. misuse of a word that sounds like the intended word
   d. emphatic interjection

   4. _____

5. The _____ gets its name from a literary character.
   a. protagonist
   b. accidental interchange of the initial sounds of words
   c. misuse of a word that sounds like the intended word
   d. indirect statement

   5. _____

6. Lewis Carroll created the concept of _____.
   a. blends   **c.** mime
   b. nonsense poetry   **d.** stereotyped words

   6. _____

7. Some portmanteau words remain _____.
   a. technical terms   **c.** informal expressions
   b. poetic   **d.** unknown

   7. _____

8. _____ are a popular way of avoiding lengthy names of organizations or inventions.
   a. Abbreviations
   b. Short introductions
   c. Words formed from the initial letters of words in a group
   d. Rhymes

   8. _____

9. _____ is a vivid and expressive method of inventing new words.
   a. Brainstorming   **c.** Using words that imitate a feeling
   b. Poetry   **d.** Using words that imitate a sound

   9. _____

10. _____ illustrate the flexibility and creativity of the language.
   a. Word games
   b. Words or sentences that read the same backward and forward
   c. Words made by transposing letters
   d. Great writers

   10. _____

Using several of the word-coining methods explained in this lesson, invent three or four words of your own. Along with each word, include a complete definition, a brief explanation of the method you used, and a sentence using the word.

LESSON 2 CARE AND PRECISION

Some tasks, such as dusting furniture or washing a car, can be performed quickly, while other tasks demand accuracy. If balancing a checkbook, following a recipe, or repairing a bicycle is not done carefully, for example, the results may be confusing, unacceptable, or even dangerous. The words in this vocabulary lesson describe different aspects of care and precision that we encounter daily.

WORD LIST

diligence
fastidious
foresight
judicious
meticulous
minutiae
prudent
punctilious
selective
systematic

DEFINITIONS

After you have studied the definitions and example for each vocabulary word, write the word on the line to the right.

1. **diligence** (dĭl'ə-jəns) *noun*   Constant and earnest effort to accomplish a task; careful attention. (From the Latin word *diligere*, meaning "to love")

   Related Words **diligent** *adjective;* **diligently** *adverb*
   Example   The study of organic chemistry requires *diligence* because one must memorize many formulas.

   1. _____

2. **fastidious** (fă-stĭd'ē-əs) *adjective*   **a.** Difficult to satisfy or please; exacting. **b.** Possessing or displaying careful attention to detail. (From the Latin word *fastidium*, meaning "loathing")

   Related Words **fastidiously** *adverb;* **fastidiousness** *noun*
   Example   Mrs. Armitage was such a *fastidious* housekeeper that she asked all visitors to remove their shoes at the front door.

   2. _____
   See *meticulous.*

3. **foresight** (fôr'sīt') *noun*   The ability to see what is likely to happen and to prepare for it accordingly; careful thought or concern for the future.

   Related Word **foresee** *verb*
   Example   Mr. Figone had the *foresight* to invest in the company when it began to produce personal computers.

   3. _____

4. **judicious** (jōō-dĭsh'əs) *adjective*   Having or exhibiting sound judgment; sensible; wise. (From the Latin word *judicium*, meaning "judgment")

   Related Word **judiciously** *adverb;* **judiciousness** *noun*
   Example   *Judicious* biographers select facts carefully and critically.

   4. _____
   USAGE NOTE: Don't confuse with *judicial*, which refers to things related to courts of law.

© Great Source DO NOT COPY

5. **meticulous** (mǐ-tǐk′yə-ləs) *adjective*   **a.** Extremely careful and precise.
   b. Excessively concerned with details. (From the Latin word *meticulosus*, meaning "timid")

   Related Words   **meticulously** *adverb;* **meticulousness** *noun*
   Example   The *meticulous* volunteer made a list of the thousands of butterfly specimens in the science museum.

6. **minutiae** (mǐ-nōō′shē-ē′, mǐ-nyōō′shē-ē′) *noun*   Minor or trivial details. (From the Latin word *minutus,* meaning "small")

   Related Words   **minute** *adjective;* **minutely** *adverb*
   Example   The *minutiae* of the company's financial report were listed in an appendix.

7. **prudent** (prōōd′nt) *adjective*   Exercising caution, good judgment, or common sense in handling practical matters; giving thought to one's actions and their consequences. (From the Latin *pro-,* meaning "forward," and *videre,* meaning "to see")

   Related Words   **prudence** *noun;* **prudently** *adverb*
   Example   *Prudent* people generally try to save part of their wages.

8. **punctilious** (pŭngk-tǐl′ē-əs) *adjective*   **a.** Attentive to the finer points of etiquette and formal conduct.   **b.** Very careful and exact.

   Related Words   **punctiliously** *adverb;* **punctiliousness** *noun*
   Example   Eric was *punctilious* in returning borrowed books.

9. **selective** (sǐ-lěk′tǐv) *adjective*   **a.** Careful in choosing; particular; discriminating.
   b. Highly specific in activity; *selective pesticides.* (From the Latin *se-,* meaning "apart," and *legere,* meaning "to choose")

   Related Words   **select** *verb;* **selectively** *adverb;* **selectiveness** *noun*
   Example   As prices for goods and services have increased, consumers have become increasingly *selective* in their purchases.

10. **systematic** (sĭs′tə-măt′ĭk) *adjective*   **a.** Having a system, method, or plan; carried out in a step-by-step procedure.   **b.** Orderly in arranging things or getting things done; purposefully regular. (From the Greek *syn-,* meaning "together," and *histanai,* meaning "to cause to stand")

    Related Words   **system** *noun,* **systematically** *adverb;* **systematize** *verb*
    Example   Biologists have a *systematic* procedure for classifying the forms of animal life.

5. _____
USAGE NOTE: *Fastidious, meticulous,* and *punctilious* all concern "fussiness." *Fastidious* suggests difficulty of being pleased, *meticulous,* anxious attention, and *punctilious,* attention even to minutiae.

6. _____
USAGE NOTE: The word *minutiae* is most often used in its plural form. The singular is *minutia.*

7. _____

8. _____
See *meticulous,* above.

9. _____

10. _____

© Great Source   DO NOT COPY

EXERCISE 1 WRITING CORRECT WORDS

On the answer line, write the word from the vocabulary list that fits each definition.

1. Constant and earnest effort to accomplish a task   1. _____

2. Difficult to please   2. _____

3. Having sound judgment; sensible   3. _____

4. Careful in choosing; discriminating   4. _____

5. Having a system, method, or plan; orderly   5. _____

6. The ability to see what is likely to happen and plan for it accordingly   6. _____

7. Minor or trivial details   7. _____

8. Attentive to the finer points of etiquette and formal conduct   8. _____

9. Exercising caution or good judgment in handling practical matters   9. _____

10. Extremely careful and precise   10. _____

EXERCISE 2 USING WORDS CORRECTLY

Each of the following questions contains an italicized vocabulary word. Choose the correct answer to the question and write *Yes* or *No* on the answer line.

1. Would a *systematic* person approach a task in a haphazard fashion?   1. _____

2. If a person is overwhelmed with *minutiae,* is he or she concerned with minor   2. _____
   details?

3. Would a good jeweler make a *meticulous* inspection of a diamond?   3. _____

4. Would a *selective* editor of a magazine automatically include every story and   4. _____
   article submitted for publication?

5. Would a *fastidious* chef be satisfied with ingredients that are not fresh?   5. _____

6. Would a *prudent* traveler go on a trip without making reservations?   6. _____

7. Would a student show *diligence* by working steadily on an assignment?   7. _____

8. If you show *foresight,* do you plan for your future?   8. _____

9. If you make *judicious* use of your spare time, do you waste it?   9. _____

10. Might a *punctilious* person know the difference between a fruit knife and a   10. _____
    butter knife?

EXERCISE 3 CHOOSING THE BEST WORD

For each italicized vocabulary word or related form in the following sentences, write the letter of the best definition on the answer line.

1. Mr. Kwong is a *fastidious* customer who likes natural fabrics and well-tailored   1. _____
   clothing.
   a. sharp   **b.** hard-to-please   **c.** memorable   **d.** hard-to-fit

2. The security guards made a *systematic* inspection of the museum.   2. _____
   a. occasional   **b.** daily   **c.** partial   **d.** orderly

3. The spy ignored the *minutiae* of the report while he concentrated on the coded message.
   a. minor details b. major flaws c. meaning d. confusion

3. _____

4. Evelyn's *diligence* was admirable; she never took a break until she had finished all of her tasks.
   a. determination c. constant effort
   b. enthusiasm d. momentary courage

4. _____

5. Before going out for a sail, John *prudently* checks to see that life jackets are on board.
   a. instinctively b. suspiciously c. repetitiously d. cautiously

5. _____

6. Mr. and Mrs. Kasabian expect *punctilious* manners at the dinner table.
   a. generous b. informal c. careful and exact d. elegant and gracious

6. _____

7. Esther had the *foresight* to provide enough copies of her outline for the entire group.
   a. request c. ability to predict the attendance
   b. idea d. ability to prepare for the future

7. _____

8. Vito always carries a book with him so that he can make *judicious* use of his time.
   a. sensible b. legal c. special d. observant

8. _____

9. The police made a *meticulous* examination of the car for clues.
   a. casual b. rapid c. precise d. hesitant

9. _____

10. The admissions counselor emphasized how *selective* private colleges can be.
    a. dependable b. particular c. unpredictable d. logical

10. _____

EXERCISE 4 IDENTIFYING SYNONYMS

Decide which word or phrase has the meaning that is closest to that of the capitalized word. Write the letter of your choice on the answer line.

1. JUDICIOUS:
   a. industrious b. pure c. foolish d. sensible

1. _____

2. PUNCTILIOUS:
   a. careless b. exacting c. prompt d. loyal

2. _____

3. FORESIGHT:
   a. balance b. endurance c. forethought d. thoughtlessness

3. _____

4. SYSTEMATIC:
   a. irregular b. responsible c. boring d. orderly

4. _____

5. METICULOUS:
   a. careful b. imaginative c. disagreeable d. sloppy

5. _____

6. DILIGENCE:
   a. logical explanation b. weakness c. ability d. constant effort

6. _____

7. PRUDENT:
   a. aggressive b. cautious c. disagreeable d. negligent

7. _____

8. SELECTIVE:
   a. discriminating b. perceptive c. offensive d. fierce

8. _____

9. MINUTIAE:
   a. misfortune b. important matters c. forgiveness d. minor details

9. _____

10. FASTIDIOUS:
    a. delighted b. moody c. particular d. unpleasant

10. _____

© Great Source DO NOT COPY

READING COMPREHENSION

Each numbered sentence in the following passage contains an italicized vocabulary word or related form. After you read the passage, you will complete an exercise.

MARY CASSATT: AMERICAN ARTIST

Mary Cassatt (1844–1926) has long been considered the United States' foremost woman artist. (1) Appreciated for her *meticulous* style, she is also notable as the only American to exhibit with the French Impressionist painters.

Mary enrolled in the Pennsylvania Academy of Fine Arts in 1856. (2) Although it was acceptable for young women to study painting for enjoyment, Mary's declaration that she wanted to be a professional artist upset her parents, who were *punctilious* in their observance of conventions. (3) Her father believed that it would not be *prudent* for a woman in traditional Philadelphia society to involve herself in such an unacceptable career.

Mary Cassatt was strong willed, however. She spent five years at the academy, where she copied plaster casts and paintings and learned the technical aspects of painting. (4) She was often bored with the *minutiae* of the curriculum but also realized the importance of learning technique. Although her family had hoped that she would outgrow her desire for a career in art, she did not. (5) Finding Philadelphia lacking in artistic inspiration, she made a *judicious* decision about her career. She went to Europe, where she lived for the rest of her life.

(6) Between 1866 and 1873, Cassatt *systematically* traveled and studied in France, Italy, Spain, and Belgium. Her genius for painting matured slowly. (7) She was a *diligent* worker, arriving in her studio by eight o'clock each morning and often painting until late at night. (8) Her efforts were rewarded in 1872 and 1873, when she had paintings accepted by the Paris Salon, a highly *selective* exhibit of the best art of the year. (9) Although Cassatt believed that the Paris Salon encouraged too much conformity in art, she was honored to have been chosen by the *fastidious* judges.

In 1874 Edgar Degas, a famous French artist, saw one of Mary's paintings in the Paris Salon. Struck by her use of light and brilliant color and her uncluttered composition, Degas invited her to join his group. The picture on this page is based on Degas's painting of Mary Cassatt.

Degas's group was called the Anonymous Society of Painters, Sculptors, and Engravers. In 1874 this group broke away from the traditional ideas of the Paris Salon. Rather than portraying the approved historical subjects, these artists wanted to capture their first impressions of ordinary objects, people, and situations. The artists earned their name, the Impressionists, from a word that a critic used contemptuously. Using separate touches of pure color, the Impressionist painters were the first to demonstrate that what matters is how an object looks, not what it is.

(10) Having the *foresight* to realize that this group would have a tremen-

dous impact on art, Mary Cassatt stopped submitting paintings to the Paris Salon and began to exhibit with the Impressionists in 1879. Because of her involvement with them, she was responsible for introducing and promoting Impressionism in the United States.

With the Impressionists, Mary Cassatt found the artistic independence she had been seeking. Her oil paintings, pastels, and etchings received international acclaim. Cassatt's portrayals of mothers and children engaged in the common activities of daily life are among the richest contributions to our artistic heritage.

Each of the following statements corresponds to a numbered sentence in the passage. Each statement contains a blank and is followed by four answer choices. Decide which choice fits best in the blank. The word or phrase that you choose must express roughly the same meaning as the italicized word in the passage. Write the letter of your choice on the answer line.

1. Mary Cassatt is appreciated for her _____ style.
   a. freehand   b. talented   c. precise   d. automatic

   1. _____

2. Mary's parents were _____ in their observance of conventions.
   a. strict   b. respectable   c. snobbish   d. embarrassed

   2. _____

3. Her father believed that it would not be _____ for a woman to be involved in an unacceptable career.
   a. creative   b. responsible   c. sensible   d. educational

   3. _____

4. She was often bored with the _____ of the curriculum.
   a. challenges   b. philosophy   c. assignments   d. trivial details

   4. _____

5. Cassatt made a(n) _____ decision about her career.
   a. wise   b. sudden   c. ridiculous   d. unusual

   5. _____

6. She traveled _____ in Europe.
   a. frequently   c. according to no plan
   b. in an organized way   d. rarely

   6. _____

7. She was a(n) _____ worker.
   a. sloppy   b. lazy   c. earnest   d. loyal

   7. _____

8. Cassatt had paintings accepted for a very _____ exhibit.
   a. discriminating   b. unusual   c. successful   d. technical

   8. _____

9. Cassatt was honored to have been chosen by the _____ judges.
   a. volunteer   b. respected   c. famous   d. exacting

   9. _____

10. Mary Cassatt had enough _____ to realize that the Impressionists would have a tremendous impact on art.
    a. understanding   c. ability to see and plan for the future
    b. historical knowledge   d. ability to analyze art trends

    10. _____

WRITING ASSIGNMENT

Suppose that you are employed by a toy and hobby manufacturer to write directions for assembling toys and models. Recently you have received several letters of complaint from people who have had difficulty in putting together an object. In reading these letters, you realize that all of these people have failed to follow the directions. Write a brief but polite response to these customers, explaining why precision in following directions is important. Use five of the vocabulary words from this lesson in your letter and underline each word that you use.

© Great Source   DO NOT COPY

Throughout history people have created rules about appropriate behavior for a variety of situations. It is important to keep in mind that what is relevant to one group of people may not be to another. For example, polite table manners, as we know them today, were hardly an important rule of behavior in Neanderthal society. In today's world, however, many societies place a high value on correct dining room etiquette. Competition is another area of behavior that differs from culture to culture. In some societies competition among people is highly encouraged. In others this type of behavior is considered rude and undesirable. The words in this lesson present different aspects of behavior and should be useful when you are called upon to describe people and their actions.

WORD LIST

beguile
civility
decorum
demeanor
foolhardy
glib
ignoble
mores
provincial
unseemly

DEFINITIONS

After you have studied the definitions and example for each vocabulary word, write the word on the line to the right.

1. **beguile** (bĭ-gīl') *trans. verb* **a.** To deceive; trick. **b.** To amuse; delight. **c.** To pass (time) pleasantly.

    Example Marianne was *beguiled* by the salesperson; as a consequence she found herself purchasing the expensive music box.

    1. _____

2. **civility** (sĭ-vĭl'ĭ-tē) *noun* **a.** Politeness; courtesy. **b.** An act or expression of courtesy.

    Related Word **civil** *adjective*
    Example Although they held opposing viewpoints, the two debaters managed to treat each other with *civility*.

    2. _____

3. **decorum** (dĭ-kôr'əm) *noun* Appropriateness of behavior or conduct; propriety. (From the Latin word *decor*, meaning "beauty" or "propriety")

    Related Word **decorous** *adjective*
    Example The young woman's refusal to curtsy to the king was a serious breach of court *decorum*.

    3. _____

4. **demeanor** (dĭ-mē'nər) *noun* The way in which one behaves or conducts oneself; deportment.

    Example The gracious *demeanor* of the hostess made us feel welcome in her home.

    4. _____

5. **foolhardy** (fo͞ol'här'dē) *adjective*   Foolishly bold or daring; rash.

    Related Word   foolhardiness *noun*

    Example   Because of the dangerous rapids, taking a white-water rafting trip seemed like a *foolhardy* venture.

5. _____

ETYMOLOGY NOTE: *Foolhardy* was borrowed long ago directly from the French *fol hardi*, meaning "bold fool."

6. **glib** (glĭb) *adjective*   **a.** Performing or performed with careless, often thoughtless, ease.   **b.** Marked by a quickness or fluency that suggests insincerity. (From the Middle German word *glibberich*, meaning "slippery")

    Related Words   glibly *adverb;* **glibness** *noun*

    Example   Paul's *glib* description of the party guests amused his friends.

6. _____

7. **ignoble** (ĭg-nō'bəl) *adjective*   **a.** Not having a noble character or purpose; dishonorable.   **b.** Not of the nobility; common. (From the Latin *in-*, meaning "not," and *nobilis*, meaning "noble")

    Related Word   **ignobly** *adverb*

    Example   The *ignoble* young man only pretended to love his fiancée while he secretly admired her large bank account.

7. _____

8. **mores** (môr'āz') *plural noun*   **a.** The accepted customs and rules of behavior of a particular social group, generally regarded by that group as essential to survival and welfare and often having the force of law.   **b.** Attitudes about proper behavior; moral conventions. (From the Latin word *mos*, meaning "custom")

    Example   The *mores* of some societies dictate that hospitality cannot be refused—even to an enemy.

8. _____

9. **provincial** (prə-vĭn'shəl) *adjective*   **a.** Characteristic of people or things away from the capital of a country; *a provincial simplicity of speech or dress.*   **b.** Limited in range or perspective; narrow; ill-informed; unsophisticated.   **c.** Of or relating to a province.

    Related Words   province *noun;* **provincialism** *noun*

    Example   The sophisticated woman commented that the casually dressed tourists behaved in a *provincial* manner.

9. _____

10. **unseemly** (ŭn-sēm'lē) *adjective*   Not in good taste; improper; unbecoming.   *adverb* In an unseemly manner. (From the Old English *un-*, meaning "not," and the Old Norse word *soemr*, meaning "fitting")

    Related Word   unseemliness *noun*

    Example   Because of Gulliver's *unseemly* table manners, his friends were reluctant to invite him to formal dinner parties.

10. _____

Word History: civility

Latin: *civis*=citizen, one who lives in a city

   Civility implies politeness and courtesy and comes from the Latin word *civis*, meaning "citizen." In ancient Roman times, citizens living in a city were regarded as more cultured and more mannerly than those living elsewhere. The sophistication and refined behavior of these ancient city-dwellers won for them a lasting following. In fact, their reputation for politeness and courtesy survives in the meaning of such modern derivatives of *civis* as *civility, civil,* and *civilized.*

© Great Source   DO NOT COPY

EXERCISE 1 WRITING CORRECT WORDS

On the answer line, write the word from the vocabulary list that fits each definition.

1. Appropriateness of behavior or conduct   1. _____

2. Characteristic of people or things away from the capital of a country   2. _____

3. Foolishly bold or daring; rash   3. _____

4. Performing or performed with careless, often thoughtless, ease   4. _____

5. The accepted customs and rules of behavior of a social group   5. _____

6. The way in which one behaves; deportment   6. _____

7. Not in good taste; improper   7. _____

8. Dishonorable   8. _____

9. Courtesy; politeness   9. _____

10. To deceive; trick   10. _____

EXERCISE 2 USING WORDS CORRECTLY

Decide whether the italicized vocabulary word has been used correctly in the sentence. On the answer line, write *Correct* for correct use and *Incorrect* for incorrect use.

1. The employee's *unseemly* behavior helped him to receive a promotion.   1. _____

2. During press receptions the feuding stars showed *civility* toward each other.   2. _____

3. The *ignoble* politician set a good example for the young people.   3. _____

4. The *provincial* visitor gaped at the paintings displayed at the city's leading art museum.   4. _____

5. Sharon complimented Rosa on her serene *demeanor*, pointing out that Rosa had behaved well under the circumstances.   5. _____

6. One of our traditional *mores* is the celebration of Thanksgiving as a national holiday.   6. _____

7. Shy and quiet Henry was a naturally *glib* speaker.   7. _____

8. Going down Niagara Falls in a barrel might be called a *foolhardy* feat.   8. _____

9. Janet maintained her sense of *decorum* by rudely telling people what she thought of them.   9. _____

10. The sorcerer cast a spell and *beguiled* the prince into trusting him.   10. _____

EXERCISE 3 CHOOSING THE BEST WORD

Decide which vocabulary word or related form best completes the sentence, and write the letter of your choice on the answer line.

1. The _____ art dealer sold the painting by misrepresenting its value.   1. _____
   a. civil   **b.** decorous   **c.** provincial   **d.** ignoble

© Great Source   DO NOT COPY

2. Martha tried to stop Ted from making a(n) _____ expedition alone on the Amazon River.

   a. foolhardy   **b.** glib   **c.** unseemly   **d.** decorous

2. _____

3. Kate specializes in writing cookbooks that feature _____ food.

   a. foolhardy   **b.** glib   **c.** provincial   **d.** ignoble

3. _____

4. The _____ with which the opposing political candidates treated each other impressed the audience.

   a. civility   **b.** foolhardiness   **c.** provincialism   **d.** unseemliness

4. _____

5. The child listened intently to the _____ story.

   a. ignoble   **b.** beguiling   **c.** civil   **d.** unseemly

5. _____

6. The tour guide spoke in a _____ manner that annoyed the tourists.

   a. decorous   **b.** civil   **c.** beguiling   **d.** glib

6. _____

7. Interested in ancient customs, the anthropologist closely studied the _____ of a primitive society.

   a. foolhardiness   **b.** provincialism   **c.** mores   **d.** glibness

7. _____

8. The class thought Alice acted in a(n) _____ manner when she interrupted Jack's speech.

   a. unseemly   **b.** beguiling   **c.** civil   **d.** decorous

8. _____

9. The guests commented that the innkeeper's _____ was pleasant and cordial.

   a. unseemliness   **b.** demeanor   **c.** foolhardiness   **d.** mores

9. _____

10. In *My Fair Lady,* Professor Higgins wants Eliza Doolittle to behave with _____.

    a. decorum   **b.** unseemliness   **c.** provincialism   **d.** foolhardiness

10. _____

EXERCISE 4 USING DIFFERENT FORMS OF WORDS

Decide which form of the vocabulary word in parentheses best completes the sentence. The form given may be correct. Write your answer on the answer line.

1. The baby sitter had trouble keeping a _____ tone in her voice when speaking to the rude children. *(civility)*

1. _____

2. At the coronation everyone behaved in a _____ manner. *(decorum)*

2. _____

3. Cynthia was eager to learn the _____ of the South Pacific islanders. *(mores)*

3. _____

4. Larry cheated and won the chess game _____. *(ignoble)*

4. _____

5. The _____ of the professor's views surprised his colleagues. *(provincial)*

5. _____

6. The _____ of the child's behavior upset her mother. *(unseemly)*

6. _____

7. Janet was _____ by her friend's vague promises. *(beguile)*

7. _____

8. "To attempt such a dangerous hike is sheer _____," Amanda scolded. *(foolhardy)*

8. _____

9. The soldier was impeccable in his _____ toward his commanding officer. *(demeanor)*

9. _____

10. Sarah talked _____ about her summer in Europe. *(glib)*

10. _____

© Great Source   DO NOT COPY

READING COMPREHENSION

Each numbered sentence in the following passage contains an italicized vocabulary word. After you read the passage, you will complete an exercise.

COURT LIFE AT ELEGANT VERSAILLES

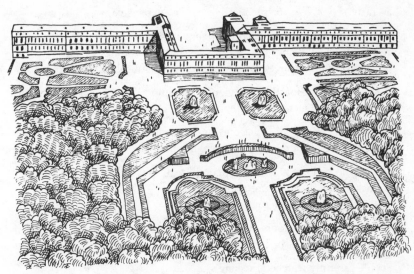

For many years the French city of Versailles, where Louis XIV held court in the late 1600s, has been identified with great wealth, luxury, and classic beauty. Upon visiting the site, one might easily imagine elegant men and women enjoying pampered lives of idleness and intrigue amid the magnificent palaces and formal gardens. (1) However, beneath the *beguiling* image of seventeenth-century life at Versailles, there was also discomfort and stress.

First and most basic, there was the matter of comfortable housing. (2) A nobleman or noblewoman could hardly refuse an invitation to live in the palace; such a denial would, indeed, have been *foolhardy.* Still, too many were invited to crowd into the small, dark rooms whose inadequate design made these chambers too hot in the summer and too cold in the winter. Frustratingly, many of the rooms had tiny windows that opened onto walls.

(3) The court of Versailles was governed by rigid rules of *decorum.* New arrivals often spent months studying the complex code. (4) The *mores* of court society dictated that being polite and showing respect for those who were socially prominent were the most important rules of all. (5) One duke exemplified this code by giving a *glib* one-hour speech of thanks to his hostess for an evening spent at her home. (6) Although the duke was an extreme case, court snobs insisted that people who had not mastered the intricate rules of politeness were hopelessly *provincial.*

What were some of these strict rules? (7) Generally, it was considered *unseemly* to knock at palace doors. Instead, one had to scratch with the nail of the little finger of one's left hand. This rule, however, did not apply to the first time one visited the home of a noble person; in that case it was preferable to knock.

If one worried about offending the nobility, the risk was much greater with the king himself. (8) The king's *demeanor* toward someone was critically important. If the king did not acknowledge someone's approach, that person might interpret this as a signal that he or she was about to lose lands and fortune. (9) If, on the other hand, a man removed his hat in the king's presence or sat down without his permission, the king might never again treat that person with *civility.* If someone greatly pleased the king, that person might be allowed to hold the royal candle or grasp the royal napkin.

The king also insisted that every courtier be extremely well dressed at all times. Any occasion—a birthday or a marriage—might motivate the king to order everyone to buy and wear expensive new clothes. For all of its frequent social occasions, life at court could be very dull. Days began early and ended late. The nobility were forced to spend their time the way the king wanted them to.

As the Duchesse d' Orleans observed in a letter to a friend: "We all troop into the billiard room, no one uttering a word until the king has finished his game. Then we all get up to go to the music room, where someone is singing an aria from some old opera which we have heard a hundred times already. After that we go to the ball. Those who, like me, do not dance have to sit there for hours without budging for an instant, and can neither see nor hear anything other than an interminable minuet."

(10) As this quotation suggests, most of the French people were thankful that they did not have to live at Versailles and master the elaborate code of behavior that often masked *ignoble* deeds.

© Great Source DO NOT COPY

Each of the following statements corresponds to a numbered sentence in the passage. Each statement contains a blank and is followed by four answer choices. Decide which choice fits best in the blank. The word or phrase that you choose must express roughly the same meaning as the italicized word in the passage. Write the letter of your choice on the answer line.

1. On the surface, life at the court of Versailles appeared _____.
   a. beautiful   **b.** delightful   **c.** attractive   **d.** expensive

   1. _____

2. Refusing to live in the palace could have been _____.
   a. rash   **b.** practical   **c.** expensive   **d.** wise

   2. _____

3. _____ was an important concern at Versailles.
   a. People's well-being   **c.** Fine dining
   b. Appropriateness of behavior   **d.** Beautiful architecture

   3. _____

4. Courteous and respectful behavior was an important _____ of this society.
   a. motivational factor   **b.** limitation   **c.** comfort   **d.** custom

   4. _____

5. A duke once gave a(n) _____ one-hour speech of thanks.
   a. boring but sincere   **b.** insincere but fluent   **c.** lengthy   **d.** tedious

   5. _____

6. Those who had not mastered the complex rules were considered _____.
   a. lucky   **c.** unsophisticated
   b. impolite   **d.** unappealing

   6. _____

7. Knocking at palace doors might be called _____ behavior.
   a. improper   **b.** informal   **c.** fitting   **d.** friendly

   7. _____

8. People carefully watched the king's _____.
   a. favors on their behalf   **c.** behavior toward them
   b. sincere compliments   **d.** daily insults

   8. _____

9. A small mistake in manners might have caused the king not to treat someone with _____.
   a. kindness   **b.** politeness   **c.** mercy   **d.** honor

   9. _____

10. Good manners sometimes hide _____ actions.
    a. sincere   **b.** dishonorable   **c.** spontaneous   **d.** thoughtless

    10. _____

Imagine that you are a book reviewer for your school or local newspaper. Choose a book that you have read recently. In two or three paragraphs, describe and explain the behavior of the important characters in the book. In your discussion use five words from this lesson and underline each one.

© Great Source   DO NOT COPY

DICTIONARY SKILLS
SYNONYM PARAGRAPHS

Words with similar meanings—such as *kind, benevolent, gracious,* and *compassionate*—are called **synonyms.** Each of these four adjectives describes a person who shows concern for others. However, synonyms almost always have slight differences in meaning. *Kind* describes an individual who is considerate and sympathetic to other people. *Benevolent* describes a person who is charitable, while *gracious* suggests a courteous, warm manner. Finally, *compassionate* describes someone who easily feels pity for others.

Dictionaries contain **synonym paragraphs** that differentiate among the related synonyms in a cluster. The paragraph first explains the similarity in meaning of the synonyms. Then, in most dictionaries, the paragraph goes on to explain the small but important differences in the meanings of the words. A synonym paragraph appears at the end of the entry for the most common word in the cluster. The paragraph is easily identifiable by the word *synonym* or its abbreviation in boldface type at the beginning. Synonym paragraphs can be useful to you in two ways.

1. *When you write, synonym paragraphs can help you choose the synonym that best expresses your meaning.* Suppose, for example, that you want a verb to use for a group of people who are trying to make a decision. At the end of the dictionary entry for the verb *ponder,* you find the following synonym paragraph. From the notes in the paragraph, you can tell that *deliberate* is the best verb to use.

Synonyms: *ponder, consider, deliberate, ruminate.* These mean to think deeply about something, usually in terms of its outcome or significance. *Ponder* suggests painstaking care and thoroughness. *Consider* is less subjective and suggests orderly evaluation. *Deliberate* can apply to the thought of a single person, but more often is used with reference to several persons engaged in seeking a decision. *Ruminate* designates a slow but less orderly process.

2. *Synonym paragraphs can help you expand your vocabulary.* The paragraph above indicates that all of the listed words mean "to think deeply about something." This shared meaning can help you remember the words as well as the special connotations of each one.

EXERCISE USING SYNONYM PARAGRAPHS

Read the synonym paragraphs at the foot of the next page. *Step 1:* Decide which of the italicized synonyms in each of the following sentences best fits the meaning of the sentence. *Step 2:* On the line labeled "BEST SYNONYM," write your choice. *Step 3:* Write a sentence of your own in which you use the word correctly.

1. Lindsay qualified for the *(accelerated, fast, rapid)* math class.

   Best Synonym _____

   Sentence _____

2. Marvin's thoughtful arguments and lively speaking style *(influenced, moved)* the audience to vote for his proposal.

   Best Synonym _____

   Sentence _____

3. As Barbara drove west, her first view of the Rockies *(struck, affected)* her in an unforgettable way.

   Best Synonym _____

   Sentence _____

4. Lee proposed an *(expeditious, accelerated)* way of running the debate.

   Best Synonym _____

   Sentence _____

5. The song about the lost dog always *(moves, touches, affects)* me.

   Best Synonym _____

   Sentence _____

6. The new restaurant offered *(fast, hasty)* but gracious service.

   Best Synonym _____

   Sentence _____

7. The pictures of the orphaned children *(moved, affected)* many viewers.

   Best Synonym _____

   Sentence _____

8. Holmes deduced from the steaming cup of hot chocolate and the uneaten piece of toast that the man had made a *(fleet, hasty, rapid)* exit.

   Best Synonym _____

   Sentence _____

9. Jennifer was *(affected, impressed)* by the candidate's views on the important issues in the campaign.

   Best Synonym _____

   Sentence _____

10. The transportation system is not noted for *(rapid, fleet)* service.

    Best Synonym _____

    Sentence _____

Synonyms: *fast, rapid, swift, fleet, speedy, quick, hasty, expeditious, accelerated.* These adjectives refer to rate of activity or movement. All but the last three are often interchangeable. *Fast* is more often applied to a person or thing, and *rapid* to the activity or movement involved; *a fast runner, rapid strides. Swift* suggests smoothness of movement, and *fleet*, lightness of movement. *Speedy* refers to velocity or, when applied to persons, to hurry or make an effort to increase progress. *Quick* also can refer to velocity; more often it applies to what takes little time or to promptness of response or action in persons. *Hasty* implies hurried action and often lack of care or thought. *Expeditious* combines the senses of rapidity and efficiency as they apply to action. *Accelerated* refers to what is increased, or stepped up, in rate of progress or motion.

Synonyms: *affect, influence, impress, touch, move, strike.* These verbs can all mean to produce a mental or emotional effect. To *affect* is to change a person's emotions in some usually specified way. *Influence* implies a degree of control over the thinking and actions, as well as the emotions, of another. To *impress* is to produce a marked, usually favorable, effect on the mind. *Touch* usually means to arouse a brief sense of pathos, wheras *move* suggests profound emotional effect capable of inciting action. *Strike* implies instantaneous mental response to a stimulus such as a sight or an idea.

© Great Source   DO NOT COPY

The root -*ject*- comes from the Latin word *jactus*, which means "thrown" or "hurled." By adding different prefixes and suffixes to this root, you can form many words that are commonly used in the English language, such as *adjective, eject, object, project,* and *projection.* This lesson provides ten more words that are formed from the root -*ject*-.

WORD LIST

abject
conjecture
dejected
injection
jetty
objectionable
projectile
reject
subjective
trajectory

DEFINITIONS

After you have studied the definitions and example for each vocabulary word, write the word on the line to the right.

1. **abject** (ăb'jĕkt', ăb-jĕkt') *adjective* **a.** Lacking all self-respect; contemptible.
    b. Very miserable; wretched. (From the Latin *ab-*, meaning "away," and *jacere*, meaning "to throw")

    Related Words **abjectly** *adverb;* **abjectness** *noun*
    Example   The *abject* coward stood by and watched as others were punished for his misdeed.

    1. _____

2. **conjecture** (kən-jĕk'chər) *noun* **a.** The act of forming an opinion from incomplete evidence; guesswork **b.** A statement or opinion based on guesswork. *trans. verb* To guess. *intrans. verb* To make a conjecture. (From the Latin *com-*, meaning "together," and *jacere*)

    Related Word **conjectural** *adjective*
    Example   There was much *conjecture* among the birthday party guests as to the contents of the packages.

    2. _____

3. **dejected** (dĭ-jĕk'tĭd) *adjective* Depressed; disheartened. (From the Latin *de-*, meaning "down," and *jacere*)

    Related Words **dejectedly** *adverb;* **dejection** *noun*
    Example   Disappointed and *dejected*, the Hartwells were forced to cancel their vacation plans.

    3. _____

4. **injection** (ĭn-jĕk'shən) *noun* **a.** The act of forcing something, generally a liquid or a gas, into something else. **b.** Something that is injected. (From the Latin *in-*, meaning "in," and *jacere*)

    Related Word **inject** *verb*
    Example   The doctor administered an *injection* of penicillin to the patient.

    4. _____

5. **jetty** (jĕt'ē) *noun*   A pier or other structure projecting into a body of water; a wharf. (From the French word *jeter*, meaning "to throw or project")

   Example   Donald stood at the end of the *jetty* and watched the fishing boat sail out of the harbor.

5. _____

6. **objectionable** (əb-jĕk'shə-nə-bəl) *adjective*   Arousing disapproval; offensive. (From the Latin *ob*, meaning "toward," and *jacere*)

   Related Words   **object** *verb;* **objection** *noun*
   Example   Barbara commented on the *objectionable* odor coming from the town dump.

6. _____

7. **projectile** (prə-jĕk'təl, prə-jĕk'tĭl') *noun*   **a.** An object, such as a bullet or an arrow, that is thrown, fired, or otherwise launched through space.   **b.** A self-propelling missile or rocket. (From the Latin *pro-*, meaning "forth," and *jacere*)

   Related Words   **project** *verb;* **projection** *noun*
   Example   The *projectile* was unable to shatter the bulletproof glass.

7. _____

8. **reject** (rĭ-jĕkt') *trans. verb*   **a.** To refuse to accept, use, grant, or consider.   **b.** To fail to give affection or love to.   **c.** To throw out; discard.
   noun   Something or someone that is rejected. (From the Latin *re-*, meaning "back," and *jacere*)

   Related Word   **rejection** *noun*
   Example   The members of the club *rejected* several old laws but suggested new ones to replace them.

8. _____

9. **subjective** (səb-jĕk'tĭv) *adjective*   Taking place within an individual's mind rather than the external environment; personal. (From the Latin *sub-*, meaning "below," and *jacere*)

   Related Words   **subjectively** *adverb;* **subjectivity** *noun*
   Example   People tend to be *subjective* in judging the talents of their friends.

9. _____

10. **trajectory** (trə-jĕk'tə-rē) *noun*   The path made by a moving body or particle, especially the flight path of a missile. (From the Latin *trans*, meaning "across," and *jacere*)

   Example   We could trace the *trajectory* of the comet by observing its long tail.

10. _____

   © Great Source   DO NOT COPY

EXERCISE I COMPLETING DEFINITIONS

On the answer line, write the word from the vocabulary list that best completes each definition.

1. A pier or a wharf is called a(n) _____ .

2. To refuse to accept something is to _____ it.

3. If something is described as coming from thoughts or feelings rather than from an outside source, it is _____ .

4. The forcing of something, such as a liquid, into something else is called a(n) _____ .

5. When someone is lacking in self-respect or is contemptible, he or she is _____ .

6. The path taken by a moving object through space is called its _____ .

7. Something that causes disapproval or is offensive is _____ .

8. Something that is shot, thrown, or fired forward is a(n) _____ .

9. The act of forming an opinion from incomplete evidence is called a(n) _____ .

10. Someone who is depressed or disheartened is also _____ .

1. _____

2. _____

3. _____

4. _____

5. _____

6. _____

7. _____

8. _____

9. _____

10. _____

EXERCISE 2 USING WORDS CORRECTLY

Each of the following questions contains an italicized vocabulary word. Choose the correct answer to the question and write *Yes* or *No* on the answer line.

1. Is a *projectile* something that takes a long time to accomplish?

2. Can you follow the *trajectory* of a rocket as it blasts into the sky?

3. Does an *abject* liar usually have honorable intentions?

4. Is a *jetty* an appropriate landing field for a large passenger aircraft?

5. Might a nurse be required to give *injections*?

6. Do pilots *reject* themselves from their aircraft when they need to escape quickly?

7. Are answers to algebra problems generally *subjective*?

8. When a reporter uses only facts, is he or she basing the story on pure *conjecture*?

9. Can a demotion cause a person to feel *dejected*?

10. Is insulting the host of a party usually considered *objectionable* by others?

1. _____

2. _____

3. _____

4. _____

5. _____

6. _____

7. _____

8. _____

9. _____

10. _____

EXERCISE 3 IDENTIFYING SYNONYMS AND ANTONYMS

Decide which word or phrase has the meaning that is the same as (a synonym) or opposite to (an antonym) that of the capitalized vocabulary word. Write the letter of your choice on the answer line.

1. ABJECT (antonym):
   a. tired   b. sorry   c. shy   d. ecstatic

1. _____

© Great Source   DO NOT COPY

2. PROJECTILE (synonym):
   a. round object
   b. self-propelling missile
   c. required subject
   d. advanced subject

2. _____

3. INJECTION (antonym):
   a. ejection   b. reflection   c. insurrection   d. election

3. _____

4. DEJECTED (synonym):
   a. careful   b. heavy   c. disheartened   d. exuberant

4. _____

5. SUBJECTIVE (synonym):
   a. personal   b. tender   c. objective   d. intellectual

5. _____

6. CONJECTURE (antonym)
   a. opinion   b. theory   c. wish   d. fact

6. _____

7. JETTY (synonym):
   a. landform   b. pier   c. train   d. island

7. _____

8. OBJECTIONABLE (antonym):
   a. subjective   b. impossible   c. pleasing   d. exact

8. _____

9. REJECT (synonym):
   a. discard   b. expect   c. except   d. exact

9. _____

10. TRAJECTORY (synonym):
    a. farm equipment
    b. obsolete machinery
    c. flight path
    d. landing spot

10. _____

EXERCISE 4 USING DIFFERENT FORMS OF WORDS

Decide which form of the vocabulary word in parentheses best completes the sentence. The form given may be correct. Write the answer on the answer line.

1. The veterinarian _____ the dog with a rabies vaccine. *(injection)*

1. _____

2. _____ about other people's business is Lawrence's favorite pastime. *(conjecture)*

2. _____

3. After calculating the possible _____ of his arrow, Robin took careful aim and shot a bull's-eye. *(trajectory)*

3. _____

4. Members of the community loudly voiced their _____ to the proposed construction project. *(objectionable)*

4. _____

5. During the depression years, many people were forced to live in _____ poverty. *(abject)*

5. _____

6. A writer often receives numerous _____ slips before having a manuscript accepted for publication. *(reject)*

6. _____

7. Students were asked to view the essay topic _____. *(subjective)*

7. _____

8. The home team walked _____ to the locker room after losing the game. *(dejected)*

8. _____

9. Three yachts were docked at the _____. *(jetty)*

9. _____

10. Gerald took careful aim, and the _____ raced through the air. *(projectile)*

10. _____

© Great Source   DO NOT COPY

READING COMPREHENSION

Each numbered sentence in the following passage contains an italicized vocabulary word or related form. After you read the passage, you will complete an exercise.

ESCAPE TO FREEDOM

From 1961 to 1989, the Berlin Wall separated the Communist-controlled east side of the city from the democratic west side. Before the city was reunited, many East Germans had to plan daring escapes to get to the west. This is the story of two such families.

For the Strelczyks and the Wetzels, life in East Germany in the late 1970s had become so intolerable that they were determined to escape to freedom in West Germany. The question they constantly asked themselves was "how?" How could eight people possibly get past the heavily fortified wall or over the closely guarded river that had divided Germany into two separate countries since 1949?

(1) The possibility of being brutally stopped by *projectiles* fired from machine guns was a very real threat. (2) Hans Peter Strelczyk, a mechanic, and Gunter Wetzel, a bricklayer, spent many hours *conjecturing* about the explosive mines and dangerous traps that were undoubtedly planted near the wall and along the river banks. (3) For example, a seemingly ordinary *jetty* could easily be rigged with explosives to stop anyone who swam near it. (4) Strelczyk and Wetzel thought of several escape plans but then later *rejected* them because they seemed too dangerous.

Finally, a television program on the history of ballooning gave the two men their answer. At one time Strelczyk had been an aircraft mechanic, and he was convinced that he and Wetzel could build a hot-air balloon that would carry their families over the wall.

After researching ballooning in the library, the families purchased over eight hundred yards of brown cotton cloth to construct the balloon. However, after the balloon was finished, it would not inflate. The cotton fabric was too porous.

(5) This unsuccessful first attempt was discouraging and caused Wetzel to feel that perhaps he was considering the escape plans from too *subjective* a viewpoint. He re-examined all the facts that he had about hot-air ballooning. (6) In doing so, he found *objections* to every possible plan. Wetzel was no longer confident that the scheme would work, and he did not want to risk his family's safety with a faulty plan.

The still-enthusiastic Strelczyk family attempted another flight in a balloon made from taffeta, a sturdier material. (7) This attempt, however, was an *abject* failure. On the evening of the liftoff, moisture from the damp, cloudy night air saturated the taffeta, causing the balloon to fall to the ground. (8) The Strelczyks were forced to abandon the balloon and quickly return home, feeling *dejected* over their second failure.

After the East German police discovered the abandoned balloon, both families knew that time was running out. The Wetzels then agreed to assist the Strelczyks in a third escape attempt. This time the two families searched the East German shops for small pieces of tightly woven cloth—too large a purchase would alert the police. This material was carefully sewed into strips, and a new balloon was constructed.

The two families selected a remote area near the border for the future liftoff and then patiently waited for a night with the correct weather conditions. (9) The wind had to be blowing from the right direction so that the balloon's *trajectory* would lead them across the border.

Finally the weather conditions were right. (10) On September 16, 1979, the two families gathered at the remote launching area and watched nervously as Strelczyk and Wetzel began the *injection* of heated air into the neck of the balloon. As the balloon began to lift, the families jumped aboard, cut the restraining ropes, and felt themselves soaring to an elevation of eight thousand feet.

The balloon began to lose altitude as it neared the border. For one frightening moment, a searchlight shone on the balloon and its passengers; but then the balloon crossed the border at about six thousand feet. At a hundred-foot altitude, Strelczyk was able to see a piece of machinery below. "I thought we were in the West then because it was a modern machine—unlike anything we have in the East," he said.

The air gave out at fifteen feet, and the balloon fell to earth, landing in a thicket. When the occupants of the balloon emerged, they were standing on West German soil. After a thirty-minute flight, they had reached freedom.

Each of the following statements corresponds to a numbered sentence in the passage. Each statement contains a blank and is followed by four answer choices. Decide which choice fits best in the blank. The word or phrase that you choose must express roughly the same meaning as the italicized word in the passage. Write the letter of your choice on the answer line.

1. To get safely over the wall into West Germany, the two families had to avoid _____.

   a. police b. spotlights c. cameras d. bullets

   1. _____

2. Strelczyk and Wetzel spent hours _____ the possible dangers.

   a. dreading b. preparing for c. planning d. guessing at

   2. _____

3. Even a(n) _____ could pose a real threat.

   a. airplane b. balloon c. hijacker d. pier

   3. _____

4. They _____ several escape plans.

   a. attempted b. imagined c. discarded d. managed

   4. _____

5. Wetzel decided that his point of view was too _____.

   a. objective b. serious c. lighthearted d. personal

   5. _____

6. He then discovered some _____.

   a. reasons for disapproval c. diverting plans
   b. boring activities d. exciting possibilities

   6. _____

7. The Strelczyk family's attempt to escape ended in _____ failure.

   a. total b. serious c. miserable d. monumental

   7. _____

8. The Strelczyks were _____ after the failure of their second escape attempt.

   a. elated b. depressed c. tired d. indifferent

   8. _____

9. Strelczyk and Wetzel needed to know the direction of the wind so they could plan the _____ of the balloon.

   a. flight path b. exact height c. launch d. final destination

   9. _____

10. On the night of the flight, they began the _____ of hot air into the balloon.

   a. ascent b. packaging c. pumping d. detouring

   10. _____

PRACTICE WITH ANALOGIES

A verbal analogy shows how two pairs of words are related. The second two words are related to each other in the same way as the first two. An analogy can be written as a sentence or with colons.

See page 79 for some strategies to use with analogies.

  Tree is to forest as star is to galaxy.
  TREE : FOREST :: star : galaxy

Directions On the answer line, write the vocabulary word or a form of it that completes each analogy.

1. ADDITION : BUILDING :: _____ : word (*Lesson 1*)

   1. _____

2. ELUSIVE : CATCH :: _____ : please (*Lesson 2*)

   2. _____

3. NEGLIGENT : CARELESS :: _____ : precise (*Lesson 2*)

   3. _____

4. BIGOT : TOLERANCE :: boor : _____ (*Lesson 3*)

   4. _____

5. ELATED : HAPPY :: _____ : depressed (*Lesson 4*)

   5. _____

6. ORBIT : PLANET :: _____ : missile (*Lesson 4*)

   6. _____

  © Great Source DO NOT COPY

How many of the following expressions do you use to describe the certain and uncertain situations you encounter?

> Rest assured
> On the horns of a dilemma
> No *ifs, and*s or *but*s
> On tenterhooks
> As sure as I live and breathe

The large number of expressions in our language that express certainty and uncertainty seems to confirm the idea that the unpredictable makes us nervous and impatient while the definite leaves us feeling more in control. Although uncertainty is sometimes exciting, people usually prefer not to be in suspense.

The vocabulary words in this lesson describe different aspects of certainty and uncertainty. By studying these words, you will know which ones are appropriate substitutions for the commonly used expressions above.

WORD LIST
apprehensive
categorical
conclusive
dubious
indeterminate
inevitable
precarious
qualm
unequivocal
vacillate

DEFINITIONS

After you have studied the definitions and example for each vocabulary word, write the word on the line to the right.

1. **apprehensive** (ăp′rĭ-hĕn′sĭv) *adjective*   Anxious or fearful about the future; uneasy.

    Related Words **apprehensively** *adverb;* **apprehensiveness** *noun*
    Example   Many students feel *apprehensive* about the first day of school.

    1. _____

2. **categorical** (kăt′ĭ-gôr′ĭ-kəl, kăt′ĭ-gŏr′ĭ-kəl) *adjective*   **a.** Without exception or qualification; positive; absolute.   **b.** Of or in a category. (From the Greek word *katēgorein*, meaning "to assert")

    Related Words **categorically** *adverb;* **category** *noun*
    Example   Alex had the habit of making *categorical* statements that stopped all conversation.

    2. _____

3. **conclusive** (kən-klōō′sĭv) *adjective*   Serving to put an end to doubt, question, or uncertainty; decisive; convincing. (From the Latin word *concludere*, meaning "to end")

    Related Words **conclusively** *adverb;* **conclusiveness** *noun*
    Example   The *conclusive* results of the medical tests indicated that Sally's operation had been successful.

    3. _____

4. **dubious** (dōō′bē-əs, dyōō′bē-əs) *adjective*   **a.** Doubtful; uncertain. **b.** Questionable as to quality or validity: *a dubious scheme.* (From the Latin word *dubius*, meaning "uncertain")

    Related Words **dubiously** *adverb;* **dubiousness** *noun*
    Example   Gretchen was *dubious* about the success of her plan.

    4. _____

© Great Source   DO NOT COPY

5. **indeterminate** (ĭn'dĭ-tûr'mə-nĭt) *adjective* **a.** Not capable of being determined or decided; not precisely known; indefinite. **b.** Lacking clarity or precision; vague: *indeterminate data*

   Example   The amethyst necklace was of an *indeterminate* age.

   5. _____

6. **inevitable** (ĭn-ĕv'ĭ-tə-bəl) *adjective* Incapable of being avoided or prevented. (From the Latin *in-,* meaning "not," and *evitare,* meaning "to avoid")

   Related Words **inevitability** *noun;* **inevitably** *adverb*
   Example   In many places mosquitoes and Japanese beetles are *inevitable* summer irritations.

   6. _____

7. **precarious** (prĭ-kâr'ē-əs) *adjective* Dangerously lacking in security or stability; unsafe; risky.

   Related Words **precariously** *adverb;* **precariousness** *noun*
   Example   After investing heavily in the stock market, Mr. Harrington found himself in a *precarious* financial position.

   7. _____

8. **qualm** (kwäm, kwôm) *noun* **a.** A sensation of doubt or misgiving; uneasiness. **b.** A pang of conscience. **c.** A sudden, brief feeling of sickness, faintness, or nausea.

   Example   The critic hadn't a *qualm* about submitting the negative review of the play.

   8. _____

9. **unequivocal** (ŭn' ĭ-kwĭv'ə-kəl) *adjective* Leaving no doubt or misunderstanding; perfectly clear.

   Related Word **unequivocally** *adverb*
   Example   Meredith answered the question with an *unequivocal* and enthusiastic "Yes!"

   9. _____

10. **vacillate** (văs'ə-lāt') *intrans. verb* To waver indecisively between one course of action or opinion and another; hesitate. (From the Latin word *vacillare,* meaning "to waver")

    Related Word **vacillation** *noun*
    Example   As he waited for the letter, Greg *vacillated* between optimism and pessimism about its contents.

    10. _____

Word History: precarious

Latin: *precari*=to beg or entreat<*prex*=prayer

If you are in a *precarious* position, your situation is risky and unsafe. The word *precarious* comes from the Latin verb *precari,* meaning "to beg or entreat," which in turn comes from the Latin noun *prex,* meaning "prayer." The ancient Romans often prayed to their gods for favors; but although these favors might be granted, they were often considered uncertain and lacking in security. This idea of uncertainty and risk, which the Romans sensed even when they received what they had prayed for, has been transmitted to the modern usage of *precarious.*

© Great Source   DO NOT COPY

EXERCISE 1 COMPLETING DEFINITIONS

On the answer line, write the word from the vocabulary list that best completes
each definition.

1. If a response leaves no doubt or misunderstanding, it is _____.

2. Something that cannot be avoided is _____.

3. Something that is indefinite or that lacks clarity is _____.

4. One who is anxious about the future is _____.

5. If you have a sensation of doubt or misgiving about a decision, you may have
a(n) _____ about it.

6. A person who expresses doubt or uncertainty is _____.

7. Approval that is without exception or qualification is _____.

8. If the results of a scientific experiment were _____, they would be decisive
and final.

9. If a person wavers indecisively between two choices, that person can be said
to _____.

10. Something dangerously lacking security or stability is _____.

1. _____

2. _____

3. _____

4. _____

5. _____

6. _____

7. _____

8. _____

9. _____

10. _____

EXERCISE 2 USING WORDS CORRECTLY

Each of the following questions contains an italicized vocabulary word. Choose the
correct answer to the question, and write *Yes* or *No* on the answer line.

1. Is tightrope-walking a *precarious* activity?

2. Is an *apprehensive* person likely to feel relaxed before giving a public performance?

3. If your answer to a question is *unequivocal,* will others misunderstand you?

4. If you *vacillate,* do you make immediate and decisive choices?

5. Is making the track team *inevitable* for an athlete who will not follow training rules?

6. Is a person who has *qualms* about taking an examination self-confident?

7. Would *categorical* approval of a loan application be likely to secure funds for the
applicant?

8. Can a dog whose breed is *indeterminate* be registered as a Labrador retriever?

9. Might someone who is *dubious* about the safety of flying avoid traveling by airplane?

10. When the results of an election are *conclusive,* is the winner known?

1. _____

2. _____

3. _____

4. _____

5. _____

6. _____

7. _____

8. _____

9. _____

10. _____

EXERCISE 3 CHOOSING THE BEST DEFINITION

For each italicized vocabulary word in the following sentences, write the letter of the
best definition on the answer line.

1. Columbus wanted to obtain *conclusive* evidence that India could be reached by
sailing west from Europe.
   a. leaving no room for doubt   c. further
   b. scientifically valuable   d. immediate

1. _____

2. The painters decided to build a scaffold rather than use the *precarious* ladder.

   a. uncomfortable   **b.** usual   **c.** well-designed   **d.** unstable

2. _____ DO NOT COPY

3. Maude's *categorical* refusal of his marriage proposal left Stanley heartbroken.

   a. immediate   **b.** absolute   **c.** conditional   **d.** uncertain

3. _____

4. People with claustrophobia, or fear of being in closed places, often feel *apprehensive* about riding in elevators.

   a. excited   **b.** determined   **c.** angry   **d.** anxious

4. _____

5. For many months the cause of Legionnaires' disease was *indeterminate*.

   a. not clearly known   **c.** widely publicized

   b. diligently pursued   **d.** under investigation

5. _____

6. After John had accepted the job offer, he had *qualms* about having to move to a new city.

   a. nightmares   **b.** visions   **c.** doubts   **d.** excuses

6. _____

7. Most historians believe that South Carolina's secession from the Union made the Civil War *inevitable*.

   a. not able to be won   **c.** able to be continued

   b. able to be fought   **d.** not able to be avoided

7. _____

8. "Don't give George his choice of movies," said Mona. "We want to make an immediate decision, and he'll *vacillate* for hours.

   a. think   **b.** complain   **c.** waver   **d.** argue

8. _____

9. Even after the Wright brothers' historic flight at Kitty Hawk, the average person was *dubious* about the future of air travel.

   a. afraid   **b.** hopeful   **c.** resigned   **d.** doubtful

9. _____

10. The store owner gave Elise the *unequivocal* guarantee that she could return the bedspread.

   a. clear   **b.** friendly   **c.** natural   **d.** written

10. _____

EXERCISE 4 USING DIFFERENT FORMS OF WORDS

Decide which form of the vocabulary word in parentheses best completes the sentence. The form given may be correct. Write your answer on the answer line.

1. Sue had _____ about borrowing her sister's blouse without asking. (*qualm*)

1. _____

2. Research has shown _____ that fluoride helps prevent tooth decay. (*conclusive*)

2. _____

3. The farther we drove on the narrow dirt road, the more our _____ increased. (*apprehensive*)

3. _____

4. The _____ of contracting certain illnesses has decreased as effective inoculations have been developed. (*inevitable*)

4. _____

5. The senator _____ refused to grant interviews with reporters during a legislative session. (*categorical*)

5. _____

6. The children looked at the magician _____ when he promised to pull a rabbit out of his hat. (*dubious*)

6. _____

7. Someone else's _____ can be extremely frustrating to a decisive person. (*vacillate*)

7. _____

8. When the runaway stagecoach came to a stop, it was perched _____ on the edge of a cliff. (*precarious*)

8. _____

9. The Renoir exhibit was _____ the best art show I've ever seen. (*unequivocal*)

9. _____

10. An _____ number of people attended the concert in the park Saturday night. (*indeterminate*)

10. _____

© Great Source DO NOT COPY

READING COMPREHENSION

Each numbered sentence in the following passage contains an italicized vocabulary word or related form. After you read the passage, you will complete an exercise.

NEW TREATMENT FOR CATARACTS

A cataract is the result of changes that hinder the passage of light through the eye's lens, a transparent capsule located behind the colored iris. The lens helps the eye to focus. Light rays pass through the lens, which bends them and causes them to focus the image on the retina, or the back layer of the eyeball. Because the lens is flexible, it can change shape to help a person focus on the objects at different distances. Thus, clear vision depends on light passing through the lens easily and on the lens focusing correctly.

A cataract begins as a small spot on the lens. Although the spot may interfere slightly with vision, special prescription glasses can correct problems during the early stages. Cataracts may cause blindness by spreading until the entire lens becomes milky white, allowing no light to penetrate.

Cataracts may be caused by injury to the eye or by certain diseases, such as diabetes. However, cataracts are most closely linked to aging. (1) In fact, doctors believe that cataracts *inevitably* cloud most people's vision to some extent by the time they reach the age of eighty.

Although prevention of cataracts is still impossible, doctors can restore sight to most patients. (2) Because of technological advances and new surgical procedures, cataract surgery, in which the clouded lens is removed, has become *unequivocally* one of the most common and successful operations in human surgery.

(3) Seventy years ago, an advanced cataract *categorically* doomed the sufferer to creeping blindness. An operation was then developed, but it was necessary to wait until the cataract was nearly mature because unclouded parts of the lens were difficult to remove. This delay placed patients in a visually disabled state for a long time before an operation could be performed.

(4) The operation itself was a source of *apprehensiveness* for many people. It involved a semi-circular incision in the cornea, after which the surgeon grasped the lens with forceps and pulled it out of the eye. (5) The results of the surgery were *dubious* because the forceps would sometimes rupture the lens, creating fragments that were too small to remove. (6) Many people *vacillated* about having the surgery when they learned that it required four to seven days in the hospital and four to eight weeks of convalescence. (7) In addition, normal vision could not be restored to an *indeterminate* number of people. After recovery, patients were fitted with thick glasses that allowed them to see well only when looking straight ahead.

(8) Few people have *qualms* about cataract surgery today. (9) Several new techniques have proved *conclusively* to be faster and safer. In the 1960s researchers perfected a device for dissolving and removing the cataract through a two- or three-millimeter incision. In the late 1970s, experiments with lasers proved effective in cataract surgery. Light energy concentrated in short, intense pulses could be used to make tiny cuts of $\frac{1}{10}$ millimeter. While the accurate and safe lasers do not remove the cataracts, they have been useful in cutting the membrane that encloses the lens. Both of these devices cause the patient less discomfort and permit the person to return to normal activity sooner than was previously possible. Current operations take approximately five minutes. (10) Thus, elderly patients, whose health may already be *precarious*, do not have the additional risk of lengthy exposure to anesthesia. In some cases the procedure can even be performed in a doctor's office under a local anesthetic.

Once the cloudy lens is out, new methods are also used to restore vision. While some patients may require the heavy glasses of the past, most can use removable contact lenses or permanent lens implants that are maintenance-free. Vision is much more accurate, and both types of lenses may even correct other vision problems. Today most people need no longer suffer from impaired vision or blindness caused by cataracts. Vision can be restored quickly and, in most cases, quite successfully.

READING COMPREHENSION EXERCISE

Each of the following statements corresponds to a numbered sentence in the passage. Each statement contains a blank and is followed by four answer choices. Decide which choice fits best in the blank. The word or phrase that you choose must express roughly the same meaning as the italicized word in the passage. Write the letter of your choice on the answer line.

1. Doctors believe that cataracts will _____ cloud most people's vision by the time they reach the age of eighty.
   a. somewhat **b.** perhaps **c.** rarely **d.** unavoidably

   1. _____

2. Cataract surgery _____ has become one of the most common and successful operations.
   a. without fear **b.** without doubt **c.** happily **d.** obviously

   2. _____

3. Seventy years ago, an advanced cataract _____ doomed the sufferer to creeping blindness.
   a. invariably **b.** statistically **c.** dramatically **d.** selectively

   3. _____

4. The operation caused _____ for many people.
   a. expense **b.** discomfort **c.** anxiety **d.** confusion

   4. _____

5. The results of the surgery were _____.
   a. predictable **b.** uncertain **c.** beneficial **d.** poor

   5. _____

6. Many people _____ about having the surgery.
   a. knew **b.** did research **c.** were angry **d.** hesitated

   6. _____

7. At one time normal vision could not be restored to a(n) _____ number of people.
   a. unknown **c.** handful
   b. small percentage **d.** large

   7. _____

8. Few people have _____ about cataract surgery today.
   a. questions **b.** certainty **c.** doubts **d.** hope

   8. _____

9. That new techniques are faster and safer has been proved _____.
   a. decisively **b.** dramatically **c.** recently **d.** suddenly

   9. _____

10. Thus, elderly patients, whose health may already be _____, do not have the additional risk of lengthy exposure to anesthesia.
    a. uncomfortable **b.** unstable **c.** deteriorated **d.** concerned

    10. _____

WRITING ASSIGNMENT

Suppose that you have just had an important job interview. As you return home, your mind is cluttered with all the questions that you were asked. Some were easy, while others caused you some hesitation. Write a letter to a favorite relative or close friend describing the interview and your reactions to it. In your letter use at least five of the vocabulary words from this lesson and underline each word that you use.

© Great Source   DO NOT COPY

To some people the words *strength* and *defense* suggest military might and war. Others think of these words in connection with sports. Still others associate *strength* and *defense* with such accomplishments as completing a difficult task or arguing for an unpopular idea. In this lesson you will learn words that refer to different aspects of strength and defense.

WORD LIST

assail
bulwark
citadel
fortitude
haven
invincible
mettle
resilient
stalwart
stamina

DEFINITIONS

After you have studied the definitions and example for each vocabulary word, write the word on the line to the right.

1. **assail** (ə-sāl′) *trans. verb* **a.** To attack; assault. **b.** To attack verbally. (From the Latin *ad-*, meaning "onto," and *salire*, meaning "to leap")

   Related Word assailant *noun*
   Example The invading army planned to *assail* the city at dawn.

   1. _____

2. **bulwark** (bŏŏl′wərk, bŭl′wərk) *noun* **a.** A defensive wall; rampart. **b.** Any protection or defense. (From the Middle High German words *bole*, meaning "plank," and *werc*, meaning "work")

   Example The knights gathered behind the *bulwark* as the invaders tried to force their way into the castle.

   2. _____

3. **citadel** (sĭt′ə-dəl, sĭt′ə-dĕl′) *noun* **a.** A fortress in or near a city. **b.** Any stronghold. (From the Latin word *civitas*, meaning "citizenry" or "city")

   Example From high atop the *citadel*, the guard could warn the townspeople of any approaching danger.

   3. _____

4. **fortitude** (fôr′tĭ-tōōd′, fôr′tĭ-tyōōd′) *noun* Strength of mind that allows one to endure pain or trouble with courage. (From the Latin word *fortis*, meaning "strong")

   Example The *fortitude* of the wheelchair athletes competing in the Special Olympics inspired the crowd.

   4. _____

5. **haven** (hā′vən) *noun* **a.** A place of rest or refuge; sanctuary. **b.** A sheltered harbor or port.

   Example The writer's *haven* was a small, comfortable cabin located in the middle of the woods.

   5. _____

6. **invincible** (ĭn-vĭn′sə-bəl) *adjective*   Too strong or great to be defeated; unconquerable. (From the Latin *in-*, meaning "not," and *vincere*, meaning "to conquer")

   Related Words **invincibility** *noun;* **invincibly** *adverb*
   Example The *invincible* football team won the play-off and took home the trophy.

   6. _____

7. **mettle** (mĕt′l) *noun*   **a.** Spirit; daring; pluck.   **b.** A strength of character or purpose equal to a test.

   Example The bold scout showed his *mettle* by riding ahead of the wagon train.

   7. _____

8. **resilient** (rĭ-zĭl′yənt) *adjective*   **a.** Recovering strength or spirits quickly.   **b.** Springing back into position or shape. (From the Latin *re-*, meaning "back," and *salire*, meaning "to leap")

   Related Words **resilience** *noun;* **resiliently** *adverb*
   Example The *resilient* patient recovered from his surgery in a surprisingly short time.

   8. _____

9. **stalwart** (stôl′wərt) *adjective*   **a.** Physically strong; sturdy; robust.   **b.** Resolute; firm.   *noun*   **a.** A sturdy, strong-willed person.   **b.** A loyal supporter.

   Related Words **stalwartly** *adverb;* **stalwartness** *noun*
   Example The *stalwart* gatekeeper successfully kept the enemy from crossing the bridge.

   9. _____

10. **stamina** (stăm′ə-nə) *noun*   Endurance; resistance to fatigue, illness, or hardship.

   Example The swimmer needed great *stamina* to complete fifty laps at the Olympic-sized pool.

   10. _____

© Great Source DO NOT COPY

EXERCISE 1 MATCHING WORDS AND DEFINITIONS

Match the definition in Column B with the word in Column A. Write the letter of the correct definition on the answer line.

Column A	Column B	
1. invincible	a. to attack physically or verbally	1. _____
2. citadel	b. courage in the face of hardship	2. _____
3. assail	c. endurance; staying power	3. _____
4. fortitude	d. a defensive wall	4. _____
5. bulwark	e. pluck or daring	5. _____
6. stamina	f. a fortress or stronghold	6. _____
7. mettle	g. recovering strength or spirits quickly; springy	7. _____
8. resilient	h. unable to be defeated	8. _____
9. haven	i. physically strong or sturdy	9. _____
10. stalwart	j. a place of rest or refuge	10. _____

EXERCISE 2 USING WORDS CORRECTLY

Each of the following statements contains an italicized vocabulary word. Decide whether the sentence is true or false, and write *True* or *False* on the answer line.

1. Because he tired so easily, the racehorse Rolling Thunder was known for his *stamina*.   1. _____

2. A boxing champion who had won one hundred consecutive matches might be described as *invincible*.   2. _____

3. If caught in a heavy storm while mountain climbing, you might look for a *haven*.   3. _____

4. Harold was quick to *assail* the bully by running in the opposite direction.   4. _____

5. The cozy *citadel* in the middle of town offered tasty early-bird dinners.   5. _____

6. *Stalwart* people are not easily swayed from their convictions.   6. _____

7. Most people avoided Jason because he always tried to *mettle* in their business.   7. _____

8. Glass shatters when hit with a hammer because it is remarkably *resilient*.   8. _____

9. The early Pilgrims needed great *fortitude* to endure their harsh living conditions. 9. _____

10. Towering *bulwarks* are popular rides at amusement parks.   10. _____

EXERCISE 3 IDENTIFYING SYNONYMS AND ANTONYMS

Decide which word or phrase has the meaning that is the same as (a synonym) or opposite to (an antonym) that of the capitalized vocabulary word. Write the letter of your choice on the answer line.

1. RESILIENT (antonym):   1. _____
   a. springy   b. soft   c. brittle   d. bumpy

2. ASSAIL (synonym):   2. _____
   a. protect   b. provoke   c. surrender   d. attack

3. FORTITUDE (antonym):
   a. courage   **b.** bravery   **c.** cowardice   **d.** indifference

3. _____

4. CITADEL (synonym):
   a. armor   **b.** fortress   **c.** skyscraper   **d.** town center

4. _____

5. INVINCIBLE (antonym):
   a. quickly forgotten   **c.** not athletic
   b. often victorious   **d.** easily defeated

5. _____

6. STAMINA (synonym):
   a. endurance   **b.** enthusiasm   **c.** incentive   **d.** ability

6. _____

7. BULWARK (synonym):
   a. rampart   **b.** breakwater   **c.** support beam   **d.** castle

7. _____

8. HAVEN (synonym):
   a. pier   **b.** sanctuary   **c.** restaurant   **d.** hotel

8. _____

9. STALWART (antonym):
   a. immobile   **b.** unending   **c.** enduring   **d.** weak

9. _____

10. METTLE (antonym):
    a. gossip   **b.** spirit   **c.** weakness   **d.** strength

10. _____

EXERCISE 4 USING DIFFERENT FORMS OF WORDS

Decide which form of the vocabulary word in parentheses best completes the sentence. The form given may be correct. Write your answer on the answer line.

1. The sheriff was successful in apprehending the masked _____. *(assail)*

1. _____

2. The human body shows great _____ in healing itself after serious injury. *(resilient)*

2. _____

3. One of the most grueling tests of _____ is the triathlon, which involves extensive swimming, bicycling, and running. *(stamina)*

3. _____

4. Touring an old _____ was the first item on the tourist's itinerary. *(citadel)*

4. _____

5. The bully's challenge tested Bobby's _____ as an athlete. *(mettle)*

5. _____

6. To earn the Congressional Medal of Honor, a soldier must show great _____. *(fortitude)*

6. _____

7. Belief in the _____ of the Spanish navy came to an abrupt end in 1588, when the British navy defeated the Spanish Armada. *(invincible)*

7. _____

8. In the Netherlands dikes are frequently used as _____ against the sea. *(bulwark)*

8. _____

9. The stray cat found a _____ in an abandoned shed. *(haven)*

9. _____

10. The old automobile ran _____ for over one hundred thousand miles before the transmission died. *(stalwart)*

10. _____

© Great Source   DO NOT COPY

READING COMPREHENSION

Each numbered sentence in the following passage contains an italicized vocabulary word or related form. After you read the passage, you will complete an exercise.

THE TROJAN HORSE

(1) According to Homer's *Odyssey*, an epic poem about the hero Odysseus' return from the Trojan War, the Greeks did not win the war by *fortitude* alone. (2) Their victory depended upon the execution of a brilliant plan devised by their *invincible* leader Odysseus.

The Trojan War began as an indirect result of a beauty competition among three goddesses. The unfortunate judge, Paris of Troy, chose the goddess Aphrodite, who promised him that the fairest woman in the world would be his. The woman was Helen, wife of Menelaus, the king of Sparta.

At Aphrodite's suggestion, Paris wangled an invitation to Menelaus' palace. He then kidnapped Helen and took her to Troy. (3) Furious at Paris' treachery, Menelaus enlisted all the able-bodied men in Greece to form an army and to *assail* Troy. Their goal was to return Helen safely to Greece.

In addition to the Greek commander-in-chief, Agamemnon, Menelaus requested the services of two great warriors, Odysseus and Achilles. (4) For different reasons both were initially reluctant to show their *mettle* in this particular war. Odysseus did not believe in the cause, and Achilles was fated to die if he ever went to Troy. In the end both Achilles and Odysseus boarded one of the thousand ships that sailed to Troy.

Although fiercely determined, the Greeks were not to have an easy victory. There were many deaths and setbacks on both sides. (5) The Greeks and Trojans were forced to battle for many years, and the *stamina* of the men on both sides declined. (6) As

they fought skirmish after skirmish, however, the *resilience* of the two armies made a decisive victory for either side impossible. The Greeks and the Trojans seemed to have reached a stalemate. (7) The Greeks could not enter Troy and storm the city because towering *bulwarks* protected it. (8) It was also at this point that the *stalwart* Greek leader Achilles was shot by an arrow and killed.

After the death of Achilles, the Greeks began to feel that they would never win the war. The course of the war changed entirely, however, when Odysseus devised the scheme of the Trojan horse. Odysseus knew that in order to defeat the Trojans, the Greek soldiers needed to get inside the city walls. To accomplish this goal, he instructed a worker to make a huge, hollow wooden horse that could hold a number of men. How to persuade the Trojans to take the horse inside the city gates was a difficult problem.

Finally, Odysseus asked one Greek soldier, Sinon, to stay behind and tell the Trojans a story that would

make them want to take the horse into the city. Sinon claimed that the horse had been left behind to appease the angry gods, who were offended by the Greek theft of a sacred image of the goddess Pallas Athena from the city of Troy. Sinon went on to say that an oracle had advised the Greeks to give up the war and return to their homeland at once. As a gesture of atonement, they had left the wooden horse behind. (9) The deluded Trojans, rejoicing in their "victory," pushed the enormous horse past the *citadel* and inside the city walls.

Later that night, when all the Trojans were asleep, the hollow belly of the horse opened and out jumped a group of Greek soldiers. (10) They quickly signaled to the remaining Greek troops who, up until this point, had been hiding in the *haven* of a nearby island. In a short time, the powerful Greeks destroyed Troy, retrieved Helen, and at last sailed toward Greece, a land that they had not seen for many years.

READING COMPREHENSION EXERCISE

Each of the following statements corresponds to a numbered sentence in the passage. Each statement contains a blank and is followed by four answer choices. Decide which choice fits best in the blank. The word or phrase that you choose must express roughly the same meaning as the italicized word in the passage. Write the letter of your choice on the answer line.

1. The Greeks were not able to win the Trojan War by _____ alone.
   a. strategy   **b.** strength of mind   **c.** excellence   **d.** battle plans

2. Their victory depended on the _____ leader Odysseus.
   a. ferocious   **b.** clever   **c.** unconquerable   **d.** unparalleled

3. Menelaus ordered the Greek army to _____ Troy.
   a. attack   **b.** trick   **c.** challenge   **d.** outwit

4. Odysseus and Achilles hesitated to show their _____ in the proposed war.
   a. cowardice   **b.** leadership   **c.** loyalty   **d.** daring

5. Before the war was over, the _____ of both sides decreased.
   a. endurance   **b.** courage   **c.** supplies   **d.** determination

6. Both armies had an unusual _____, however.
   a. number of casualties   **c.** ability to recover quickly
   b. number of reserves   **d.** overconfidence

7. Troy was protected by tall _____.
   a. defensive walls   **b.** watery moats   **c.** cannons   **d.** trees

8. The _____ Greek leader Achilles was killed.
   a. friendly   **b.** inspiring   **c.** resolute   **d.** headstrong

9. The Greeks tricked the Trojans into pulling the wooden horse past the _____.
   a. entrance   **b.** fortress   **c.** shipyard   **d.** arsenal

10. A nearby island had provided a(n) _____ for the Greek troops.
    a. location   **b.** vacation   **c.** refuge   **d.** opportunity

1. _____
2. _____
3. _____
4. _____
5. _____
6. _____
7. _____
8. _____
9. _____
10. _____

WRITING ASSIGNMENT

In your study of history, you have probably learned about the warfare that has gone on between people throughout the ages. Take the point of view of a textbook writer and select a period of history that interests you. Find an important battle within this period. As concisely as you can, relate the highlights of this conflict. Use five words from this lesson and underline each one.

VOCABULARY ENRICHMENT

Stamina, which appears in this lesson, is the plural of the Latin word *stamen*, which means "thread." This word has its ancient origins in the terminology of weaving. In Roman times the *stamen* was the warp, or lengthwise thread, in an upright loom. Because of its supporting position in the loom, the *stamen* had to be very strong. As time went by, people metaphorically associated *stamen* with the idea of strength. Today we use *stamina* in this same way to mean "endurance or strength that lasts."

Activity Using your dictionary, look up the following words and write their principal meanings and their Latin roots. Then, in a sentence or two, explain the connection between the root and the meaning.

1. linear   2. filament   3. filigree   4. acumen   5. acute

© Great Source   DO NOT COPY

TEST-TAKING SKILLS
ANTONYM TEST ITEMS

Standardized tests, as well as classroom vocabulary tests, often contain sections on antonyms. **Antonyms** are words whose meanings are opposite or nearly opposite. Examples are *sad* and *happy,* and *modest* and *arrogant.* Answering antonym test items requires careful thought, for you often need to know slight differences in word meanings in order to select the correct answer. The strategies below will help you.

STRATEGIES

1. *Read all of the answer choices and eliminate those that are incorrect.* The first possible answer may not be the best choice.

2. *Be sure to eliminate answer choices that are synonyms.* To mislead you, a synonym, a word similar in meaning to the given word, is sometimes offered as an answer. The following test item illustrates the use of misleading answer choices.

   VAPID: (A) vigilant   (B) dry   (C) lifeless   (D) lively   (E) likely

   Vapid is an adjective meaning "lacking liveliness, zest, or interest." The third choice, *lifeless,* is a synonym of *vapid* and must therefore be eliminated.

3. *Watch for other misleading choices.* Tests often contain other incorrect answers that may fool you if you are not on the alert for them. In the sample item above, choice B, *dry,* suggests that *vapid* might mean "having vapor"; however, *vapid* does not have this meaning. Furthermore, choices D and E look very much alike and could mislead a student who is working too quickly.

4. *Choose the word most opposite in meaning to the given word.* Test items may include more than one possible antonym. The sample test item includes both *vigilant,* "on the alert; watchful," and *lively,* "full of life, energy, or activity; vigorous." *Lively* is more nearly opposite in meaning to *vapid* than is the word *vigilant.* It is, therefore, the correct answer.

5. *Use your knowledge of prefixes, suffixes, and roots.* What you know about word parts may help you figure out the meanings of words about which you are doubtful. For example, if you did not already know the meaning of *lifeless,* you could recall that *-less* means "without" and use this knowledge to help you eliminate that answer choice. It is never a good idea to guess wildly, but guessing may be sensible when you have a reasonable basis for eliminating one or more answer choices.

In each of the following items, select the word that is most nearly opposite in meaning to the word in capital letters. Write the letter of your choice on the answer line. Use your dictionary as needed.

1. ABSTRACT: (A) general   (B) absolute   (C) concrete   (D) conclusive   (E) apathetic   1. _____

2. BLEAK: (A) stark   (B) inscrutable   (C) cherished   (D) cheerful   (E) concrete   2. _____

3. CHAOTIC: (A) confused   (B) quite   (C) ornate   (D) bedraggled   (E) orderly   3. _____

4. AMBIGUOUS: (A) amenable   (B) straightforward   (C) devious   (D) dishonest   (E) orthodox   4. _____

5. IMPOVERISHED: (A) affluent   (B) abandoned   (C) impressionable   (D) transparent   (E) needy   5. _____

6. EXPEDITE: (A) convoke   (B) proceed   (C) facilitate   (D) disavow   (E) hamper   6. _____

7. DEVOUT: (A) pious   (B) attentive   (C) conservative   (D) irreverent   (E) irrelevant   7. _____

8. DISPARAGE: (A) depreciate   (B) esteem   (C) belittle   (D) scatter   (E) criticize   8. _____

9. VETERAN: (A) novice   (B) old   (C) experienced   (D) military   (E) nomadic   9. _____

10. JEOPARDY: (A) hazard   (B) jubilation   (C) safety   (D) envy   (E) comedy   10. _____

11. LOATHE: (A) attract   (B) love   (C) shackle   (D) detest   (E) vilify   11. _____

12. MERITORIOUS: (A) notorious   (B) public   (C) noteworthy   (D) praiseworthy   (E) blameworthy   12. _____

13. MALICIOUS: (A) tasty   (B) kind   (C) hostile   (D) unsavory   (E) false   13. _____

14. FASTIDIOUS: (A) slovenly   (B) solitary   (C) retarded   (D) meticulous   (E) ugly   14. _____

15. DEARTH: (A) cleanliness   (B) bounty   (C) plethora   (D) life   (E) disease   15. _____

© Great Source DO NOT COPY

The Latin root -*cred*- serves as the core of many of our English words. Words such as *credit*, which can refer to belief in a buyer's ability to fulfill financial obligations, and *credible*, which means "capable of being believed," come from the Latin verb *credere*, meaning "to believe." In this lesson you will learn other words that are derived from -*cred*- and are connected in some way with believing.

WORD LIST

accredit
credence
credential
credibility
creditable
credulous
creed
discredit
incredible
miscreant

DEFINITIONS

After you have studied the definitions and example for each vocabulary word, write the word on the line to the right.

1. **accredit** (ə-krĕd′ĭt) *trans. verb*   **a.** To recognize as having met official standards. **b.** To ascribe or attribute to; credit with: *accredit Galileo with the invention of the pendulum.*   **c.** To authorize: *accredit an ambassador.* (From the Latin *ad-*, meaning "to," and *credere,* meaning "to believe")

   Related Word   **accreditation** *noun*
   Example   The state board of education had the power to *accredit* all schools in the county.

   1. _____

2. **credence** (krēd′ns) *noun*   **a.** Acceptance as true or valid; belief.   **b.** Claim to acceptance; trustworthiness. (From the Latin word *credere*)

   Example   Mrs. Payne always reminds us not to give *credence* to gossip.

   2. _____

3. **credential** (krĭ-dĕn′shəl) *noun*   **a.** Something that entitles a person to confidence, credit, or authority.   **b.** A letter or other written evidence of a person's qualifications or status; a reference. (From the Latin word *credere*)

   Example   The Days lacked the *credentials* for a large business loan.

   3. _____

4. **credibility** (krĕd′ə-bĭl′ĭ-tē) *noun*   **a.** The quality of deserving confidence; plausibility; reliability.   **b.** Readiness to believe: *challenges the reader's credibility.* (From the Latin word *credere*)

   Related Word   **credible** *adjective*
   Example   The magazine article lacked *credibility* because of its many factual errors.

   4. _____
   See *credulous.*

5. **creditable** (krĕd′ĭ-tə-bəl) *adjective* Deserving commendation; praiseworthy. (From the Latin word *credere*)

   Related Words **creditability** *noun* **creditably** *adverb*
   Example Although she lacked experience as a diplomat, she did a *creditable* job of defending the interests of her country.

5. _____

6. **credulous** (krĕj′ə-ləs) *adjective* Tending to believe too readily; easily deceived; gullible. (From the Latin word *credere*)

   Related Words **credulity** *noun;* **credulously** *adverb*
   Example When "War of the Worlds" was first heard on radio, many *credulous* people were convinced that Earth was being invaded by Martians.

6. _____

USAGE NOTE: Don't confuse *credible*, "believable," with *credulous*, "believing too readily."

7. **creed** (krēd) *noun* Any statement or system of belief, principles, or opinions that guides a person's actions. (From the Latin word *credo*, meaning "I believe")

7. _____

8. **discredit** (dĭs-krĕd′ĭt) *trans. verb* **a.** To cast doubt on; destroy belief, faith, or trust in. **b.** To damage in reputation; disgrace. **c.** To refuse to believe in. *noun* **a.** Doubt; lack of belief or trust. **b.** Loss or damage to one's reputation. **c.** Something that brings disgrace or distrust. (From the Latin *dis-*, meaning "not," and *credere*)

   Example A substantial body of scientific evidence has *discredited* the theory that human skull size is related to intelligence.

8. _____

9. **incredible** (ĭn-krĕd′ə-bəl) *adjective* **a.** Too extraordinary to be possible. **b.** Astonishing; amazing. (From the Latin *in-*, meaning "not," and *credere*)

   Related Word **incredibly** *adverb*
   Example Pam's *incredible* talent for computer programming enabled her to write sophisticated programs after only three weeks of training.

9. _____

10. **miscreant** (mĭs′krē-ənt) *noun* A person who behaves badly or criminally; villain. *adjective* Wicked; base. (From the Old French word *mescreant*, meaning "heretic," which is derived from the Latin words *minus*, meaning "less" or "lacking," and *credere*)

    Example The police searched for the *miscreant* who had committed the robberies.

10. _____

© Great Source   DO NOT COPY

EXERCISE 1 WRITING CORRECT WORDS

On the answer line, write the word from the vocabulary list that fits each definition.

1. A system of beliefs of principles that guides a person's actions

2. Something that entitles a person to confidence, credit, or authority; written evidence of a person's qualifications

3. Tending to believe too readily; gullible

4. A person who behaves badly or criminally; villain

5. Acceptance as true or valid; trustworthiness

6. Too extraordinary to be possible; astonishing

7. The quality of deserving confidence; readiness to believe

8. To recognize as having met official standards; attribute to

9. To cast doubt on; disgrace

10. Deserving commendation; praiseworthy

1. _____

2. _____

3. _____

4. _____

5. _____

6. _____

7. _____

8. _____

9. _____

10. _____

EXERCISE 2 USING WORDS CORRECTLY

Decide whether the italicized vocabulary word has been used correctly in the sentence. On the answer line, write *Correct* for correct use or *Incorrect* for incorrect use.

1. The lawyer was unable to *discredit* either the witness or her testimony.

2. Before you select a doctor, you should thoroughly check his or her *credentials*.

3. The *credence* of the ocean pulled Kevin's boat farther out to sea.

4. Self-discipline was an important aspect of the ancient Spartan *creed*.

5. Gerry has a *creditable* and chairs set up in the game room.

6. Shirley's father refuses to carry *accredit* card.

7. Only an expert can tell if this mushroom is the *incredible* kind that won't make people sick.

8. The judge fined the *miscreants* for damaging city property.

9. Jay brought samples of Mesozoic and *credulous* rock formations to class.

10. Once April had established her *credibility*, she was the most respected reporter on the newspaper staff.

1. _____

2. _____

3. _____

4. _____

5. _____

6. _____

7. _____

8. _____

9. _____

10. _____

EXERCISE 3 CHOOSING THE BEST WORD

Decide which vocabulary word or related form best expresses the meaning of the italicized word or phrase in the sentence. On the answer line, write the letter of the correct choice.

1. Rolfe lives by a *system of beliefs* from which he never deviates.
   a. credence   b. miscreant   c. creed   d. credential

1. _____

2. Adam, my three-year-old brother, is an *easily deceived* little boy.

   a. credulous   **b.** accredited   **c.** incredible   **d.** discredited

   2. _____

3. Using quotations from reference books gives *validity* to the term papers that you write.

   a. credence   **b.** creed   **c.** accreditation   **d.** credulity

   3. _____

4. Louisa lost her *ability to be believed* when she kept "crying wolf" about how sick she was.

   a. miscreants   **b.** credibility   **c.** credentials   **d.** creed

   4. _____

5. Darnell *cast doubt on* Dr. Stabrose's theory by proving that birds can communicate through the use of symbols.

   a. accredited   **b.** miscreant   **c.** credence   **d.** discredited

   5. _____

6. Michael is compiling his *qualifications* for his first job interview.

   a. credence   **b.** credentials   **c.** accreditation   **d.** discredit

   6. _____

7. Although the poor folk of Nottingham thought Robin Hood was a hero, the sheriff thought he was a *villain*.

   a. credence   **b.** credential   **c.** miscreant   **d.** creed

   7. _____

8. Joshua read an *astonishing* account of a man who survived a fall from an airplane.

   a. creditable   **b.** credulous   **c.** discredited   **d.** incredible

   8. _____

9. The committee was proud to *authorize* the institute's program of studies.

   a. credence   **b.** accredit   **c.** credential   **d.** discredit

   9. _____

10. Celia's intentions are *worthy of praise;* let's hope she succeeds.

   a. creditable   **b.** incredible   **c.** credulous   **d.** credible

   10. _____

EXERCISE 4 USING DIFFERENT FORMS OF WORDS

Decide which form of the vocabulary word in parentheses best completes the sentence. The form given may be correct. Write your answer on the answer line.

1. The college lost its _____ when the committee learned that graduate teaching assistants were not supervised. *(accredit)*

   1. _____

2. Barbara's _____ make her an ideal applicant for this job. *(credential)*

   2. _____

3. The historian spoke _____ about the Civil War. *(creditable)*

   3. _____

4. Even though she was only a freshman, Willa made the varsity track team because she was an _____ fast runner. *(incredible)*

   4. _____

5. "Do unto others as you would have them do unto you" is the _____ known as the golden rule. *(creed)*

   5. _____

6. The type of rock formations found in Idaho give _____ to the theory that a volcano once erupted there. *(credence)*

   6. _____

7. Your short story would be more _____ if you left out a few of the coincidental meetings. *(credibility)*

   7. _____

8. The Aztecs' _____ allowed Cortés to be treated as a god at first. *(credulous)*

   8. _____

9. Consumers need someone to _____ the false claims of advertisers. *(discredit)*

   9. _____

10. When you are in a crowd, watch out for the _____ who pick pockets. *(miscreant)*

   10. _____

READING COMPREHENSION

Each numbered sentence in the following passage contains an italicized vocabulary word or related form. After you read the passage, you will complete an exercise.

HEROINES OF THE AMERICAN REVOLUTION

"You may destroy all the men in America, and we will still have enough to do to defeat the women." (1) With these words a British army officer paid tribute to the *incredible* heroism of the women who took part in the Revolutionary War. (2) After British policies of limiting economic freedom and self-government had been *discredited* by the colonists, women fought long and hard in a variety of ways for the cause of independence.

(3) Some women did a *creditable* job of supporting the Revolutionary War simply by encouraging men to support it. (4) In Lancaster, Pennsylvania, for example, women formed an association, pledging that they would marry only those men who believed in the revolutionary *creed* and served in the army. (5) It is said that no traitor to the Revolution ever dared to challenge the *credibility* of any of the women by proposing marriage.

Many women played typical but important roles in the Revolution. They mended uniforms, carried water, and nursed the wounded. As they watched the men and their families go off to war, they assumed responsibility for running their farms and plantations. Sometimes these women used hatchets, muskets, farm implements, and even such improvised weapons as pots of boiling lye to defend their families from British troops. (6) When the British raided Nancy Hale's home in Georgia, for example, she held the *miscreants* at gunpoint until American troops arrived.

Although they stayed at home, many women exhibited unusual bravery. Emily Geiger of South Carolina was stopped by British soldiers while carrying a message to an American general. Having memorized the message, she tore it into pieces and swallowed it before the soldiers noticed. (7) Thinking that she meant no harm, the *credulous* British let her pass, and she successfully delivered the information. (8) The story of fifteen-year-old Susanna Bolling of Virginia lends *credence* to the fact that young people did their best to support the cause. When she overheard British troops discussing military strategy, Susanna crossed the Appomattox River to deliver the information to General de Lafayette.

(9) A few women earned their *credentials* as heroines on the battlefield. Deborah Sampson of Massachusetts was the first female soldier in the American army. Disguising herself as a man, she enlisted in the army under the name of Robert Shurtleff. Sampson served for over a year in the Fourth Massachusetts regiment and was commended as an outstanding soldier. She reputedly removed a musketball from her own thigh with a penknife rather than risk discovery by allowing a doctor to do it.

Mary Ludwig Hays McCauley and Margaret Cochran Corbin followed their husbands to war. At first both women cooked, nursed the wounded, and carried water. In fact, Mary McCauley earned her nickname "Molly Pitcher" by bringing pitchers of water to the thirsty troops. Both women observed gun drill so carefully that they were capable gunners when circumstances forced them to become artillerywomen. (10) As a reward for her bravery in the Battle of Monmouth, George Washington *accredited* Molly Pitcher as a noncommissioned officer. Margaret Corbin, wounded in battle, was the first woman to collect a federal pension as compensation for her disability. She was also the only veteran of the Revolution to be buried at West Point.

The women of the Revolutionary War were true heroines. With strength, courage, and dedication, they helped the struggling colonies to win independence.

Each of the following statements corresponds to a numbered sentence in the passage. Each statement contains a blank and is followed by four answer choices. Decide which choice fits best in the blank. The word or phrase that you choose must express roughly the same meaning as the italicized word in the passage. Write the letter of your choice on the answer line.

1. A British officer paid tribute to the _____ heroism of the women who took part in the Revolutionary War.
   a. rare **b.** astonishing **c.** famous **d.** typical

 1. _____

2. The colonists _____ British policies of limiting economic freedom and self-government.
   a. cast doubt on **c.** adopted
   b. overturned **d.** remained loyal to

 2. _____

3. Some women did a _____ job of supporting the Revolutionary War.
   a. sophisticated **b.** generous **c.** predictable **d.** praiseworthy

 3. _____

4. Women in Lancaster, Pennsylvania, pledged that they would marry only men who believed in the revolutionary _____ .
   a. war **b.** policy of rebellion **c.** ideal **d.** system of belief

 4. _____

5. Traitors to the Revolution never challenged the women's _____ .
   a. decisions **c.** capacity for enthusiasm
   b. reliability **d.** reservations

 5. _____

6. Nancy Hale held the _____ at gunpoint.
   a. British **b.** spies **c.** villains **d.** robbers

 6. _____

7. The _____ British let Emily Geiger deliver her message.
   a. gullible **b.** courageous **c.** hostile **d.** innocent

 7. _____

8. The story of Susanna Bolling gives _____ to the idea that young people supported the cause.
   a. excitement **b.** interest **c.** validity **d.** perspective

 8. _____

9. A few women earned their heroic _____ on the battlefields.
   a. awards **b.** status **c.** salaries **d.** evaluations

 9. _____

10. George Washington _____ Molly Pitcher as a noncommissioned officer.
    a. happily recognized **c.** courageously recognized
    b. officially recognized **d.** once recognized

 10. _____

PRACTICE WITH ANALOGIES

See page 79 for some strategies to use with analogies.

Directions Write the vocabulary word or a form of it that completes each analogy.

1. CREDIBLE : BELIEVABLE :: _____ : absolute *(Lesson 5)*

 1. _____

2. CONQUER : INVINCIBLE :: avoid : _____ *(Lesson 5)*

 2. _____

3. REFUGEE : ASYLUM :: ship : _____ *(Lesson 6)*

 3. _____

4. ADHERENT : PARTY :: _____ : cause *(Lesson 6)*

 4. _____

5. SHATTER : MYTH :: _____ : belief *(Lesson 7)*

 5. _____

6. LOAFER : LAZY :: _____ : wicked *(Lesson 7)*

 6. _____

7. EXPLORER : CURIOUS :: skeptic : _____ *(Lesson 5)*

 7. _____

8. SCHEMER : DEVIOUS :: simpleton : _____ *(Lesson 7)*

 8. _____

© Great Source DO NOT COPY

How do you spend your time on a warm summer day? Would you prefer to lie in a hammock and read a mystery novel or take a bike trip? Would you rather have an animated conversation with a group of friends or think quietly by yourself?

Your answers to these questions depend on the situation and your mood. Although everyone has his or her preferences for particular pastimes, most people tend to enjoy both vigorous and less active pursuits. The words in this lesson will help you to express the degree of movement that you encounter.

WORD LIST

alacrity
composure
ennui
imperturbable
impetuous
incite
indolent
inert
pandemonium
serenity

DEFINITIONS

After you have studied the definitions and example for each vocabulary word, write the word on the line to the right.

1. **alacrity** (ə-lăk′rĭ-tē) *noun*   Speed and willingness in acting or responding; cheerful readiness; eagerness. (From the Latin word *alacritas*, meaning "lively")

   Example   Carmella accepted our invitation with *alacrity*.

   1. _____

2. **composure** (kəm-pō′zhər) *noun*   Control over one's emotions; steadiness of manner; tranquility. (From the Latin *com-*, meaning "together," and *ponere*, meaning "to put")

   Related Words **compose** *verb;* **composed** *adjective*
   Example   Theodore Roosevelt was famous for his *composure* in stressful situations.

   2. _____

3. **ennui** (ŏn-wē′, ŏn′wē) *noun*   Listlessness and dissatisfaction resulting from inactivity or lack of interest; boredom. (From the French word *ennui*, meaning "boredom")

   Example   Mrs. Keller suggested finger painting as a way to relieve the children's rainy-day *ennui*.

   3. _____

4. **imperturbable** (ĭm′pər-tûr′bə-bəl) *adjective*   Not easily disturbed or excited; unshakably calm and collected.

   Related Words **imperturbability** *noun;* **imperturbably** *adverb*
   Example   The *imperturbable* cat slept in the sun, ignoring butterflies and bees that flew around it.

   4. _____

5. **impetuous** (ĭm-pĕch′ oo-əs) *adjective*   Tending toward suddenness and boldness of action; impulsive; hasty. (From the Latin *in-*, meaning "against," and *petere,* meaning "to go toward" or "to seek")

   Related Words **impetuously** *adverb;* **impetuousness** *noun*
   Example   Dirk's *impetuous* decisions often get him into trouble.

   5. _____

6. **incite** (ĭn-sīt′) *trans. verb*   To provoke to action; rouse; stir up or urge on. (From the Latin word *incitare,* meaning "to urge forward")

   Related Word   **incitement** *noun*
   Example   The cheerleaders and fans *incited* the football team to victory.

   6. _____

7. **indolent** (ĭn′də-lənt) *adjective*   **a.** Reluctant to exert oneself; habitually lazy. **b.** Suggesting a calm idleness and ease. (From the Latin *in-*, meaning "not," and *dolere,* meaning "to feel pain")

   Related Words **indolence** *noun;* **indolently** *adverb*
   Example   Margaret gave an *indolent* sigh as she stretched out in the deck chair.

   7. _____

8. **inert** (ĭn-ûrt′) *adjective*   **a.** Having no power to move or act; lifeless. **b.** Exhibiting no chemical activity. (From the Latin *in-*, meaning "not," and *ars,* meaning "skill")

   Related Words **inertia** *noun;* **inertly** *adverb*
   Example   The new mayor had no patience with the *inert* city council.

   8. _____

9. **pandemonium** (păn′ də-mō′nē-əm) *noun*   **a.** Wild uproar or noise; tumult. **b.** A place of wild disorder and confusion. (Coined by the poet John Milton from the Greek *pan-*, meaning "all," and *daimon,* meaning "spirit" or "demon")

   Example   *Pandemonium* occurred at Leslie's house when a family of five raccoons got in through the attic.

   9. _____

10. **serenity** (sə-rĕn′ĭ-tē) *noun*   The quality of being untroubled or unruffled; peacefulness. (From the Latin word *serenus,* meaning "clear")

    Related Words **serene** *adjective;* **serenely** *adverb*
    Example   The painting of the landscape conveyed a sense of *serenity.*

    10. _____

© Great Source   DO NOT COPY

EXERCISE 1 COMPLETING DEFINITIONS

On the answer line, write the word from the vocabulary list that best completes each definition.

1. The quality of being unruffled or untroubled is _____ .

2. To provoke to action or to urge on is to _____ .

3. If something lacks the power to move or act, it is _____ .

4. Control of one's emotions is _____ .

5. Speed and willingness in acting or responding is _____ .

6. Listlessness from inactivity or lack of interest is _____ .

7. Someone who tends toward suddenness and boldness of action is _____ .

8. Wild uproar or loud noise is called _____ .

9. Someone who is not easily disturbed or excited is _____ .

10. Someone who is reluctant to exert himself or herself is _____ .

1. _____

2. _____

3. _____

4. _____

5. _____

6. _____

7. _____

8. _____

9. _____

10. _____

EXERCISE 2 USING WORDS CORRECTLY

Each of the following statements contains an italicized vocabulary word. Decide whether the sentence is true or false and write *True* or *False* on the answer line.

1. An *impetuous* person gives careful thought to each decision.

2. Firefighters respond with *alacrity* to every alarm.

3. Most children would be filled with *ennui* at an amusement park.

4. *Pandemonium* might occur if a tiger escaped from the zoo.

5. An *indolent* person is highly energetic.

6. A spinning top is an *inert* object.

7. An orator who *incites* an audience calms it.

8. A goalie with *composure* would remain calm even when failing to block a shot.

9. A poet who describes the *serenity* of a facial expression is describing its peacefulness.

10. A newscaster who is easily disturbed by activity in the newsroom can be said to be *imperturbable*.

1. _____

2. _____

3. _____

4. _____

5. _____

6. _____

7. _____

8. _____

9. _____

10. _____

EXERCISE 3 CHOOSING THE BEST WORD

Decide which vocabulary word or related form best expresses the meaning of the italicized word or phrase in the sentence. On the answer line, write the letter of the correct choice.

1. *A wild uproar* greeted the announcement that the math team had won the state championship.
   a. Serenity   **b.** Ennui   **c.** Pandemonium   **d.** Alacrity

1. _____

© Great Source   DO NOT COPY   Activity and Inactivity   **49**

2. Helium is an *inactive* gas.
   a. inert   **b.** indolent   **c.** serene   **d.** impetuous

2. _____

3. People sometimes regret *impulsive* actions.
   a. indolent   **b.** impetuous   **c.** composed   **d.** inert

3. _____

4. The *peacefulness* of the beach in late afternoon was suddenly disturbed by the cries of sea gulls.
   a. inertia   **b.** pandemonium   **c.** composure   **d.** serenity

4. _____

5. *Spurred on* by the excited voice of the jockey, Classic Damsel crossed the finish line several lengths ahead of the other horses.
   a. Impetuous   **b.** Indolent   **c.** Incited   **d.** Serene

5. _____

6. Overcome with *listlessness*, Everett waited for a strong breeze to fill the sails of the boat.
   a. pandemonium   **b.** ennui   **c.** composure   **d.** alacrity

6. _____

7. Mrs. Rassias volunteered with *cheerful willingness* to read to the patients in local hospitals.
   a. alacrity   **b.** indolence   **c.** ennui   **d.** composure

7. _____

8. Grandmother's favorite reminder for any task is "*Habitual laziness* never won the war."
   a. Serenity   **b.** Composure   **c.** Pandemonium   **d.** Indolence

8. _____

9. Sidney's *emotional control* was momentarily shaken by a shout of "Surprise!"
   a. serenity   **b.** ennui   **c.** composure   **d.** alacrity

9. _____

10. The people who live next to the kennel are *calm and collected:* no amount of noise disturbs them.
    a. inert   **b.** imperturbable   **c.** impetuous   **d.** indolent

10. _____

EXERCISE 4   USING DIFFERENT FORMS OF WORDS

Decide which form of the word in parentheses best completes the sentence. The form given may be correct. Write your answer on the answer line.

1. _____ greeted the performers as they walked onto the stage. (*pandemonium*)

1. _____

2. Darlene glanced _____ at the height of the hurdles. (*imperturbable*)

2. _____

3. In spite of his one mistake, Luke remained _____ throughout his performance. (*composure*)

3. _____

4. While reading a poem by Robert Frost, Charlie could picture the _____ of the snow-covered forest. (*serenity*)

4. _____

5. Because of Kelly's _____ in neglecting to water the flowers, they withered and died. (*indolent*)

5. _____

6. The campaign for a new bridge died of _____. (*inert*)

6. _____

7. Scott _____ chose a kiwi even though the fruit wasn't on his shopping list. (*impetuous*)

7. _____

8. We were overcome with _____ while waiting in line for three hours. (*ennui*)

8. _____

9. Mr. Kim accepted our ideas with _____. (*alacrity*)

9. _____

10. For fans of the rival team, losing the game was enough of an _____ to riot. (*incite*)

10. _____

© Great Source   DO NOT COPY

READING COMPREHENSION

Each numbered sentence in the following passage contains an italicized vocabulary word or related form. After you read the passage, you will complete an exercise.

MARY McLEOD BETHUNE: DEDICATED CRUSADER

Mary McLeod Bethune (1875–1955) was an educator and public administrator who devoted her life to improving social and economic opportunities for African Americans. By giving generously of her time to organizations working for the promotion of racial understanding, this wise, patient, and persuasive woman became something of a legend in her lifetime.

Mary McLeod was born in Mayesville, South Carolina, the youngest of the seventeen children of former slaves. (1) *Indolence* was unknown to Mary, who picked two hundred pounds of cotton a day and walked ten miles to and from school by the time she was twelve years old. (2) Even after these exhausting days, if someone in her family asked her to teach them, she would agree with *alacrity.* Her energy and passion for learning earned her scholarships to both high school and college.

After graduating from college, Mary McLeod planned to become a missionary in Africa. (3) When she learned that she was too young to get a placement, the *imperturbable* Mary McLeod made other plans. She found, instead, an equally important mission in the United States—teaching. McLeod was a superb teacher who electrified her students with her personality, enthusiasm, and imagination. (4) With her oratorical ability, she could quiet the *pandemonium* in any classroom. (5) None of her students ever suffered *ennui.* In addition to the usual curriculum, she taught industrial and home-making

skills. McLeod believed that everyone should be employable and self-sufficient.

While teaching in Georgia, South Carolina, and Florida, Mary McLeod observed the inadequacies of the existing schools. She and her husband, Albert, also a teacher, decided to open a school for African American girls in Daytona Beach, Florida. (6) This was somewhat *impetuous,* for they had only $1.50 in cash. Although her first five students had only charcoal for pencils and crushed elderberries for ink, nothing could stop Mary Bethune. To raise money, she baked sweet potato pies and sold them door to door. She peddled fried fish, sang in local hotels, wrote articles, and made speeches at meetings. (7) She missed no opportunity to *incite* people to action. The Daytona Educational Industrial Training School soon grew into a flourishing coeducational secondary school and in 1916 became Bethune-Cookman College.

Bethune's reputation as an educator, fund raiser, and school founder brought her national attention. She was in wide demand as a speaker, using her eloquence to plead for interracial good will and the dignity and respect due every human being. (8) Her *composure* was adequate for any situation. (9) She could meet the anger of an adversary or the stubbornness of an *inert* bureaucrat with the same steadiness. (10) The *serene* woman became the diplomatic link between whites and blacks under four presidential administrations.

In 1935 Mary Bethune was appointed by Franklin Roosevelt to a youth advisory board. The following year she became the director of the Division of Negro Affairs, the first African American woman to head a federal agency. Under her leadership her department funded 150,000 high-school and 60,000 college graduate school students and provided countless jobs and training courses.

Bethune was active in other areas as well. She started the National Council for Negro Women, an organization whose goal was to improve opportunities in all areas of life. During World War II, she assisted the Secretary of War in selecting officer candidates for the Women's Army Corps. Finally, she served as the consultant on interracial relations at the San Francisco conference, which organized the United Nations in 1945. Her death in 1955 brought to a close an unrelenting sixty-year struggle for African American progress and opportunity.

Each of the following statements corresponds to a numbered sentence in the passage. Each statement contains a blank and is followed by four answer choices. Decide which choice fits best in the blank. The word or phrase that you choose must express roughly the same meaning as the italicized word in the passage. Write the letter of your choice on the answer line.

1. _____ was unknown to Mary.
   a. Fear   **b.** Confusion   **c.** Entertainment   **d.** Idleness

   1. _____

2. If someone in her family asked her to teach them, she would agree with _____ .
   a. reluctance   **b.** regret   **c.** alarm   **d.** eagerness

   2. _____

3. Too young to be a missionary, the _____ Mary McLeod made other plans.
   a. undisturbable   **b.** annoyed   **c.** satisfied   **d.** uncooperative

   3. _____

4. She could quiet the _____ in any classroom.
   a. complaints   **b.** enthusiasm   **c.** students   **d.** disorder

   4. _____

5. None of her students ever experienced _____ .
   a. education   **b.** boredom   **c.** gratitude   **d.** joy

   5. _____

6. This was somewhat _____, for they had only $1.50 in cash.
   a. accidental   **b.** automatic   **c.** impulsive   **d.** feared

   6. _____

7. She missed no opportunity to _____ people to contribute money.
   a. beg   **b.** rouse   **c.** group   **d.** order

   7. _____

8. Her _____ seemed adequate for any situation.
   a. attitude   **b.** appearance   **c.** manners   **d.** control

   8. _____

9. She would meet the stubbornness of a(n) _____ bureaucrat with steadiness.
   a. angry   **b.** nervous   **c.** lifeless   **d.** bored

   9. _____

10. The _____ woman became the diplomatic link between whites and blacks.
    a. unruffled   **b.** dedicated   **c.** competent   **d.** formal

    10. _____

WRITING ASSIGNMENT

Choose a magazine photograph that portrays people involved in any type of activity—a child's birthday party, for example. Write a paragraph that describes the scene from the point of view of one of the people in the picture. Use a least five of the vocabulary words from this lesson and underline each one.

VOCABULARY ENRICHMENT

The word *pandemonium* was invented by John Milton for his epic poem *Paradise Lost*. Pandemonium is the name of the capital city of Hell. In the poem it is the scene of a great argument among the fallen angels, who have gathered to consider their defeat and their future prospects. Today the word means "great noise and confusion." *Pandemonium* comes from the Greek *pan-*, meaning "all," and *daimon*, meaning "divine power." In time *daimon* came to mean "an evil supernatural power or being," and it is also the source of the English word *demon*.

Activity   Many names for places have been borrowed from Latin and Greek. In a dictionary look up the etymologies of each of the following words. Without looking at the definition, write a brief explanation of each place. Then see whether your explanation matches the definition.

1. arboretum   2. gymnasium   3. auditorium   4. solarium

© Great Source   DO NOT COPY

The words in this lesson deal with the common human traits of boldness and mildness. While most people tend to be either bold or mild, an occasional individual manages to combine these two characteristics. Mohandas Ghandi, one of the great leaders of the twentieth century, proved that mildness can actually inspire boldness. Ghandi led a powerful movement that brought India and Pakistan independence from Great Britain in the 1950s. In keeping with the mildness that characterized his personal life, he lived simply, eating only vegetarian foods and even weaving his own clothing. In fact, he refused to injure any living thing. But Ghandi used his mildness in a bold way, fostering the concept of nonviolent resistance against oppression. When he and his followers were attacked in political protests, they simply refused to fight back. In this way, they maintained personal dignity and showed the justice of their cause. This arresting response awakened the conscience of the world, and had a profound influence both on the fate of India and Pakistan and, later, on civil rights movements throughout the world.

WORD LIST

brazen
complaisant
conspicuous
docile
flamboyant
intrepid
pacific
reserved
strident
unabashed

DEFINITIONS

After you have studied the definitions and example for each vocabulary word, write the word on the line to the right.

1. **brazen** (brā′zən) *adjective* Rudely bold; insolent. *trans. verb* To face or undergo with bold or brash self-assurance.

   Related Words **brazenly** *adverb;* **brazenness** *noun*
   Example Tom made a *brazen* remark about the unattractive color of Tiffany's dress.

   1. _____

2. **complaisant** (kəm-plā′sənt) *adjective* Showing a desire or willingness to please; cheerfully obliging; amiable. (From the Old French word *complaire,* meaning "to please")

   Related Words **complaisance** *noun;* **complaisantly** *adverb*
   Example Miriam's *complaisant* attitude made her an easy person to work with.

   2. _____
   USAGE NOTE: Compare *complacent.* Like *complaisant, complacent* means "eager to please," but it also means "contented to a fault; self-satisfied and unconcerned."

3. **conspicuous** (kən-spĭk′yoo-əs) *adjective* **a.** Easy to notice; obvious. **b.** Attracting attention by being unusual or remarkable. (From the Latin *com-,* an intensive prefix, and *specere,* meaning "to look")

   Related Words **conspicuously** *adverb;* **conspicuousness** *noun*
   Example The last to arrive, Patricia made a *conspicuous* entrance at the formal dinner party.

   3. _____

4. **docile** (dŏs′əl) *adjective* Easily managed or taught; gentle. (From the Latin word *docere,* meaning "to teach")

   Related Word **docilely** *adverb*
   Example Because the puppy was unusually *docile,* the Ayalas chose him as a pet for their four-year-old.

   4. _____

5. **flamboyant** (flăm-boi′ənt) *adjective* **a.** Exaggerated or high-flown in style or manner; showy. **b.** Highly elaborate; ornate. **c.** Richly colored; vivid. (From the Latin word *flamma*, meaning "flame")

Related Words flamboyance *noun;* flamboyantly *adverb*
Example The journalist was criticized for his *flamboyant* writing style.

5. _____

6. **intrepid** (ĭn-trĕp′ĭd) *adjective* Courageous; fearless; bold. (From the Latin *in-*, meaning "not," and *trepidus*, meaning "alarmed")

Related Words intrepidly *adverb;* intrepidness *noun*
Example The *intrepid* adventurer risked her life exploring the jungles along the Amazon River.

6. _____

USAGE NOTE: *Trepid*, meaning "timid" or "apprehensive," is a seldom-used antonym of *intrepid*.

7. **pacific** (pə-sĭf′ĭk) *adjective* Promoting peace; peaceful; tranquil; serene. (From the Latin words *pax*, meaning "peace," and *facere*, meaning "to make")

Example The powerful nation's *pacific* statements were reassuring to its weaker neighbor.

7. _____

8. **reserved** (rĭ-zûrvd′) *adjective* **a.** Quiet and restrained in manner. **b.** Held for a particular person or persons. (From the Latin word *reservare*, meaning "to keep back")

Related Words reservation *noun;* reserve *verb*
Example Instead of reacting angrily to the insulting remark, Meg answered Ted in a *reserved* way.

8. _____

9. **strident** (strīd′nt) *adjective* Having a shrill, harsh, and grating sound or effect. (From the Latin word *stridere*, meaning "to make harsh sounds")

Related Words stridency *noun;* stridently *adverb*
Example The speaker's *strident* voice irritated many members of the audience.

9. _____

10. **unabashed** (ŭn′ə-băsht′) *adjective* Not embarrassed or ashamed.

Related Word unabashedly *adverb*
Example Forgetting his lines for the second time, Paul remained *unabashed*.

10. _____

USAGE NOTE: An antonym of *unabashed* is *abashed*, meaning "disconcerted," "uneasy," or "ashamed."

© Great Source   DO NOT COPY

EXERCISE I COMPLETING DEFINITIONS

On the answer line, write the word from the vocabulary list that best completes each definition.

1. Someone who shows a desire or willingness to please is _____.

2. A rudely bold or insolent person is _____.

3. A courageous or fearless person is _____.

4. A peaceful person is _____.

5. Something that is easy to notice or that attracts attention is _____.

6. Something that is exaggerated or showy is _____.

7. An _____ person is not easily embarrassed.

8. To have a shrill, harsh, or grating sound or effect is to be _____.

9. Someone who is quiet and restrained in manner is _____.

10. An easily managed person is _____.

1. _____
2. _____
3. _____
4. _____
5. _____
6. _____
7. _____
8. _____
9. _____
10. _____

EXERCISE 2 USING WORDS CORRECTLY

Decide whether the italicized vocabulary word has been used correctly in the sentence. On the answer line, write *Correct* for correct use and *Incorrect* for incorrect use.

1. Wanting to please his aunt, Jerry made a series of *brazen* remarks.

2. People sometimes overlook Suzanne because she is such a *reserved* person.

3. Because of her *pacific* nature, Linda was often called upon to settle her friends' arguments.

4. Henry's dark gray suit seemed *flamboyant* next to Anna's bright red dress.

5. David Livingstone, the *intrepid* explorer responsible for some of the first maps of central Africa, followed the Zambezi River to Victoria Falls in 1855.

6. Turning bright red and stammering helplessly, Felicia continued her recitation, totally *unabashed*.

7. As the speaker became angrier, a *strident* tone crept into his voice.

8. Duane's extreme height made him *conspicuous*—even on the basketball team.

9. Wilma's stubbornness was the reason that her employer described her as having a *docile* personality.

10. In a *complaisant* frame of mind, Michelle mowed the lawn even before her father asked her to.

1. _____
2. _____
3. _____
4. _____
5. _____
6. _____
7. _____
8. _____
9. _____
10. _____

EXERCISE 3 IDENTIFYING SYNONYMS AND ANTONYMS

Decide which word or phrase has the meaning that is the same as (a synonym) or opposite to (an antonym) that of the capitalized vocabulary word. Write the letter of your choice on the answer line.

1. CONSPICUOUS (antonym):
   a. invisible   **b.** obvious   **c.** shy   **d.** faint

1. _____

© Great Source DO NOT COPY   Boldness and Mildness **55**

2. UNABASHED (synonym):
   a. displeased   **b.** absent   **c.** uninspired   **d.** unembarrassed

2. _____

3. INTREPID (antonym):
   a. bold   **b.** modest   **c.** fearful   **d.** aggressive

3. _____

4. STRIDENT (synonym):
   a. mellow   **b.** adventurous   **c.** harsh   **d.** sweet

4. _____

5. DOCILE (antonym):
   a. mild   **b.** stubborn   **c.** clownish   **d.** ill-mannered

5. _____

6. FLAMBOYANT (synonym):
   a. showy   **b.** dull   **c.** neat   **d.** conservative

6. _____

7. PACIFIC (antonym):
   a. colorful   **b.** mild   **c.** outrageous   **d.** turbulent

7. _____

8. COMPLAISANT (synonym):
   a. sincere   **b.** unfriendly   **c.** talkative   **d.** amiable

8. _____

9. RESERVED (antonym):
   a. quiet   **b.** optimistic   **c.** outspoken   **d.** joyful

9. _____

10. BRAZEN (synonym):
    a. shy   **b.** proud   **c.** brash   **d.** polite

10. _____

EXERCISE 4 USING DIFFERENT FORMS OF WORDS

Decide which form of the vocabulary word in parentheses best completes the sentence.
The form given may be correct. Write your answer on the answer line.

1. The _____ of the talk-show host's voice discouraged many listeners from calling in. *(strident)*

1. _____

2. The groom's parents were _____ absent from the wedding ceremony. *(conspicuous)*

2. _____

3. The baby sitter prided herself on her _____ attitude toward the squabbling four-year-olds. *(pacific)*

3. _____

4. Without a deposit the hotel clerk would not accept a _____ for Labor Day weekend. *(reserved)*

4. _____

5. Elsa Schiaparelli (1890–1973) was a fashion designer known for the _____ of her design. *(flamboyant)*

5. _____

6. The tour guide _____ led the tourists through the ancient stone ruins. *(complaisant)*

6. _____

7. Sir Edmund Hillary, a New Zealander, climbed _____ to the top of Mt. Everest in 1953. *(intrepid)*

7. _____

8. Hoping for a fish, the trained seal _____ clapped his flippers three times. *(docile)*

8. _____

9. Jeremy walked _____ into the teachers' cafeteria to look for the coach. *(brazen)*

9. _____

10. The young man smiled _____ as the store detective accused him of shoplifting. *(unabashed)*

10. _____

© Great Source   DO NOT COPY

READING COMPREHENSION

Each numbered sentence in the following passage contains an italicized vocabulary word or related form. After you read the passage, you will complete an exercise.

FASHIONS OF THE PAST AND THOSE WHO BROKE TRADITIONS

Clothing customs of bygone ages reveal the important role that fashion can play in society. In ancient Rome, for example, complex customs and laws governed the wearing of the "toga," a sort of draped cloth. (1) Purple togas with gold embroidery were *reserved* for victorious generals returning from war. Candidates for office wore togas rubbed in white chalk. (2) This *conspicuous* outfit, which actually shone in the sunlight, symbolized integrity.

From antiquity into the early middle ages, men and women tended to wear formal clothing that was, like the toga, loose fitting and draped. Then, in about A.D. 1200, a major fashion innovation, originating in war, changed men's outfits. Before 1200, knights had worn chain-mail armor, which hung straight from arms and legs. (3) Colored and decorated tunics, put over the mail, added some *flamboyance* to the outfit and permitted the knight to be identified in combat. The outfit was heavy and awkward, but protected the fighter.

Then, Europeans developed a new "plate" armor, fitted to arms, legs, and torso. It was lighter and more flexible, but since it did not cover the entire body, additional clothing was needed. "Linen armor,"

at first created to be worn under this plate armor, soon became fashionable and men started to wear it even without covering it in armor. The new outfit was form-fitting, consisting of tights and a shirt. When worn without armor, short pants, a jacket, and a formal coat were added. Once this attire was adopted, men had clothes that made movement easier.

Despite these changes for men, women continued to wear heavy, loose, draped clothing and headdresses. This heavy attire made movement difficult. (4) Thus, while new fashions gave men freedom, women's clothing continued to support the *docility* that was expected of them by society.

An occasional woman, however, broke the rules. Joan of Arc, born in 1412, was a simple French peasant child. In quieter times she would have lived the simple life of her village, lost to history. (5) But the times were not *pacific,* for the English were attacking France. Possessed by overwhelming patriotism, she decided to fight for the French prince, Charles. Her success as a soldier was phenomenal. Her first battle began suddenly, when she stood up and announced that she must attack the English immediately. (6) The *intrepid* Joan, so dedicated that she

returned to the fight after she was wounded, led the battle that recaptured the city of Orleans. After several more victories, she saw Charles crowned as the French king. Joan was a heroine!

Joan did other things unheard of for women. She courted the adoration of the crowd. Armed for combat, she dressed as a man. (7) Even more *brazenly,* she also used the male attire developed from linen-armor in everyday life.

(8) *Unabashed* by any sense that she was violating customs, she appeared with form-fitting outfits and an uncovered head. (9) Other women, more *complaisant,* continued to drag heavy skirts and balance tall headgear.

Later, when Joan was captured by the English and put on trial, her clothing was used as evidence against her. (10) The *stridency* of their complaints shows how difficult it was for women to break the barriers that held them. In the end, Joan was condemned to death.

In today's modern world, informality and freedom govern our appearance. Yet lessons from the past show that clothing customs and laws can be used to shape and govern our lives. Those who dared to break these, like Joan of Arc, often have suffered.

READING COMPREHENSION EXERCISE

Each of the following statements corresponds to a numbered sentence in the passage. Each statement contains a blank and is followed by four answer choices. Decide which choice fits best in the blank. The word or phrase that you choose must express roughly the same meaning as the italicized word in the passage. Write the letter of your choice on the answer line.

1. Purple togas with gold embroidery were _____ for victorious generals returning from war.
   a. held   **b.** hoped   **c.** opened   **d.** worked

   1. _____

2. This _____ outfit, which actually shone in the sunlight, symbolized integrity.
   a. bright   **b.** impractical   **c.** heavy   **d.** noticeable

   2. _____

3. Colored and decorated tunics, put over the mail, added some _____ to the outfit and permitted the knight to be identified in combat.
   a. curiosity   **b.** vividness   **c.** identity   **d.** weight

   3. _____

4. Thus, while new fashions gave men freedom, women's clothing continued to support the _____ that was expected of them by society.
   a. gentleness   **b.** goodness   **c.** slowness   **d.** hopelessness

   4. _____

5. But the times were not _____, for the English were attacking France.
   a. normal   **b.** peaceful   **c.** interesting   **d.** frightening

   5. _____

6. The _____ Joan, so dedicated that she returned to the fight after she was wounded, led the battle that recaptured the city of Orleans.
   a. foolish   **b.** well-armed   **c.** cautious   **d.** brave

   6. _____

7. Even more _____, she also used the male attire developed from linen-armor in everyday life.
   a. insolently   **b.** snobbishly   **c.** controversially   **d.** dangerously

   7. _____

8. _____ by any sense that she was violating customs, she appeared with form-fitting outfits and an uncovered head.
   a. Not shamed   **c.** Not made bold
   b. Not made fearful   **d.** Not stopped

   8. _____

9. Other women, more _____, continued to drag heavy skirts and balance tall headgear.
   a. willing to suffer   **c.** willing to be uncomfortable
   b. willing to please   **d.** willing to complain

   9. _____

10. The _____ of their complaints shows how difficult it was for women to break the barriers that held them.
    a. righteousness   **b.** frequency   **c.** shrillness   **d.** miserableness

    10. _____

WRITING ASSIGNMENT

The words in this lesson can be used to describe two different types of personality—bold and mild. Probably you have known people of each type. Imagine yourself as a writer for your community newspaper. Your assignment is to write a one-page feature story about either a bold person or a mild-mannered person. Explain how the character trait helped the person in a difficult situation. If you cannot think of a real person, invent one. Use at least four words from this lesson and underline each one.

© Great Source   DO NOT COPY

TEST-TAKING SKILLS
SENTENCE-COMPLETION TEST ITEMS

You are probably familiar with tests of sentence completion by this time. Sentence-completion test items form one section of the verbal part of the Preliminary Scholastic Assessment Test (PSAT). The following procedure will help you to choose correct answers for sentence-completion questions.

PROCEDURE

1. *Read the entire sentence, noting where the missing word or words are.* Each test item consists of a single sentence with one or two blanks, followed by five answer choices. Each answer choice is a single word or a pair of words. Your task is to select the word or words that make sense in the sentence. A sample test item follows.

   History has - - - - hundreds of instances of - - - - rule throughout the centuries, from the Byzantine emperors to the tsars of Russia.
   (A) ignored . . benevolent   (D) obscured . . tyrannical
   (B) seen . . popular   (E) witnessed . . democratic
   (C) recorded . . absolute

2. *Analyze the structure of the sentence, searching the context for clues to the overall meaning.* A sentence may offer reasons or examples, present a contrast, or give a definition. The sample test item contains two examples of harsh, repressive governments in which the common people had no say.

3. *Eliminate the incorrect answer choices.* In the sample sentence, choices A, B, and E can be eliminated because the second word in each pair does not characterize the governments as harsh and repressive.

4. *Substitute the remaining answer choices in the sentence, and select the better one.* If choice D is substituted, the sense is faulty: the Byzantine emperors and Russian tsars are *not* obscure historical figures. Choice C makes sense: the rule of both the emperors and czars was absolute, and history has indeed recorded the reigns of these rulers. Choice C is therefore correct.

EXERCISE ANSWERING SENTENCE-COMPLETION TEST ITEMS

Select the word or pair of words that best completes each of the following sentences. Write the letter of your choice on the answer line. Use your dictionary as needed.

1. After years of anxiety and - - - -, Copernicus finally agreed to publish his theory that the earth was not the center of the solar system.
   (A) apprehension   (D) indolence
   (B) boredom   (E) flamboyance
   (C) serenity

   1. _____

2. In sharp contrast to the numerous errors contained in the first draft, the final version of the report was based upon - - - - research that even the most severe critics could not - - - -.
   (A) careless .. attack   (D) credible .. commend
   (B) dubious .. condemn   (E) meticulous .. assail
   (C) fraudulent .. endorse

   2. _____

3. The - - - - of Peter the Great impressed his contemporaries: he clearly understood that Russia needed to build a warm-water port in order to become a great power.
   (A) vacillation
   (B) inactivity
   (C) indifference
   (D) negligence
   (E) foresight

   3. _____

4. The emergency squad reacted to the frantic call for help with great - - - -, arriving just in time to revive the heart-attack victim.
   (A) diligence
   (B) apprehension
   (C) alacrity
   (D) decorum
   (E) vacillation

   4. _____

5. Diplomats hoped for a quick resolution of the conflict, but on-the-scene reporters were - - - - because both sides still refused to hold meaningful talks.
   (A) docile
   (B) impetuous
   (C) dubious
   (D) conspicuous
   (E) decorous

   5. _____

6. Susan's distinguishing trait is her - - - -, she always seems to bounce back from adversity.
   (A) alacrity
   (B) impulsiveness
   (C) elegance
   (D) resilience
   (E) deviousness

   6. _____

7. She was always - - - - in performing dangerous missions, remaining calm and collected in the face of great perils.
   (A) agitated
   (B) composed
   (C) incompetent
   (D) apprehensive
   (E) punctual

   7. _____

8. Claire argued that since extrasensory experiences are by their very nature - - - -, they are not observable and cannot, therefore, be - - - - scientifically.
   (A) strident .. rejected
   (B) subjective .. proven
   (C) ignoble .. discredited
   (D) beguiling .. judged
   (E) flamboyant .. confirmed

   8. _____

9. For the masquerade ball, the fashion designer created an elaborate costume too - - - - for even the most extravagant celebrity.
   (A) flamboyant
   (B) serene
   (C) meticulous
   (D) judicious
   (E) decorous

   9. _____

10. Lenin and other Communist revolutionaries wrote - - - - pamphlets filled with inflammatory language as part of their campaign to - - - - workers to overthrow Czar Nicholas II.
    (A) strident .. incite
    (B) serene .. agitate
    (C) indecent .. inspire
    (D) equivocal .. convince
    (E) dejected .. rally

    10. _____

11. The model was of an - - - - age: youthful but sophisticated, she might have been twenty-five or thirty-five.
    (A) indolent
    (B) intrepid
    (C) invincible
    (D) imperturbable
    (E) indeterminate

    11. _____

12. While - - - - explorers such as Marco Polo and Ibn Battuta faced risks courageously, they were not - - - -, choosing instead to avoid needless dangers.
    (A) provincial .. prudent
    (B) intolerant .. docile
    (C) punctual .. apprehension
    (D) intrepid .. foolhardy
    (E) indolent .. systematic

    12. _____

© Great Source   DO NOT COPY

<table>
<tr><td>

Derived from the Latin words and *versare,* meaning "to turn," the word elements *-vert-* and *-vers-* occur in many English words. For example, *adverse* weather is weather that has turned, or changed. Water that is *converted* to ice has been turned to another state. The *obverse* of a coin is the face because that is the part that is most often turned toward the observer. To *advertise* a product involves turning it toward prospective buyers. In this lesson you will learn other words that refer to turning.

</td></tr>
</table>

WORD LIST
avert
diversify
diversion
inadvertent
incontrovertible
invert
irreversible
revert
versatile
vertigo

DEFINITIONS

After you have studied the definitions and example for each vocabulary word, write the word on the line to the right.

1. **avert** (ə-vûrt′) *trans. verb* **a.** To turn away or aside. **b.** To prevent from happening: *avert disaster.* (From the Latin *ab-*, meaning "away," and *vertere,* meaning "to turn")

   Example　　　Sandra *averted* her eyes during the frightening parts of the horror movie.

   1. _____

2. **diversify** (dĭ-vûr′sə-fī′, dī-vûr′sə-fī) *trans. verb* **a.** To give variety to; vary. **b.** To extend (activities) into distinct fields. *intrans. verb* To spread out activities or investments, as a business. (From the Latin *dis-*, meaning "apart," *vertere,* and *facere,* meaning "to make")

   Related Word　**diversification** *noun*
   Example　　　The restaurant *diversified* the menu by adding some new beef and chicken dishes

   2. _____

3. **diversion** (dĭ-vûr′zhən, dī-vûr′zhən) *noun* **a.** Something that relaxes or entertains; recreation. **b.** The act of turning aside from a course or direction. **c.** The act of drawing the attention from one thing to another.

   Related Word　**divert** *verb*
   Example　　　Going for a walk was a welcome *diversion* after long hours of studying.

   3. _____

4. **inadvertent** (ĭn′əd-vûr′tnt) *adjective* **a.** Accidental; unintentional. **b.** Not duly attentive. (From the Latin *in-*, meaning "not," *ad-*, meaning "toward," and *vertere*)

   Related Word　**inadvertently** *adverb*
   Example　　　Henry's *inadvertent* omission of his signature caused the bank teller to refuse his check.

   4. _____

5. **incontrovertible** (ĭn-kŏn′trə-vûr′tə-bəl) *adjective*   Indisputable; unquestionable. (From the Latin *in-*, meaning "not," *contra-*, meaning "against," and *vertere*)

>   **Related Word**   **incontrovertibly** *adverb*
>   **Example**   The *incontrovertible* evidence caused the jury to find the defendant guilty.

5. _____

6. **invert** (ĭn-vûrt′) *trans. verb*   **a.** To turn inside out or upside down.   **b.** To reverse the position, order, or condition of. (From the Latin *in-*, meaning "in," and *vertere*)

>   **Related Word**   **inversion** *noun*
>   **Example**   If you *invert* a glass filled with water, the liquid will spill out.

6. _____

7. **irreversible** (ĭr′ĭ-vûr′sə-bəl) *adjective*   Incapable of being reversed. (From the Latin *in-*, meaning "not," *re-*, meaning "back," and *vertere*)

>   **Example**   Muscle loss in the elderly was once thought to be *irreversible*, but researchers have discovered that muscular tissue can be rebuilt.

7. _____

8. **revert** (rĭ-vûrt′) *intrans. verb*   To return to a former condition, practice, or belief. (From the Latin *re-*, meaning "back," and *vertere*)

>   **Related Word**   **reversion** *noun*
>   **Example**   When they were frightened, the children *reverted* to babyish behavior.

8. _____

9. **versatile** (vûr′sə-təl, vûr′sə-tīl′) *adjective*   **a.** Capable of doing many things competently.   **b.** Having varied uses or functions. (From the Latin word *versare*, meaning "to turn")

>   **Related Word**   **versatility** *noun*
>   **Example**   The *versatile* mechanic was able to discover and correct any kind of car problem.

9. _____

10. **vertigo** (vûr′tĭ-gō′) *noun*   The sensation of dizziness and the feeling that oneself or one's environment is whirling about. (From the Latin word *vertere*)

>   **Example**   When Harvey stood on the high bridge and glanced at the water below, he began to experience *vertigo*.

10. _____

© Great Source   DO NOT COPY

EXERCISE 1 MATCHING WORDS AND DEFINITIONS

Match the definition in Column B with the word in Column A. Write the letter of the correct definition on the answer line.

Column A

1. incontrovertible
2. diversion
3. avert
4. vertigo
5. inadvertent
6. diversify
7. irreversible
8. versatile
9. invert
10. revert

Column B

a. to return to a former condition or belief
b. to turn away; prevent from happening
c. able to do many things well
d. accidental or unintentional
e. indisputable; unquestionable
f. not capable of being reversed
g. a sensation of dizziness
h. to turn inside out or upside down
i. to give variety to or vary
j. something that relaxes or entertains; the act of turning aside

1. _____
2. _____
3. _____
4. _____
5. _____
6. _____
7. _____
8. _____
9. _____
10. _____

EXERCISE 2 USING WORDS CORRECTLY

Each of the following questions contains an italicized vocabulary word or related form. Choose the correct answer to the question and write *Yes* or *No* on the answer line.

1. If you *inadvertently* broke an antique vase, would you have done it on purpose?

2. Does the numerator become the denominator when you *invert* the numbers of a fraction?

3. If you *diversified* the colors in a picture you were painting, would you use more than one color?

4. Would you be likely to introduce a new topic of conversation if you always *reverted* to old ideas?

5. To *avert* an accident, would you skate on thin ice?

6. If a decision is *irreversible*, can it be changed?

7. Is the statement "the earth is round" *incontrovertible*?

8. Might someone suffering from *vertigo* have trouble with swiftly spinning rides at an amusement park?

9. Do employees often consider afternoon breaks as *diversions*?

10. Would you be able to run a variety of programs on a *versatile* computer?

1. _____
2. _____
3. _____
4. _____
5. _____
6. _____
7. _____
8. _____
9. _____
10. _____

EXERCISE 3 CHOOSING THE BEST WORD

Decide which vocabulary word or related form best completes the sentence, and write the letter of your choice on the answer line.

1. The high school hoped to _____ its program of elective courses.
    a. revert   b. diversify   c. avert   d. invert

1. _____

2. The fast-thinking forest ranger was able to _____ what could have been a real disaster.

   a. invert   **b.** revert   **c.** diversify   **d.** avert

   2. _____

3. Miniature golf was a(n) _____ for Laura and her friends.

   a. inversion   **b.** diversion   **c.** versatility   **d.** diversification

   3. _____

4. The dancers tried to correct the errors in their routines, but in their next performance they _____ to their old mistakes.

   a. averted   **b.** diversified   **c.** reverted   **d.** diverted

   4. _____

5. As a result of the _____ evidence in her argument, Jill won the debate.

   a. inadvertent   **b.** inverted   **c.** versatile   **d.** incontrovertible

   5. _____

6. "Once you move your chess piece, that action is _____," John told Sidney.

   a. irreversible   **b.** versatile   **c.** inverted   **d.** inadvertent

   6. _____

7. After spinning on Super Jet Spin, Patsy experienced _____ .

   a. vertigo   **b.** versatility   **c.** reversion   **d.** diversification

   7. _____

8. Jonathan greatly regretted his _____ remark.

   a. versatile   **b.** inverted   **c.** inadvertent   **d.** diversified

   8. _____

9. Capable of playing the piano and the cello, Oscar is a(n) _____ musician.

   a. versatile   **b.** incontrovertible   **c.** irreversible   **d.** inadvertent

   9. _____

10. The child filled the _____ party hat with newly acquired prizes.

    a. diverting   **b.** averted   **c.** incontrovertible   **d.** inverted

    10. _____

EXERCISE 4 USING DIFFERENT FORMS OF WORDS

Decide which form of the vocabulary word in parentheses best completes the sentence. The form given may be correct. Write your answer on the answer line.

1. The carpenter showed great _____ because he could make fine furniture and also renovate old houses. *(versatile)*

   1. _____

2. The process of erosion caused _____ damage to the cliffs along the ocean. *(irreversible)*

   2. _____

3. _____ war is a goal of most countries. *(avert)*

   3. _____

4. Alexis was unable to complete her homework because she _____ had left her history book at school. *(inadvertent)*

   4. _____

5. Ted's _____ to his former relaxed and friendly self was a welcome change. *(revert)*

   5. _____

6. A _____ of the exhibits at the museum increased the number of visitors. *(diversify)*

   6. _____

7. The veterinarian was delighted to discover that the medicine had _____ cured the sick monkey. *(incontrovertible)*

   7. _____

8. At the circus the clown _____ the audience. *(diversion)*

   8. _____

9. The geologist studied the patterns of _____ in the rock formation. *(invert)*

   9. _____

10. Max's inner-ear infection caused him to experience _____ . *(vertigo)*

    10. _____

 © Great Source   DO NOT COPY

READING COMPREHENSION

Each numbered sentence in the following passage contains an italicized vocabulary word or related form. After you read the passage, you will complete an exercise.

WALKING A TIGHTROPE

Seventy feet above the ground, the high-wire walker pauses on the platform. As thousands watch, he takes a step, only a half-inch of wire separating him from disaster. (1) Moving cautiously, to *avert* an accident, he walks, dances, or even bike rides to the end of the path. (2) Breathless audience members gasp, imagining the *vertigo* they would suffer looking down from such heights. How does he do it?

(3) High-wire walking is based on *incontrovertible* principles of physics that pertain to a center of gravity. Imagine that the wire is an axis, and that the bodily mass (roughly, the weight) of the walker can rotate around it. If the weight is balanced directly above the wire, the performer can proceed. But if the weight shifts to one side, the forces will become unequal, and the unfortunate walker will start to rotate around the axis. (4) Theoretically, the performer could actually *invert*, but of course, he would fall to the ground long before he got to this position. Even the most skilled tightrope walkers find that their weight shifts from side to side. (5) They must correct these shifts before the effect is *irreversible* and they lose balance.

Performers carry balancing poles to help them correct these shifts. These poles may be up to 40 feet in length and weigh as much as 70 pounds. When walkers feel their weight shifting, they can correct the imbalance immediately, using the weight of the pole. Then they can adjust their body weight. (6) Thus, the pole allows the performer more time to *revert* to a balanced position. Of course, the entire process takes only a few seconds.

(7) Now mainly a *diversion* provided at circuses, highwire walking dates back several thousand years. In ancient China, it was performed over knives! (8) The high-wire artists of today have developed increasingly *diversified* acts. Balanced on a thin wire rope, performers ride bicycles and unicycles, balance on each other's shoulders, and even build human pyramids in the air.

In addition to high-wire walking, performers can perform on slack wire ropes. These are generally closer to the ground, so that they do not have to use a balancing pole. With their hands free, they can juggle clubs, rings, balls, and even flaming torches! (9) Some *versatile* artists are also gymnasts. They combine wire walking with trapeze performance, featuring twists and somersaults in midair.

Since accidents can still happen, performers train for years to develop their skills. To minimize risks, they constantly check their equipment. (10) Even slight defects may lead to *inadvertent* disaster. Some use safety precautions, such as nets, in their acts. It takes constant attention, a sense of perfectionism, and knowledge of the laws of physics to maintain the safety of this thrilling sport.

READING COMPREHENSION EXERCISE

Each of the following statements corresponds to a numbered sentence in the passage. Each statement contains a blank and is followed by four answer choices. Decide which choice fits best in the blank. The word or phrase that you choose must express roughly the same meaning as the italicized word in the passage. Write the letter of your choice on the answer line.

1. Moving cautiously to _____ an accident, he walks, dances, or even bike rides to the end of the path.
   a. manage   **b.** prevent   **c.** control   **d.** ensure

1. _____

2. Breathless audience members gasp, imagining the _____ they would suffer looking down from such heights.
   a. fear   **b.** helplessness   **c.** tension   **d.** dizziness

2. _____

3. High-wire walking is based on _____ principles of physics that pertain to the center of gravity.
   a. physical   **b.** helpful   **c.** indisputable   **d.** complex

3. _____

4. Theoretically, the performer could actually _____, but of course, he would fall to the ground long before he got to this position.
   a. bounce around   **b.** fly in the air   **c.** fall weightless   **d.** turn upside down

4. _____

5. They must correct these shifts before the effect is _____ and they lose balance.
   a. dangerous to audience members   **c.** out of control
   b. not capable of being turned back   **d.** contrary to safety principles

5. _____

6. Thus, the pole allows the performer more time to _____ to a balanced position.
   a. return   **b.** fly   **c.** change   **d.** look forward

6. _____

7. Now mainly a(n) _____ provided at circuses, high-wire walking dates back several thousand years.
   a. sport   **b.** laugh   **c.** entertainment   **d.** contest

7. _____

8. The high-wire artists of today have developed increasingly _____ acts.
   a. dangerous   **b.** varied   **c.** amusing   **d.** lengthy

8. _____

9. Some _____ performers are also gymnasts.
   a. competent in everything   **c.** competent in many things
   b. competent in sports   **d.** competent in entertaining

9. _____

10. Even slight defects may lead to _____ disaster.
    a. accidental   **b.** great   **c.** tragic   **d.** hopeless

10. _____

PRACTICE WITH ANALOGIES

See page 79 for some strategies to use with analogies.

Directions On the answer line, write the vocabulary word or a form of it that completes each analogy.

1. UNSTABLE : TOPPLE :: _____ : manage (*Lesson 9*)

1. _____

2. COWARD : FEARFUL :: hothead : _____ (*Lesson 8*)

2. _____

3. OBVIOUS : PROVE :: _____ : notice (*Lesson 9*)

3. _____

4. ORNATE : BUILDING :: _____ : clothing (*Lesson 9*)

4. _____

5. MERCILESS : COMPASSION :: _____ : fear (*Lesson 9*)

5. _____

6. ELATION : HAPPINESS :: _____ : dizziness (*Lesson 10*)

6. _____

7. PERPETUAL : STOP :: _____ : work (*Lesson 8*)

7. _____

8. AIMLESS : PURPOSE :: _____ : motion (*Lesson 8*)

8. _____

© Great Source   DO NOT COPY

Most of us are intrigued with things that are hidden. Mystery or secrecy awakens in us a desire to grasp the unknown. We hunt treasure, read between the lines, explore new places, and delve beneath the surfaces of things. We often ignore that which is plainly in view as commonplace, uninteresting, or obvious.

At the same time, we respect and welcome things that are open. We expect our public officials to be accessible and forthright. We are suspicious when facts are concealed. When we are open to new experiences, we are unrestrained in learning and profiting from them. We may greet someone with open arms or regard something with an open mind.

The concepts of openness and concealment have many dimensions. The words in this lesson will help you to understand the range of meanings within these two broad areas.

WORD LIST
flagrant
flaunt
furtive
latent
ostensible
salient
sequester
subterfuge
surreptitious
unobtrusive

DEFINITIONS

After you have studied the definitions and example for each vocabulary word, write the word on the line to the right.

1. **flagrant** (flā′grənt) *adjective*   Extremely or deliberately noticeable; glaring. (From the Latin word *flagare*, meaning "to burn")

    Related Words **flagrancy** *noun;* **flagrantly** *adverb*
    Example   Residents of Squirrel Falls believed that the mayor's actions represented a *flagrant* abuse of his power.

1. _____

2. **flaunt** (flônt) *trans. verb*   To show off in order to impress others; display boastfully.

    Related Word **flauntingly** *adverb*
    Example   When she returned to her hometown, the movie star *flaunted* her wealth, arriving in a limousine and wearing diamond bracelets.

2. _____
    USAGE NOTE: Do not confuse *flaunt*, meaning "to show off," with *flout*, meaning "to defy openly."

3. **furtive** (fûr′tĭv) *adjective*   Done quickly and with stealth; sly. (From the Latin word *furtum*, meaning "theft")

    Related Words **furtively** *adverb;* **furtiveness** *noun*
    Example   The cat appeared to give a *furtive* look behind her before leaping onto the kitchen counter.

3. _____

4. **latent** (lāt′nt) *adjective*   Present or capable of coming into existence but not evident, active, or visible. (From the Latin word *latere*, meaning "to lie hidden")

    Related Words **latency** *noun;* **latently** *adverb*
    Example   Jeremy's *latent* creativity was discovered when he took an aptitude test.

4. _____

5. **ostensible** (ŏ-stĕn'sə-bəl) *adjective*   Represented or appearing a certain way, but often not actually so; seeming; professed. (From the Latin *ob-*, meaning "before," and *tendere*, meaning "to stretch")

Related Word   ostensible *adverb*
Example   The *ostensible* purpose of Ms. Meader's trip is business, but she plans to spend much of the time visiting her grandchild.

5. _____

6. **salient** (sā'lē-ənt, sāl'yənt) *adjective*   **a.** Standing out and attracting attention; noticeable; prominent.   **b.** Projecting or jutting beyond a line or surface; protruding up or out: *a salient shelf of rock.* (From the Latin world *salire*, meaning "to leap")

Related Word   saliently *adverb*
Example   Kathryn and Tim explained the *salient* features of their plan.

6. _____

7. **sequester** (sĭ-kwĕs'tər) *trans. verb*   To remove or withdraw from public view; seclude; set apart.

Related Word   sequestration *noun*
Example   Mr. Ludlum *sequestered* himself for almost a year so that he could finish writing his book on Michelangelo.

7. _____

8. **subterfuge** (sŭb'tər-fyo͞oj') *noun*   **a.** Deception by means of a strategy or device.   **b.** A deceptive strategy or device. (From the Latin words *subter*, meaning "secretly," and *fugere*, meaning "to flee")

Example   Elaine occasionally uses *subterfuge* to get her own way.

8. _____

9. **surreptitious** (sûr'əp-tĭsh'əs) *adjective*   Done or acting in secret; sneaky. (From the Latin *sub-*, meaning "secretly," and *rapere*, meaning "to seize")

Related Words   surreptitiously *adverb;* surreptitiousness *noun*
Example   As his uncle continued to lecture him, Nathan cast a *surreptitious* glance at his watch.

9. _____

10. **unobtrusive** (ŭn'əb-tro͞o'sĭv) *adjective*   **a.** Not readily noticeable; inconspicuous.   **b.** Not aggressive; discreet. (From the English *un-*, meaning "not," the Latin *ob-*, meaning "against," and the Latin word *trudere*, meaning "to thrust")

Related Words   unobtrusively *adverb;* unobtrusiveness *noun*
Example   Although *unobtrusive* in the classroom, Carole was usually the center of attention at home.

10. _____

© Great Source   DO NOT COPY

EXERCISE I WRITING CORRECT WORDS

On the answer line, write the word from the vocabulary list that best completes each definition.

1. Appearing a certain way, but not actually so; professed

2. Done or acting in secret; sneaky

3. Extremely noticeable; glaring

4. Standing out and attracting attention; prominent

5. Deception by means of a strategy or a device; a deceptive strategy or device

6. To show off in order to impress others

7. Not readily noticeable; inconspicuous

8. To remove or withdraw from public view; seclude

9. Done quickly and with stealth; sly

10. Capable of coming into existence but not visible

1. _____

2. _____

3. _____

4. _____

5. _____

6. _____

7. _____

8. _____

9. _____

10. _____

EXERCISE 2 USING WORDS CORRECTLY

Decide whether the italicized vocabulary word has been used correctly in the sentence. On the answer line, write *Correct* for correct use and *Incorrect* for incorrect use.

1. Clara's *ostensible* reason for coming to the house was to return our lawn mower, but she really wanted to meet our cousins.

2. *Flagrant* parking violations are rewarded by the police.

3. Because the case was so sensational, the judge *sequestered* the jury.

4. The pirates announced their arrival with an *unobtrusive* blast from their cannon.

5. The boy's *furtive* manner made people trust him instinctively.

6. Ella's aches and pains were only a *subterfuge* to avoid going shopping.

7. Kevin decided to tell the complete story by eliminating the *salient* details.

8. Shy and embarrassed, Elise *flaunted* her discomfort by sitting quietly in a corner.

9. Hercules' strength was hardly *latent* in childhood; he was said to have strangled two snakes in his cradle when he was a baby.

10. McDonald conducted a *surreptitious* search for a new job so that his supervisor wouldn't find out.

1. _____

2. _____

3. _____

4. _____

5. _____

6. _____

7. _____

8. _____

9. _____

10. _____

EXERCISE 3 IDENTIFYING SYNONYMS AND ANTONYMS

Decide which word or phrase has the meaning that is the same as (a synonym) or opposite to (an antonym) that of the capitalized vocabulary word. Write the letter of your choice on the answer line.

1. SALIENT (synonym):
   a. hidden   **b.** striking   **c.** covered   **d.** sarcastic

1. _____

2. FURTIVE (antonym):
   a. forthright   b. offensive   c. stealthy   d. furrowed

   2. _____

3. FLAUNT (synonym):
   a. disregard   b. display   c. antagonize   d. waver

   3. _____

4. SEQUESTER (synonym):
   a. bring forth   b. follow   c. line up   d. set apart

   4. _____

5. LATENT (antonym):
   a. perceptible   b. abundant   c. riotous   d. quiet

   5. _____

6. FLAGRANT (synonym):
   a. fluent   b. affectionate   c. outrageous   d. courteous

   6. _____

7. OSTENSIBLE (antonym):
   a. violent   b. peculiar   c. infamous   d. actual

   7. _____

8. SUBTERFUGE (synonym):
   a. reserve   b. trick   c. puzzle   d. solution

   8. _____

9. UNOBTRUSIVE (antonym):
   a. subtle   b. obvious   c. exceptional   d. insincere

   9. _____

10. SURREPTITIOUS (synonym):
    a. overt   b. acute   c. secretive   d. noticeable

    10. _____

EXERCISE 4 USING DIFFERENT FORMS OF WORDS

Decide which form of the vocabulary word in parentheses best completes the sentence. The form given may be correct. Write your answer on the answer line.

1. The depiction of the effect of light on objects was a _____ feature of Impressionist paintings. *(salient)*

   1. _____

2. The _____ of Lillian's lies astonished her friends. *(flagrant)*

   2. _____

3. The cat crept _____ toward the goldfish bowl. *(furtive)*

   3. _____

4. By choosing to join a certain kind of religious order, a nun can live in _____. *(sequester)*

   4. _____

5. The detective entered the room _____ and was able to hear and see a great deal before being noticed. *(unobtrusive)*

   5. _____

6. The thief entered the darkened house _____ but was surprised by the detective, who was waiting for him. *(surreptitious)*

   6. _____

7. Lucy antagonized her friends by _____ Ed's school ring, which she wore on a chain around her neck. *(flaunt)*

   7. _____

8. Gary was _____ truthful, but Millicent was still suspicious. *(ostensible)*

   8. _____

9. Sandy won the prize by _____ but then felt guilty about it. *(subterfuge)*

   9. _____

10. Chicken pox is infectious during its _____. *(latent)*

    10. _____

© Great Source   DO NOT COPY

READING COMPREHENSION

Each numbered sentence in the following passage contains an italicized vocabulary word or related form. After you read the passage, you will complete an exercise.

THE TREASURE OF OAK ISLAND

Over the past two hundred years, treasure hunters have flocked to Oak Island, off the coast of the Canadian province of Nova Scotia. Millions of dollars have been spent in attempts to excavate a 170-foot pit, where submerged wooden chests filled with precious jewels and gold coins await someone with the genius to remove them. (1) But so far, no efforts, whether concealed by *subterfuge* or pursued openly by teams of engineers, have succeeded.

According to legend Oak Island was put under a curse in 1720. During that year mainlanders saw strange, flickering lights on the island. Several people ventured close enough to see huge bonfires and large groups of pirates hard at work. (2) These people were said to have died mysteriously after reporting the *surreptitious* activity. (3) Two men who rowed in to inspect the pirates' activity were not *furtive* enough; they were never seen again. (4) Rumors of *flagrantly* illegal activity were circulated but were never proved. (5) The pirates had *sequestered* themselves and their activities quite well.

The curse remained until 1795, when three young men landed on Oak Island. Out for a day of canoeing and exploring, they soon noticed a pulley device from an old ship that was nailed to the trunk of a large oak tree. (6) The most *salient* feature of the pulley was its position directly over a depressed square of earth. Daniel McInnes, Jack Smith, and Tony Vaughan were convinced that they had found the site of pirate treasure.

The next day the three returned to Oak Island with shovels, axes, and picks. They found and old, clay-lined shaft, seven feet wide and refilled with loose dirt. Shoveling out tons of dirt, they also discovered platforms of heavy oak planks located at ten, twenty, and thirty feet. Thirty feet beneath the surface, they were no closer to a bottom of any sort. After weeks of digging, the young men were forced to return to their farming.

McInnes, Smith, and Vaughan had not given up their dream, however. (7) They still believed that they had found a *latent* source of incredible wealth. (8) By making *unobtrusive* inquiries, they found Dr. John Lynds, who, inspired by their enthusiastic tales, raised capital to buy equipment and hire labor. Working furiously, the diggers excavated to one hundred feet below the surface. When they struck a solid layer, they believed that they had found the last barrier to the treasure. (9) Deciding to rest until morning, the excited treasure hunters dreamed of *flaunting* their riches to their neighbors. Their expectations were shattered, however. The next morning the shaft was filled with sixty feet of water. No amount of bailing or pumping could reduce the level of the water, which seemed to flow into the shaft through some underground source.

Since the Oak Island treasure pit was discovered in 1795, thirty to forty separate expeditions have been mounted to try to unearth the treasure. All of the work done over the years has yielded only a bone whistle shaped like a violin and three heavy links of a gold chain. (10) Engineers have *ostensibly* come to understand the construction of the tunnels and shafts; however, the sophisticated drilling equipment, hydraulic pumps, metal detectors, dynamite blasts, and bulldozers that they have used have failed to reveal what lies buried in what has come to be known as the "Money Pit."

Whether the treasure turns out to be the gold of the Incas, the loot of the pirate Captain Kidd, the plunder of Spanish explorers, or the never-recovered jewels of Marie Antoinette, treasure hunters are sure of one thing: The treasure must be extraordinarily valuable to have warranted the conception and construction of a hiding place that has defied the best talents of the modern engineering world.

READING COMPREHENSION EXERCISE

Each of the following statements corresponds to a numbered sentence in the passage. Each statement contains a blank and is followed by four answer choices. Decide which choice fits best in the blank. The word or phrase that you choose must express roughly the same meaning as the italicized word in the passage. Write the letter of your choice on the answer line.

1. But so far, no efforts, whether concealed by _____ or pursued openly by teams of engineers, have succeeded.
   a. darkness   b. deception   c. weather   d. mystery

  1. _____

2. They were said to have died mysteriously after reporting the _____ activity.
   a. pirates'   b. illegal   c. secretive   d. fascinating

  2. _____

3. Two men were not _____ enough.
   a. imaginative   b. sly   c. graceful   d. skillful

  3. _____

4. Rumors of _____ illegal activity were never proved.
   a. glaringly   b. humorously   c. supposedly   d. purposefully

  4. _____

5. The pirates had _____ themselves and their activities quite well.
   a. encouraged   b. stopped   c. secluded   d. covered

  5. _____

6. The most _____ feature of the ship's pulley was that it hung over a depression in the ground.
   a. interesting   b. confusing   c. reasonable   d. noticeable

  6. _____

7. The three young men still believed that they had found a _____ source of wealth.
   a. challenging   b. glamorous   c. concealed   d. endless

  7. _____

8. They located Dr. John Lynds by making _____ inquiries.
   a. discreet   b. written   c. public   d. disorganized

  8. _____

9. They dreamed of _____ their riches to their neighbors.
   a. creatively describing   c. giving clues about
   b. boastfully displaying   d. voluntarily explaining

  9. _____

10. Engineers have _____ come to understand the construction of the money pit.
   a. not   b. almost   c. definitely   d. seemingly

  10. _____

WRITING ASSIGNMENT

Suppose that you are planning a surprise party for a close friend. You are extremely excited about the party—so excited, in fact, that you are having a difficult time keeping the secret from your friend. You decide that you will write a letter about the party to a relative or another friend. This way, you can communicate the details without giving away the secret. Using at least five of the words from this lesson and underlining each word that you use, write a letter in which you explain how you will handle the party.

© Great Source   DO NOT COPY

12

WORD LIST

didactic
edify
elucidate
erudite
explicit
imbue
indoctrinate
instill
pedagogy
pedantic

The American philosopher and historian Henry Adams once said, "A teacher affects eternity. He can never tell where his influence stops." Adams was a university professor, but he knew that teaching takes place everywhere and at all stages of life. Imparting knowledge is not only one of the most common kinds of communication, but it is also one of the most important. The words in this lesson will help you to distinguish different kinds of teaching and explaining as well as different attitudes toward them.

DEFINITIONS

After you have studied the definitions and example for each vocabulary word, write the word on the line to the right.

1. **didactic** (dī-dăk′tĭk, dĭ-dăk′tĭk) *adjective* **a.** Intended to teach or instruct. **b.** Teaching a moral lesson. **c.** Inclined to teach or moralize too much. (From the Greek word *didaktos*, meaning "taught")

   Related Words **didactically** *adverb*; **didacticism** *noun*
   Example Some poems, such as alphabet jingles and counting rhymes, have a *didactic* purpose.

   1. _____

2. **edify** (ĕd′ə-fī′) *trans. verb* To instruct in order to bring about intellectual, moral, or spiritual improvement. (From the Latin words *aedis*, meaning "a building," and *facere*, meaning "to make")

   Related Word **edification** *noun*
   Example The new teacher considered it his job not just to teach his pupils but to *edify* them.

   2. _____

3. **elucidate** (ĭ-lōō′sĭ-dāt′) *trans. verb* To make clear or plain. *intrans. verb* To give an explanation that makes something clear. (From the Latin *ex-*, an intensive prefix, and *lucidus*, meaning "bright")

   Related Word **elucidation** *noun*
   Example The footnotes contain essential information that helps to *elucidate* the author's argument.

   3. _____

4. **erudite** (ĕr′yə-dīt′, ĕr′ə-dīt′) *adjective* **a.** Possessing deep and extensive learning, especially learning gotten from books; learned: *an erudite scholar.* **b.** Showing or marked by extensive learning or knowledge: *an erudite treatise.* (From the Latin *ex-*, meaning "out," and *rudis*, meaning "uncivilized" or "ignorant")

   Related Word **erudition** *noun*
   Example The *erudite* professor could read seven ancient languages.

   4. _____

5. **explicit** (ĭk-splĭs'ĭt) *adjective*   **a.** Expressed clearly and precisely, without any possibility of misunderstanding.   **b.** Forthright and unambiguous in expression. (From the Latin *ex-*, meaning "out," and *plicare*, meaning "to fold")

   Related Words   **explicitly** *adverb;* **explicitness** *noun*
   Example   One teacher believed that students learn best from *explicit* criticism of their work.

5. _____
USAGE NOTE: An antonym of *explicit* is *implicit*, "implied or understood although not directly expressed."

6. **imbue** (ĭm-byoo') *trans. verb*   **a.** To pervade or permeate as if with a dye or stain. **b.** To dye or stain intensely. (From the Latin word *imbuere*, meaning "to moisten" or "to stain")

   Example   The political rally was *imbued* with the fervor of reform.

6. _____

7. **indoctrinate** (ĭn-dŏk'trə-nāt') *trans. verb*   **a.** To instruct in the beliefs or principles of a party, sect, or other special group.   **b.** To teach a body of doctrine to.

   Related Word   **indoctrination** *noun*
   Example   The English boarding school *indoctrinated* students with the ideals of patriotism and public service.

7. _____

8. **instill** (ĭn-stĭl') *trans. verb*   To introduce gradually. (From the Latin *in-*, meaning "in," and *stilla*, meaning "drop")

   Related Word   **instillation** *noun*
   Example   Good teachers do not only impart knowledge but also *instill* in their pupils a desire to learn.

8. _____

9. **pedagogy** (pĕd'ə-gō'jē, pĕd'ə-gōj'ē) *noun*   The art or profession of teaching. (From the Greek words *pais*, meaning "boy," and *agein*, meaning "to lead")

   Related Words   **pedagogical** *adjective;* **pedagogically** *adverb;* **pedagogue** *noun*
   Example   Mathematical *pedagogy* in the United States has benefited from strategies used in Eastern Europe and Russia.

9. _____
See *pedantic.*

10. **pedantic** (pə-dăn'tĭk) *adjective*   **a.** Marked by a concern for minute, often unimportant and uninteresting details.   **b.** Making a show of scholarship of book learning.

    Related Words   **pedantically** *adverb;* **pedantry** *noun*
    Example   Professor Marcus's *pedantic* approach to literature takes all the fun out of reading.

10. _____
ETYMOLOGY NOTE:
The noun *pedant* originally meant "schoolmaster" and later "one who shows off his learning"; thus *pedantic* is related to *pedagogy.*

© Great Source   DO NOT COPY

EXERCISE 1 MATCHING WORDS AND DEFINITIONS

Match the definition in Column B with the word in Column A. Write the letter of the correct definition on the answer line.

Column A	Column B	
1. explicit	a. to make clear or plain	1. _____
2. didactic	b. possessing deep and extensive learning	2. _____
3. pedantic	c. to pervade as if with a dye	3. _____
4. erudite	d. expressed clearly and precisely	4. _____
5. pedagogy	e. intended to teach	5. _____
6. edify	f. to instruct in the beliefs of a special group	6. _____
7. indoctrinate	g. to introduce gradually	7. _____
8. instill	h. the art of teaching	8. _____
9. elucidate	i. marked by a concern for minute details	9. _____
10. imbue	j. to instruct in order to improve	10. _____

EXERCISE 2 USING WORDS CORRECTLY

Decide whether the italicized vocabulary word has been used correctly in the sentence. On the answer line, write *Correct* for correct use and *Incorrect* for incorrect use.

1. Professor Susan Lee is considered the most *erudite* member of the mathematics department at the university.   1. _____

2. Lawyers have to study *pedagogy* to learn their profession.   2. _____

3. The instructions for building her dune buggy were so *explicit* that Rita could not figure out where the engine should go.   3. _____

4. Mr. Baldwin gave his class an *edifying* talk about the importance of neatness, punctuality, and good manners.   4. _____

5. Ever since he fell down the stairs, Uncle Fred has walked at a *pedantic* pace and used a cane.   5. _____

6. In *Brave New World*, Aldous Huxley envisions a society whose members have been *indoctrinated* with materialistic values.   6. _____

7. Ms. Harris's conversations are more *didactic* than entertaining.   7. _____

8. The general's strategy was to *elucidate* the enemy and capture the bluffs overlooking the ford.   8. _____

9. The princess's tutors tried to *instill* in her a sense of the great responsibilities and obligations that she would have when she was queen.   9. _____

10. The auditorium was so *imbued* with early arrivals that we could not find a seat, although we came on time.   10. _____

EXERCISE 3 CHOOSING THE BEST WORD

Decide which vocabulary word or related form best expresses the meaning of the italicized word or phrase in the sentence. On the answer line, write the letter of the correct choice.

1. The article about archaeology on the island of Crete that I am reading has some merit as a travelogue, but it is not *marked by extensive learning*.
   a. explicit   **b.** pedagogical   **c.** erudite   **d.** imbued

   1. _____

2. After the coach's pep talk, the team was thoroughly *filled* with the desire to win.
   a. elucidated   **b.** imbued   **c.** indoctrinated   **d.** edified

   2. _____

3. I like television programs about current issues, but any show that is *inclined to moralize too much* gets turned off.
   a. didactic   **b.** pedantic   **c.** explicit   **d.** erudite

   3. _____

4. Lisa is *too concerned with the smallest details* about the rules of even the silliest games.
   a. explicit   **b.** pedagogical   **c.** erudite   **d.** pedantic

   4. _____

5. Charlemagne's court included men of learning and scholarship, for he was as concerned with the *intellectual improvement* of his people as with their governance.
   a. edification   **b.** elucidation   **c.** indoctrination   **d.** instillation

   5. _____

6. The person who copied this medieval manuscript made many marginal comments that help to *clarify* the text.
   a. edify   **b.** elucidate   **c.** imbue   **d.** indoctrinate

   6. _____

7. This booklet contains a concise, *clearly expressed* statement of the candidate's position.
   a. pedantic   **b.** pedagogical   **c.** explicit   **d.** erudite

   7. _____

8. *With respect to the art of teaching,* this method of learning to read is not sound.
   a. Pedagogically   **b.** Didactically   **c.** Pedantically   **d.** Explicitly

   8. _____

9. Parents influence their children by *gradually introducing* their own principles and beliefs.
   a. edifying   **b.** imbuing   **c.** indoctrinating   **d.** instilling

   9. _____

10. Gerald quit the economics club because he regarded the discussions as a subtle form of *instruction in the principles of a special group.*
    a. pedantry   **b.** indoctrination   **c.** explicitness   **d.** pedagogy

    10. _____

EXERCISE 4 USING DIFFERENT FORMS OF WORDS

Each sentence contains an italicized vocabulary word or related word in a form that does not fit the sentence. On the answer line, write the form of that word that does fit the sentence.

1. In his later years, Samuel Johnson had a brilliant career as *pedagogy* to a nation.

   1. _____

2. Mara is unusual among students at our school for the *explicit* of her opinions.

   2. _____

3. The unfortunate citizens were *indoctrinate* with a hatred of foreigners in the vain hope that this would keep them loyal to the ruling party.

   3. _____

4. The American Transcendalists believed that all natural things were *imbue* with a force or spirit that united them into a greater whole.

   4. _____

5. Modern writers may dismiss the centuries following the fall of Rome as the Dark Ages, but many men of great *erudite* lived during those times.

   5. _____

© Great Source   DO NOT COPY

6. Morals and manners are best taught by *instill* them in children from a very young age.

6. _____

7. Professor Grandison was once a brilliant scholar and an inspired teacher, but the years have worn his teaching and learning down to mere *pedantic*.

7. _____

8. In the revised edition, the author offers several new examples in *elucidate* of her main points.

8. _____

9. Her poetry is a curious blend of *didactic* and satire that appeals to a small but devoted audience.

9. _____

10. The painters said that they were trying to *edification* their patrons through art.

10. _____

READING COMPREHENSION

Each numbered sentence in the following passage contains an italicized vocabulary word or related form. After you read the passage, you will complete an exercise.

ENGLISH, THE INTERNATIONAL LANGUAGE

In order to be a high-level secretary in Mexico City or Taiwan, you must know more than typing and short-hand—you must also know English! This is because English is used by executives, scientists, and other professionals around the world. For example, English is the language of international scientific meetings. (1) Business people, computer designers, chemists, and doctors in many countries have *explicitly* stated that an understanding of English is essential to their work. In short, for many people English is becoming the standard international language.

It is estimated that over a billion people speak English as their first or second language, and the number is growing every day. Even in countries where English is not an official or native language, many people are exposed to English. (2) Popular songs, movies, and television programs *instill* a sense of the prestige of English in children, teenagers, and adults. (3) Popular culture does not have a *didactic* purpose, however, and the importance of English is reinforced by formal instruction in the language.

Courses in English have become common throughout the non-English-speaking world for students of all ages. (4) English is often part of the regular curriculum in elementary schools, for *pedagogical* research has shown that a second language is best learned by young children. Adults learn English through several different methods. One technique is the immersion method, in which the students hear only English from the moment a class begins. (5) Sometimes the students live among English-speaking people, in an environment thoroughly *imbued* with the language. Immersion is a method that stresses conversation and meaning. (6) However, it often omits more *pedantic* instruction in vocabulary and grammar. (7) This grammatical knowledge is necessary for *elucidating* unfamiliar sentences, and without it students may not be able to understand much of what they read or hear.

The spread of English has raised doubts among the leaders of some countries where English is not normally spoken. (8) Some fear that the popularity and prestige of English will detract from the *erudite* and often ancient traditions of their own languages. (9) Some do not consider learning English to be a way of *edifying* their people and making them better able to succeed economically and politically in the modern world. (10) Some think that instruction in English is a kind of *indoctrination* in an alien culture and alien values and is therefore not in the best interests of their countries. On more than one occasion, journalists have reported that English courses had been temporarily suspended by the authorities. Despite these reactions, however, English has become the language that allows the world to communicate, and the demand to learn it continues to grow.

Each of the following statements corresponds to a numbered sentence in the passage. Each statement contains a blank and is followed by four answer choices. Decide which choice fits best in the blank. The word or phrase that you choose must express roughly the same meaning as the italicized word in the passage. Write the letter of your choice on the answer line.

1. Many people in non-English-speaking countries have _____ stated that a knowledge of English is necessary for their work.
   a. angrily   b. often   c. clearly   d. ambiguously

   1. _____

2. Popular culture _____ a sense of the importance of English to people who do not speak it.
   a. introduces   b. emphasized   c. denies   d. exposes

   2. _____

3. Popular culture is not _____.
   a. important   b. formal   c. entertaining   d. intended to teach

   3. _____

4. Research _____ shows that young children learn a second language best.
   a. done by children
   b. in the art of teaching
   c. that has been done recently
   d. funded by the UN

   4. _____

5. Some students of English must live in an environment _____ the language.
   a. permeated with
   b. uncontaminated by
   c. isolated from
   d. supportive of

   5. _____

6. The immersion method often omits instruction in grammar and vocabulary that is more _____.
   a. instructive
   b. precise
   c. concerned with details
   d. popular with teachers

   6. _____

7. Knowledge of grammar and vocabulary is needed for _____ unfamiliar sentences.
   a. making up   b. reading   c. avoiding   d. clarifying

   7. _____

8. Some people who do not speak English are afraid that learning English will detract from their own _____ traditions.
   a. literary   b. learned   c. formal   d. written

   8. _____

9. Some leaders do not consider learning English to be a way of _____ their people.
   a. improving   b. teaching   c. helping   d. understanding

   9. _____

10. Some people think that teaching English is a kind of _____.
   a. experience of practical affairs
   b. instruction in special beliefs
   c. introduction to popular culture
   d. alien communication

   10. _____

WRITING ASSIGNMENT

You belong to a group of students who provide tutoring for elementary school students in your area. The group is writing guidelines for students who are interested in joining but who have never tutored before. You have been asked to contribute a paragraph. Using at least five words from this lesson and underlining each word that you use, write an explanation of your approach to tutoring a younger student in the subject of your choice.

© Great Source   DO NOT COPY

TEST-TAKING SKILLS

ANALOGY TEST ITEMS

Analogy questions appear on many standardized tests, such as the Preliminary Scholastic Assessment Test (PSAT). An **analogy** is a similarity between things that are otherwise dissimilar. An analogy test item gives a pair of words. To answer correctly, you must identify another pair of words that has a relationship similar to the one between the given pair. The following procedure will help you to select the correct answer for an analogy test item.

PROCEDURE

1. *Determine the relationship between the given pair of words.* To find the correct answer, you must understand the relationship between the given words. Study the following sample test item:

   MUSICIAN : BAND :: (A) stage : dancers   (B) alphabet : letter
   (C) student : faculty   (D) actor : company   (E) principal : school

   A musician is a part of a band. Thus, the relationship between the two stem words is of part to whole. An analogy test will frequently use such relationships as part to whole. Here are some examples of other often used relationships:

Relationship	Example
Is a Type of	coal : fuel
Is a Place Where	pharmacy : medicine
Is Used to	scale : weight
Is Characteristic of	sage : wisdom
Antonym	trivial : significance
Definitional	elusive : catch
Degree	angry : infuriated

2. *Eliminate the word pairs that have different relationships.* Knowing that you are looking for a part/whole relationship, you can eliminate choices A, C, and E in the sample test item. Choice A expresses a place/where relationship (stage-dancers), Choice C expresses a false part/whole relationship (a student is not part of a faculty), and Choice E expresses a definitional analogy (a principal is in charge of a school).

3. *Find the pair of words that has the correct relationship.* Watch for answer choices that reverse the relationship. Analogy test items often include such misleading answer choices. In the sample item above, *alphabet : letter* is similar to *musician : band* because a letter is part of an alphabet. However, the relationship is whole/part rather than part/whole. Only Choice D, *actor : company*, has the correct part/whole relationship.

EXERCISE ANSWERING ANALOGY TEST ITEMS

In each of the following items, select the lettered pair of words that best expresses a relationship similar to that expressed by the two capitalized words. Write the letter of your choice on the answer line. Use your dictionary as needed.

1. SILVER : METAL :: (A) wave : hand   (B) thunder : lightning
   (C) kitten : cat   (D) coal : fuel   (E) passenger : bus

   1. _____

2. TEMPERATURE : THERMOMETER :: (A) exposure : camera
   (B) weight : scale   (C) reflection : telescope   (D) mold : plastic
   (E) boat : barge

   2. _____

3. CHOIR : SINGER :: (A) election : voter   (B) anthology : poet
   (C) cast : actor   (D) orchestra : composer   (E) convention : organizer

   3. _____

4. DOCTOR : HOSPITAL :: (A) artist : studio   (B) patient : ward
   (C) commuter : car   (D) spectator : auditorium   (E) diner : restaurant

   4. _____

5. PEA : LEGUME :: (A) crust : pie   (B) wheat : grain
   (C) watermelon : seed   (D) root : tree   (E) apple : core

   5. _____

6. BLIZZARD : FLURRY :: (A) rumble : thunder   (B) freeze : thaw
   (C) deluge : shower   (D) desert : oasis   (E) breathe : inhale

   6. _____

7. DEJECTED : SAD :: (A) astounded : surprised   (B) repulsed : interested
   (C) bored : curious   (D) frustrated : patient   (E) encouraged : hindered

   7. _____

8. MICROSCOPE : SMALL :: (A) monocle : single   (B) telescope : distant
   (C) drill : depth   (D) elevator : height   (E) horoscope : truth

   8. _____

9. CREST : WAVE :: (A) slope : hill   (B) base : triangle   (C) peak : roof
   (D) rim : glass   (E) bank : river

   9. _____

10. PILGRIM : PIETY :: (A) extrovert : reserve   (B) explorer : curiosity
    (C) traitor : loyalty   (D) acrobat : popularity   (E) daredevil : caution

    10. _____

11. ABBREVIATE : WORD :: (A) avoid : controversy   (B) condense : story
    (C) duplicate : page   (D) introduce : speaker   (E) communicate : idea

    11. _____

12. ANONYMOUS : NAME :: (A) informal : style   (B) vast : area
    (C) analogous : parallel   (D) aimless : goal   (E) fleeting : fame

    12. _____

13. VETERAN : EXPERIENCE :: (A) soldier : bravery   (B) child : curiosity
    (C) physician : practice   (D) expert : skill   (E) actor : fame

    13. _____

14. JUVENILE : MATURITY :: (A) barren : fertility   (B) cautious : timidity
    (C) inhuman : cruelty   (D) spontaneous : originality
    (E) ambitious : inferiority

    14. _____

15. PREAMBLE : LAW :: (A) suffix : word   (B) climax : story
    (C) chapter : book   (D) location : address   (E) prologue : play

    15. _____

© Great Source   DO NOT COPY

The word root -*cur*- is derived from the Latin verb *currere*, meaning "to run."
Many English words are derived from Latin and from other European
languages, such as Spanish, French, and Rumanian, that are themselves
descended from Latin. In medieval French, the verb "to run" was *courre*.
Thus, the root is spelled as *cor*, as well as *cur*, in modern English. Common
words that contain this root include *current*, which means "something in
continuous, running motion" or, in another sense, belonging to or "running"
at the present time. Similarly, a *corridor* "runs" along a set of rooms. Even the
word "currency," money currently circulating, or, more metaphorically, "in
running movement" derives from *currere*. This lesson introduces ten
additional words that contain the root -*cur*-.

WORD LIST

concurrent
courier
cursory
discursive
incur
incursion
precursor
recourse
recurrent
succor

DEFINITIONS

After you have studied the definitions and example for each vocabulary word, write
the word on the line to the right.

1. **concurrent** (kən-kûr′ənt) *adjective*   Occurring at the same time; simultaneous.
   (From the Latin word *concurrens*, meaning "running together")

   Related Word   **concurrently** *adverb*
   Example   The judge sentenced the defendant to two *concurrent* six-month
                      terms in jail.

1. _____

2. **courier** (ko͝or′ē-ər) *noun*   A messenger, particularly one involved in a diplomatic
   transaction.

   Example   The *courier* carried copies of the treaty from Washington to
                      Geneva.

2. _____

3. **cursory** (kûr′sə-rē) *adjective*   **a.** Hasty.   **b.** Not thorough. (From the Latin word
   cursor, meaning "runner")

   Example   We learned very little from our *cursory* inspection of the hospitals.

3. _____

4. **discursive** (dĭ-skûr′sĭv) *adjective*   **a.** Rambling; digressive.   **b.** Covering a wide
   range of subjects. (From the Latin word *discursus*, meaning "running back and
   forth")

   Related Words **discourse** *noun;* **discursively** *adverb*
   Example   Mrs. Flagstad's *discursive* talk had some interesting points but was
                      hard to follow.

4. _____

5. **incur** (ĭn-kûr′) *trans. verb* To bring something upon oneself; become subject to. (From the Latin *in-*, meaning "in," and *currere*, meaning "to run")

5. _____

   Example Drusilla *incurred* considerable expense when she began planning her sixteenth birthday.

6. **incursion** (ĭn-kûr′zhən) *noun* **a.** An attack on or an invasion of enemy territory; a raid. **b.** An act of entering another's territory or domain.

6. _____

   Example In the 1500s Scottish outlaws often made *incursions* into England to pillage rich farms.

7. **precursor** (prĭ-kûr′sər, prē′kûr′sər) *noun* Someone or something that precedes something else; a forerunner. (From the Latin word *praecursor*, meaning "forerunner")

7. _____

   Example Blaise Pascal's seventeenth-century digital calculator was a *precursor* of our modern computers.

8. **recourse** (rē′kôrs′, rĭ-kôrs′) *noun* **a.** A turning to someone or something for aid or support. **b.** A source of help or strength. (From the Latin *re-*, meaning "back," and *currere*, meaning "to run")

8. _____

   Example Landlords have *recourse* to civil courts when tenants fail to pay their rent.

9. **recurrent** (rĭ-kûr′ənt) *adjective* Happening repeatedly; occurring over and over again.

9. _____

   Related Words recur *verb*; recurrence *noun*
   Example The highway has *recurrent* problems with flooding from the nearby lake.

10. **succor** (sŭk′ər) *noun* Help in time of distress. *trans. verb* To give aid and comfort in time of distress.

10. _____

   Example Florence Nightingale, the founder of the nursing profession, provided *succor* to soldiers wounded in the Crimean War (1853–1856).

© Great Source   DO NOT COPY

EXERCISE 1 WRITING CORRECT WORDS

On the answer line, write the word from the vocabulary list that best fits
each definition.

1. Simultaneous

2. An attack on or an invasion of enemy territory; a raid

3. A turning to someone or something for aid or support

4. Hasty; not thorough

5. Help in time of distress

6. Someone or something that precedes something else

7. Occurring repeatedly

8. To bring something upon oneself

9. A messenger

10. Rambling; covering many subjects

1. _____

2. _____

3. _____

4. _____

5. _____

6. _____

7. _____

8. _____

9. _____

10. _____

EXERCISE 2 USING WORDS CORRECTLY

Each of the following statements contains an italicized vocabulary word. Decide
whether the sentence is true or false, and write *True* or *False* on the answer line.

1. Handwriting in which all letters are connected is *discursive* writing.

2. A *courier* might take a declaration of war from one monarch to another.

3. The rooster crowing before sunrise is a *precursor* of the dawn.

4. A master chef has highly developed *cursory* skills.

5. By sending warriors into Northumbria, the king of Wessex made an *incursion* into that kingdom.

6. Someone who continually makes up bizarre excuses for not doing homework is being *concurrent*.

7. Thoroughbred horses walk around a *recourse* after competing in big races.

8. A *succor* is a fool.

9. The pull of the tide after a wave breaks on the shore is called *recurrent*.

10. When you anger people, you *incur* their wrath.

1. _____

2. _____

3. _____

4. _____

5. _____

6. _____

7. _____

8. _____

9. _____

10. _____

EXERCISE 3 CHOOSING THE BEST DEFINITION

For each italicized vocabulary word or related form in the following sentences, write
the letter of the best definition on the answer line.

1. Attila the Hun made many *incursions* into eastern Europe.
   a. geological surveys   **b.** religious quests   **c.** pleasure trips   **d.** raids

2. I have a *recurrent* nightmare about a spider that lives in my basement.
   a. frightening   **b.** harmless   **c.** short   **d.** repeating

1. _____

2. _____

3. Danny cast a *cursory* glance at the scoreboard and then shot his free throws.   3. _____
   a. worried   b. hasty   c. menacing   d. prolonged

4. Professor Alfred's *discursive* style of lecturing is confusing.   4. _____
   a. focused   b. learned   c. long-winded   d. rambling

5. Antony sent his answer to the Emperor by *courier*.   5. _____
   a. messenger   b. midday   c. telegram   d. cavalry

6. The doctor's responsibility is to offer *succor* to the ill.   6. _____
   a. referral   b. help   c. bills   d. money

7. The chamber-music concert and the opera were staged *concurrently* in two   7. _____
   adjoining theaters.
   a. dramatically   b. simultaneously   c. recently   d. appropriately

8. Mrs. Hodgkiss Barnes was unfortunate enough to *incur* her neighbors'   8. _____
   displeasure.
   a. beg for   c. bring upon herself
   b. seek out   d. reciprocate

9. This storm is just a *precursor* of the hurricane approaching our shores.   9. _____
   a. forerunner   b. example   c. symbol   d. consequence

10. Chumley had no *recourse* for information but the local library.
   a. organization   b. possibility   c. source of help   d. place to gather   10. _____

EXERCISE 4 USING DIFFERENT FORMS OF WORDS

Decide which form of the vocabulary word in parentheses best completes the sentence. The form given may be correct. Write your answer on the answer line.

1. The dental examination was only _____. *(cursory)*   1. _____

2. The interest on this loan is to be paid off _____ with the principal. *(concurrent)*   2. _____

3. You can always count on Mr. Mendez to offer _____ to those who need comfort. *(succor)*   3. _____

4. This author writes _____ but powerfully. *(discursive)*   4. _____

5. Look for my answer to reach you by _____ tomorrow. *(courier)*   5. _____

6. I promise you, Mrs. Larson, that this problem will never _____. *(recurrent)*   6. _____

7. Cervantes's *Don Quixote* and Sterne's *Tristram Shandy* are _____ of the modern novel. *(precursor)*   7. _____

8. Franklin's only _____ was to use the money that he had worked so hard to save. *(recourse)*   8. _____

9. Why are you always _____ unnecessary obligations? *(incur)*   9. _____

10. Maestro Alder is an accomplished conductor, but his _____ into the realm of composing has not been successful. *(incursion)*   10. _____

© Great Source   DO NOT COPY

READING COMPREHENSION

Each numbered sentence in the following passage contains an italicized vocabulary word or related form. After you read the passage, you will complete an exercise.

CHINA AND THE DAWN OF SCIENTIFIC CULTURE

(1) Even the most *cursory* survey of the history of science reveals that, from the second century B.C. until the sixteenth century A.D., China's technological achievements were without equal. (2) Many of the discoveries that were to transform Europe in the sixteenth century had *precursors* in China. Francis Bacon, the English philosopher of the early seventeenth century, considered three Chinese discoveries—the magnetic compass, the printing press, and gunpowder—to be the most powerful and influential discoveries ever made.

(3) By looking at the *recurrent* themes that emerge from the Chinese observation of nature, we can evaluate the Chinese attitude toward scientific discovery. Chinese natural philosophy had its basis in the magic and alchemy of Chinese Taoist religion. Taoist books of the ninth century, for example, warn against mixing charcoal, saltpeter, and sulphur. (4) Doing so might cause one to *incur* the wrath of nature in the form of an explosion, for these three substances are the components of gunpowder. (5) By the eleventh century, however, this magical compound had found strategic application, making *incursions* into enemy territory both easier and more efficient. Two centuries would pass before Europe adopted the use of gunpowder and refashioned its social structure entirely by making the defense of the traditional European stronghold, the castle, nearly impossible.

Bacon's choice of the most influential discoveries gives only a hint of the breadth of Chinese achievement

in science. Efficient harnesses for horses, iron and steel technology, stern-post rudders on ships, and a primitive form of vaccination are just a few of the scientific inventions and discoveries made in China.

(6) Interestingly, however, the great European scientists of the Renaissance had no *recourse* to the advances in science and technology made in China, for few of these were known in the West. Contact between China and Europe was limited for the most part to trade in luxury goods, primarily silks and spices. (7) *Concurrent* research in astronomy, for example, would have taken place with neither side aware of the findings of the other. (8) European scholars had no access to *discursive* tracts on the Chinese concept of the universe as infinite space, a concept that

would have fascinated Galileo. (9) Nor were they any *couriers* carrying news of Galileo's discoveries to the Imperial court astronomers in Peking. In post-Renaissance Europe, scientists developed seismographs, precision instruments used to measure earthquakes. They were completely unaware of seismographs that had been used in China from the second to the seventh centuries.

Fortunately, such an occurrence is not likely to happen today with improved communications and collaboration between scientists in the East and West. (10) To cite just one example, Western doctors are beginning to look seriously at Eastern therapeutic practices, such as herbal remedies and acupuncture, as methods of bringing *succor* to the sick and the suffering.

© Great Source   DO NOT COPY

Each of the following statements corresponds to a numbered sentence in the passage. Each statement contains a blank and is followed by four answer choices. Decide which choice fits best in the blank. The word or phrase that you choose must express roughly the same meaning as the italicized word in the passage. Write the letter of your choice on the answer line.

1. Even the most _____ survey of the history of science reveals that China's technological achievements were without equal.
   a. routine   **b.** thorough   **c.** hasty   **d.** doubting

1. _____

2. Many modern European discoveries had _____ in China.
   a. success   **b.** forerunners   **c.** messengers   **d.** help

2. _____

3. We can evaluate the Chinese attitude toward discovery by analyzing the _____ themes of their scientific observations.
   a. simultaneous   **b.** important   **c.** repeating   **d.** interesting

3. _____

4. By making gunpowder, one is apt to _____ the wrath of nature.
   a. give thanks for   **b.** stir up   **c.** outfit oneself with   **d.** bring upon oneself

4. _____

5. Gunpowder made _____ into enemy territory easy and efficient.
   a. raids   **c.** traveling
   b. sending messages   **d.** introducing technology

5. _____

6. Fifteenth- and sixteenth-century European scientists could not _____ the scientific advances made in China.
   a. get interested in   **c.** pay attention to
   b. understand   **d.** turn for support to

6. _____

7. _____ scientific research took place in mutual ignorance.
   a. Timely   **b.** High-level   **c.** Simultaneous   **d.** Supporting

7. _____

8. There were no _____ writings on astronomy.
   a. scientific   **b.** wide-ranging   **c.** accurate   **d.** simultaneous

8. _____

9. No _____ carried news of Galileo's discoveries to China.
   a. telegraphs   **b.** messengers   **c.** mail trains   **d.** one known

9. _____

10. Chinese medical technology has brought _____ to the sick and suffering.
    a. help   **b.** herbs and spices   **c.** cures   **d.** suffering

10. _____

See page 79 for some strategies to use with analogies.

Directions   Write the letter of the phrase that best completes the analogy.

1. SCHOLAR : ERUDITE :: (A) speaker : monotonous
   (B) miscreant : wicked   (C) patriot : truthful   (D) truant : prompt
   (E) bungler : skillful

1. _____

2. FABLE : EDIFY :: (A) poem : brief   (B) gossip : truthful
   (C) play : acclaimed   (D) comedy : amuse   (E) complaint : valid

2. _____

3. COURIER : MESSAGE :: (A) general : battle   (B) athlete : victory
   (C) student : average   (D) oracle : prophecy   (E) employee : salary

3. _____

4. ELUCIDATE : CLEAR :: (A) renovate : new   (B) indoctrinate : obscure
   (C) abbreviate : lengthy   (D) conciliate : angry   (E) vacillate : certain

4. _____

5. FLAGRANT : NOTICEABLE :: (A) terrified : calm   (B) sincere : popular
   (C) obtrusive : evident   (D) salient : blurred   (E) explicit : vague

5. _____

© Great Source   DO NOT COPY

WORD LIST

acrimonious
chastise
derogatory
disparage
harass
impugn
innuendo
invective
reprove
vilify

To criticize does not always mean "to find fault." Criticism can refer to judging the merits of something as well as its defects. For example, critics of books, plays, movies, and music offer judgments of the strengths and weaknesses of current works or performances. Rightly or wrongly, however, we most often use the words *criticism, criticize,* and *critical* to refer to negative comments. Whether it comes from family members, from friends, or from coworkers, negative criticism can be valuable: it can provide insight and make change possible.

The way in which criticism is communicated is extremely important. No one reacts well to judgments that are delivered angrily and insultingly. If criticism is to be valuable, it needs to be expressed neutrally and kindly. In the words of Frank A. Clark, "Criticism, like rain, should be gentle enough to nourish . . . growth without destroying . . . roots." This lesson will help you to become aware of the range of words used to refer to unfair or abusive criticism; the lesson will also help you to distinguish such words from those used to denote constructive criticism.

DEFINITIONS

After you have studied the definitions and example for each vocabulary word, write the word on the line to the right.

1. **acrimonious** (ăk′rə-mō′nē-əs) *adjective*   Bitter and ill-natured in language or tone. (From the Latin word *acer,* meaning "sharp")

   Related Words   **acrimoniously** *adverb;* **acrimony** *noun*
   Example   The *acrimonious* remarks of the coach upset the entire basketball team.

1. _____

MEMORY CUE: *Acrimonious* is related to *acrid,* meaning "harsh to the taste or smell" and "caustic in language or tone."

2. **chastise** (chăs-tīz′) *trans. verb*   **a.** To punish for misbehavior or wrongdoing. **b.** To criticize severely. (From the Latin word *castigare,* meaning "to correct")

   Related Word   **chastisement** *noun*
   Example   The parents *chastised* their children for playing tag in the neighbor's yard.

2. _____

3. **derogatory** (dĭ-rŏg′ə-tôr′ē) *adjective*   Detracting from the character or standing of someone or something; expressive of a low opinion; disdainful. (From the Latin *de-,* meaning "away," and *rogare,* meaning "to ask")

   Example   Not realizing that Dwayne was standing behind her, Ella made several *derogatory* comments about him.

3. _____

4. **disparage** (dĭ-spăr′ĭj) *trans. verb*   **a.** To speak of as unimportant or inferior; belittle.   **b.** To lower in rank or reputation. (From the Old French *des-,* meaning "apart," and *parage,* meaning "rank")

   Related Words   **disparagement** *noun;* **disparagingly** *adverb*
   Example   The architect *disparaged* the cluttered designs of her competitors.

4. _____

5. **harass** (hə-răs′, hăr′əs) *trans. verb*   **a.** To bother or torment repeatedly and persistently.   **b.** To carry out repeated attacks or raids against: *harass the enemy.* (From the Old French word *harer,* meaning "to set a dog on")

   Related Word   harassment *noun*
   Example   The unknown caller *harassed* the family by phoning late at night and then hanging up.

6. **impugn** (ĭm-pyo͞on′) *trans. verb*   **a.** To criticize or refute by argumentation.   **b.** To oppose as false or worthless; cast doubt on. (From the Latin *in-,* meaning "against," and *pugnare,* meaning "to fight")

   Example   In five minutes of cross-examination, the attorney had *impugned* the testimony of the star witness.

7. **innuendo** (ĭn′yo͞o-ĕn′dō) *noun*   **a.** A roundabout, often spiteful reference to someone or something not named; an insinuation.   **b.** An indirect suggestion meant to discredit a person. (From the Latin word *innuendo,* meaning "by hinting")

   Example   Many Hollywood gossip columnists spread scandal by *innuendo.*

8. **invective** (ĭn-vĕk′tĭv) *noun*   Sharp, harsh, insulting words used to attack; violent denunciation or abuse. (From the Latin word *invectivus,* meaning "reproachful")

   Example   We were shocked at the reviewer's *invective* about the new film by our favorite director.

9. **reprove** (rĭ-pro͞ov′) *trans. verb*   **a.** To scold or correct, usually gently and with kindly intent.   **b.** To express disapproval of. (From the Latin *re-,* meaning "not," and *approbare,* meaning "to approve")

   Related Words   reproof *noun;* reprovingly *adverb*
   Example   Norton *reproved* the puppies for tracking mud into the kitchen.

10. **vilify** (vĭl′ə-fī′) *trans. verb*   To utter slanderous and abusive statements against; defame; speak evil of. (From the Latin words *vilis,* meaning "worthless," and *facere,* meaning "to make")

    Related Word   vilification *noun*
    Example   The local newspaper *vilified* Senator Gilbart for his position on taxes and the economy.

5. _____

6. _____

7. _____

8. _____

9. _____

10. _____

Word History: acrimonious

Latin: *acer*=sharp

   Someone's *acrimonious* remarks might upset you since they are bitter and ill-natured in tone. *Acrimonious* comes from the Latin word *acer,* meaning "sharp," and often occurs in English derivatives that have to do with bitterness or sharpness. An unusual derivative of *acer* is the word *vinegar* from the Latin *vinum,* "wine," plus *acer,* "bitter," adapted from the Old French *vin aigre* "sour wine." Since *vinegar* is actually wine that has become bitter or sour in the process of grape fermentation, its root *acer* "flavors" its meaning significantly.

© Great Source   DO NOT COPY

EXERCISE 1 MATCHING WORDS AND DEFINITIONS

Match the definition in Column B with the word in Column A. Write the letter of the correct definition on the answer line.

Column A

1. innuendo
2. acrimonious
3. impugn
4. disparage
5. invective
6. reprove
7. harass
8. chastise
9. derogatory
10. vilify

Column B

a. to punish for wrongdoing; criticize severely

b. to scold or correct with kindly intent; express disapproval of

c. bitter and ill-natured in language or tone

d. detracting from the character or standing of; expressive of a low opinion

e. to criticize by argumentation; oppose as false or worthless

f. to speak of as unimportant or inferior; belittle

g. to utter slanderous and abusive statements against; defame

h. a roundabout and often spiteful reference to someone or something not named; an insinuation

i. insulting words used to attack; violent denunciation or abuse

j. to irritate or torment persistently; carry out repeated attacks

1. _____
2. _____
3. _____
4. _____
5. _____
6. _____
7. _____
8. _____
9. _____
10. _____

EXERCISE 2 USING WORDS CORRECTLY

Decide whether the italicized vocabulary word has been used correctly in the sentence. On the answer line, write *Correct* for correct use and *Incorrect* for incorrect use.

1. By questioning the authenticity of the Vermeer painting, Mrs. Carlisle *impugned* the reputation of the museum director who had purchased it.

2. Anthony's baby sitter *chastised* him for taking his stuffed animals into the bathtub with him.

3. Katherine's *derogatory* remarks about Jack's pet parrot made Jack beam with pride.

4. "Confront me directly," said Gilbert. "I will not defend myself against anonymous accusations and *innuendo*."

5. After the debate the two candidates shook hands, smiled at each other, and exchanged *acrimonious* remarks.

6. Minna glowed with pleasure whenever *invectives* were lavished upon her.

7. In one of Aesop's fables, a hare *disparages* a tortoise's slow speed.

8. Because of her good grades, Stella was *reproved* and made class speaker for graduation.

9. Yasuko *harassed* her little brother by tickling him.

10. Everyone in the neighborhood *vilified* the driver of the car that caused a fatal accident.

1. _____
2. _____
3. _____
4. _____
5. _____
6. _____
7. _____
8. _____
9. _____
10. _____

EXERCISE 3 CHOOSING THE BEST DEFINITION

For each italicized vocabulary word in the following sentences, write the letter of the best definition on the answer line.

1. The *acrimonious* bickering of our neighbors seemed to go on for hours.
   a. foolish   **b.** ill-natured   **c.** feeble   **d.** outrageous

   1. _____

2. As the crowd *harassed* him with whistles and shouts, the speaker's voice rose louder and louder.
   a. applauded   **b.** educated   **c.** tormented   **d.** rushed

   2. _____

3. Anne *disparages* the work of abstract painters like Jasper Johns.
   a. belittles   **b.** approves of   **c.** imitates   **d.** notices

   3. _____

4. Mary Queen of Scots *impugned* Elizabeth I's right to the throne of England.
   a. supported as logical   **b.** challenged as false   **c.** favored   **d.** emphasized

   4. _____

5. Although he expected praise for his cooking, Hank received only *derogatory* comments from his brother and sisters.
   a. joking   **b.** positive   **c.** angry   **d.** degrading

   5. _____

6. Monica still can't seem to get to work on time even though her boss has *reproved* her for lateness.
   a. gently scolded   **b.** harshly punished   **c.** criticized   **d.** demoted

   6. _____

7. Hernandez realized that *innuendo* had no effect on Derek.
   a. spiteful insinuation   **c.** constructive suggestion
   b. an irregular idea   **d.** pleading

   7. _____

8. *Chastised* for overturning the plant, the cat huddled by its owner's chair, waiting to be forgiven.
   a. Praised   **b.** Punished   **c.** Encouraged   **d.** Chased

   8. _____

9. The general's *invective* had the intended effect: the recruits were instantly quiet.
   a. speech   **b.** charming approach   **c.** analysis   **d.** insulting attack

   9. _____

10. The politician gave up his hopes of re-election after being *vilified* by his constituents.
    a. complimented   **b.** defamed   **c.** criticized   **d.** rewarded

    10. _____

EXERCISE 4 USING DIFFERENT FORMS OF WORDS

Decide which form of the vocabulary word in parentheses best completes the sentence. The form given may be correct. Write the answer on the answer line.

1. The children, who just moments before had been speaking _____ to one another, were again playing happily. *(acrimonious)*

   1. _____

2. "_____ my character won't build your own," Carla angrily told Rick. *(impugn)*

   2. _____

3. Ralph's feelings were hurt by Millicent's _____ comments. *(derogatory)*

   3. _____

4. The candidate spoke _____ of his opponent's voting record. *(disparage)*

   4. _____

5. Apologetic for yesterday's _____, Harrison made a special effort to be complimentary. *(invective)*

   5. _____

6. The children forgot their mother's _____ in half an hour. *(reprove)*

   6. _____

7. The children's forgetfulness brought them further _____. *(chastise)*

   7. _____

8. Casey didn't realize that the director's _____ were directed against his performance. *(innuendo)*

   8. _____

9. The man was taken to court on charges of _____. *(harass)*

   9. _____

10. The author ignored the _____ of her recent novel. *(vilify)*

    10. _____

© Great Source   DO NOT COPY

READING COMPREHENSION

Each numbered sentence in the following passage contains an italicized vocabulary word or related form. After you read the passage, you will complete an exercise.

THE ORIGIN OF THE SEASONS

The ancient Greeks attributed the cycle of summer and winter to the gods. The myth of Demeter, goddess of grain and fertility, and her daughter Persephone explains the reasons for the changing seasons and the death and renewal of vegetation.

Persephone, the daughter of Demeter and Zeus, was a beautiful girl who reminded everyone of the youth and joy of spring. The god of the underworld, Hades, fell in love with Persephone as he watched her play in the meadows and pick flowers. Believing that she would bring beauty and gaiety to his gloomy kingdom, he went to Olympus to ask Zeus for permission to marry her. (1) Zeus was afraid of offending his eldest brother with an outright refusal, but he also knew that Demeter would *impugn* his judgment if he gave his permission. (2) Responding to Hades' *harassment,* Zeus answered shrewdly that he could neither give nor withhold his consent. (3) Hades, certain that he would not be *reproved* by Zeus, made plans to abduct Persephone.

One day, as Persephone was picking flowers with her handmaidens, she strayed from the group. Suddenly the earth opened in front of her, and she found herself swept into a golden chariot by Hades. Before she could call out to the others, the earth closed over her.

When Demeter heard of her daughter's mysterious disappearance, she was grief-stricken. (4) *Chastising* Persephone's handmaidens was useless; they had no idea what had happened to her. (5) For nine days Demeter searched everywhere and

acrimoniously questioned all whom she met. The response was always the same; neither gods nor humans had seen Persephone.

Finally, Demeter went to Phoebus Apollo, god of the sun, who saw everything. When she learned from him what had transpired between Hades and Zeus, she was both furious and despairing. She knew that returning to Olympus was out of the question. (6) She would not be able to prevent herself from hurling *invective* at Zeus and might anger him. Instead, she continued to wander the earth, giving no thought to her duties as the harvest goddess.

The earth suffered as Demeter suffered. Nothing grew, and even offerings to the gods were neglected by people who could not spare anything from their dwindling supplies. When famine threatened the earth, Zeus knew he would have to do something. Ashamed to visit Demeter himself, he sent Iris, the rainbow goddess, to persuade her to do her duty. (7) Although Iris urged her with

messages from Zeus and offerings of gifts, Demeter responded only with *innuendoes* about the king of the gods. She would neither return to Olympus nor let vegetation grow until Persephone was returned to her.

(8) Although the other gods and goddesses had begun to speak of Demeter in a *derogatory* way, Zeus accepted the responsibility for the situation and sent Hermes, messenger of the gods, to bring Persephone back. (9) Although Hades *disparaged* Zeus' power, he could not disobey his younger brother's commands. The god of the underworld was crafty, however. Before Persephone left with Hermes, Hades pressed Persephone to celebrate her departure with him by drinking and eating. Persephone was eager to leave, but to avoid argument and further delay, she ate seven seeds of a pomegranate.

The joyous reunion of Demeter and Persephone was marred only by the information that Persephone had eaten part of the pomegranate, thereby magically binding herself to Hades. (10) When Demeter heard this, she *vilified* both Zeus and Hades for their tricks. Although Zeus worked out a compromise that Persephone would dwell in the underworld for seven months and return to her mother for five, Demeter vowed that the earth would be barren while her daughter was gone. Only when Persephone returned would Demeter permit trees to bloom, plants to flower, and crops to grow. Thus, every spring and summer the earth rejoices along with Demeter when Persephone reappears from the land of the dead.

Each of the following statements corresponds to a numbered sentence in the passage. Each statement contains a blank and is followed by four answer choices. Decide which choice fits best in the blank. The word or phrase that you choose must express roughly the same meaning as the italicized word in the passage. Write the letter of your choice on the answer line.

1. Zeus knew that Demeter would _____ his judgment if he gave Hades permission to marry Persephone.
   a. refuse to accept   **b.** criticize   **c.** support   **d.** rebel against

1. _____

2. Reacting to Hades' _____, Zeus neither gave nor withheld his consent.
   a. logical arguments   **c.** persistent bothering
   b. sorrowful pleas   **d.** angry threats

2. _____

3. Hades was sure that he would not be _____ by Zeus.
   a. protected   **b.** punished   **c.** congratulated   **d.** scolded

3. _____

4. Demeter could not _____ Persephone's handmaidens because they had no idea what had happened to her.
   a. punish   **b.** thank   **c.** resent   **d.** respect

4. _____

5. Demeter searched everywhere for Persephone and _____ questioned all whom she met.
   a. painfully   **b.** bitterly   **c.** sadly   **d.** proudly

5. _____

6. Demeter worried that she could not prevent herself from hurling _____ at Zeus.
   a. boulders   **b.** accusations   **c.** sarcasm   **d.** verbal attacks

6. _____

7. Turning down gifts, Demeter responded with _____ about the king of the gods.
   a. insinuations   **b.** sarcasm   **c.** gossip   **d.** compliments

7. _____

8. The other gods and goddesses had begun to speak of Demeter in a _____ way.
   a. suspicious   **b.** proud   **c.** disdainful   **d.** timid

8. _____

9. Hades _____ Zeus' power.
   a. mourned   **b.** belittled   **c.** celebrated   **d.** ignored

9. _____

10. Because of their tricks, Demeter _____ Zeus and Hades.
    a. made abusive statements about   **c.** questioned the rights of
    b. complained about   **d.** argued with

10. _____

You have recently observed an incident that disturbed or irritated you. For example, you might have witnessed an example of poor sportsmanship at a hockey match or an impolite audience at a school assembly. Write a letter to the editor of your school newspaper in which you criticize the actions of the people involved in the incident. Use at least five of the vocabulary words from this lesson in your letter and underline each word that you use.

© Great Source   DO NOT COPY

By helping others or by improving the way something is done, we can have a positive impact on the world. Whether the help or improvement is as simple as one traveler giving directions to another or as involved as one nation helping another to develop its agriculture, people can make a difference in other people's lives. The words in this lesson will enable you to understand and describe the aid you give or receive.

WORD LIST

aegis
amends
conciliatory
conducive
extricate
foster
importune
mediate
mitigate
rectify

DEFINITIONS

After you have studied the definitions and example for each vocabulary word, write the word on the line to the right.

1. **aegis** (ē′jĭs) *noun* **a.** Sponsorship. **b.** Protection. (From the Greek word *aigis*, the name of the shield used by Zeus and Athena)

   Example   The group of Japanese scientists toured the United States under the *aegis* of the State Department.

   1. _____
   USAGE NOTE: *Aegis* is often part of the idiomatic expression *under the aegis of.*

2. **amends** (ə-měndz′) *noun*   Compensation given as satisfaction for insult, loss, or injury. **To make amends**   To make up (to someone) for an insult or injury. (From the Old French word *amendes*, meaning "penalties" or "reparations")

   Example   Carl was ashamed of his behavior and wanted to make *amends* to his parents.

   2. _____
   USAGE NOTE: The noun *amends* is always used in the plural.

3. **conciliatory** (kən-sĭl′ē-ə-tôr′ē) *adjective*   Tending to win over or soothe; attempting to overcome distrust or anger. (From the Latin word *concilium*, meaning "a meeting")

   Related Words   conciliate *verb;* **conciliation** *noun*
   Example   Realizing how angry she sounded, Amanda adopted a more *conciliatory* tone of voice.

   3. _____
   ETYMOLOGY NOTE: *Conciliate* has the same root as *reconcile*, which means "to reestablish friendship between" and "to settle or resolve."

4. **conducive** (kən-dōō′sĭv, kən-dyōō′sĭv) *adjective*   **a.** Tending to cause, promote, or help bring about. **b.** Helpful; favorable. (From the Latin *com-*, meaning "together," and *ducere*, meaning "to lead")

   Related Word   conduciveness *noun*
   Example   The ranger explained that the dryness of the summer was *conducive* to forest fires.

   4. _____

5. **extricate** (ĕk'strĭ-kāt') *trans. verb*   To free or release from an entanglement or difficulty; disengage. (From the Latin *ex-*, meaning "out," and *tricae*, meaning "hindrances")

   Related Word   extrication *noun*
   Example   Wesley *extricated* the lobster traps from the tangled lines.

   5. _____

6. **foster** (fô'stər, fŏs'tər) *trans. verb*   **a.** To promote the development or growth of; cultivate.   **b.** To bring up; rear: *to foster a child.*   *adjective*   Receiving or giving parental care although not related through legal or blood ties: *foster parents.* (From the Old English word *fostor*, meaning "food")

   Example   Moderate rain *fosters* the growth of such important crops as corn and wheat.

   6. _____

7. **importune** (ĭm'-pôr-tōōn', ĭm'pôr-tyōōn', ĭm-pôr'chən) *trans. verb*   To press with repeated and insistent requests; beg urgently. (From the Medieval Latin word *importunari*, meaning "to be troublesome")

   Related Word   importunate *adjective*
   Example   Five-year-old Diane *importuned* her grandparents for weeks until they gave in and bought her a camera.

   7. _____

8. **mediate** (mē'dē-āt') *trans. verb*   **a.** To help the opposing sides in a dispute come to an agreement by hearing their arguments and proposing a compromise. **b.** To settle by intervening in this way: *to mediate a boundary dispute.*   *intrans. verb* To intervene between disputing parties to bring about an agreement: *to mediate between the two of you.* (From the Latin word *mediare*, meaning "to be in the middle")

   Related Words   mediation *noun;* **mediator** *noun*
   Example   Mrs. Sevigny often *mediates* salary disputes between workers and their employers.

   8. _____

9. **mitigate** (mĭt'ĭ-gāt') *trans. verb*   To make less severe or intense; moderate. (From the Latin word *mitis*, meaning "soft")

   Related Word   mitigation *noun*
   Example   The editor's complimentary letter *mitigated* Lou's disappointment at having his short story rejected by the magazine.

   9. _____

10. **rectify** (rĕk'tə-fī') *trans. verb*   **a.** To set right; remedy.   **b.** To correct by calculation or adjustment: *to rectify the schedule.* (From the Medieval Latin word *rectus*, meaning "right," and the Latin word *facere*, meaning "to make")

    Related Words   rectifiable *adjective;* **rectification** *noun*
    Example   The accountant *rectified* the errors in the tax form.

    10. _____

© Great Source   DO NOT COPY

EXERCISE 1 WRITING CORRECT WORDS

On the answer line, write the word from the vocabulary list that best fits
each definition.

1. To promote the development of; bring up or rear

2. To press with insistent requests

3. To remedy; correct by adjustment

4. Tending to cause or help bring about; favorable

5. Compensation for loss or insult

6. To make less severe or intense; moderate

7. Tending to win over or soothe

8. Sponsorship or protection

9. To help the opposing sides in a dispute come to an agreement

10. To release from entanglement

1. _____

2. _____

3. _____

4. _____

5. _____

6. _____

7. _____

8. _____

9. _____

10. _____

EXERCISE 2 USING WORDS CORRECTLY

Decide whether the italicized vocabulary word has been used correctly in the sentence.
On the answer line, write *Correct* for correct use and *Incorrect* for incorrect use.

1. Doctors generally agree that exercise is *conducive* to good health.

2. The judge *mitigated* the criminal's prison term by adding five years to it.

3. Jordan's *conciliatory* manner was evident in his stubborn refusal to leave the room.

4. Zoo keepers *foster* the well-being of animals under their care.

5. Much medical research is conducted under the *aegis* of the federal government.

6. Rob intended to *rectify* his oversight by continuing to ignore the problem.

7. Lynn *extricated* herself from the situation with a reasonable excuse.

8. The volunteer *importuned* everyone in the community to contribute to the famine-
relief fund.

9. A person can *mediate* a dispute by taking sides.

10. Theodora made *amends* to her neighbor by paying for the broken window.

1. _____

2. _____

3. _____

4. _____

5. _____

6. _____

7. _____

8. _____

9. _____

10. _____

EXERCISE 3 CHOOSING THE BEST WORD

Decide which vocabulary word or related form best completes the sentence, and write
the letter of your choice on the answer line.

1. Training and good nutrition are _____ to athletic excellence.
   a. rectifiable   **b.** importunate   **c.** conducive   **d.** conciliatory

2. The Secretary of State was asked to _____ the trade dispute between the two
nations.
   a. mediate   **b.** extricate   **c.** foster   **d.** importune

1. _____

2. _____

3. Although Guido _____ her daily to return his jacket, it was two weeks before Sally remembered to take it to school.

    a. mediated   **b.** rectified   **c.** extricated   **d.** importuned

3. _____

4. During the Italian Renaissance, many talented artists worked under the _____ of the Medici family.

    a. aegis   **b.** amends   **c.** conciliation   **d.** mediation

4. _____

5. Lisa hoped that her apologetic letter to the Perezes would make _____ for her lack of hospitality during their visit.

    a. mitigation   **b.** amends   c aegis   **d.** conciliation

5. _____

6. Sam's weekly allergy shots helped to _____ his uncomfortable symptoms.

    a. conciliate   **b.** extricate   **c.** foster   **d.** mitigate

6. _____

7. By giving the roses special plant food, the gardener _____ their growth.

    a. extricated   **b.** conciliated   **c.** fostered   **d.** mediated

7. _____

8. Carrie attempted to _____ a belt from the pile of clothing.

    a. importune   **b.** rectify   **c.** mitigate   **d.** extricate

8. _____

9. Jesse soon realized that the computer program was not _____; he would have to start over.

    a. conducive   **b.** rectifiable   **c.** conciliatory   **d.** fostered

9. _____

10. Wanda tried to _____ her mother by doing extra chores around the house.

    a. extricate   **b.** foster   **c.** mitigate   **d.** conciliate

10. _____

EXERCISE 4 USING DIFFERENT FORMS OF WORDS

Decide which form of the vocabulary word in parentheses best completes the sentence. The form given may be correct. Write your answer on the answer line.

1. The United Nations is the official _____ of conflicts between member states. *(mediate)*

1. _____

2. Tina tried to _____ her angry brother by giving him a present. *(conciliatory)*

2. _____

3. With patience and care, Felicia managed the _____ of her jacket from the barbed wire. *(extricate)*

3. _____

4. The _____ of the weather to outdoor activities pleased the tourists, who planned to spend the day hiking in the mountains. *(conducive)*

4. _____

5. Their delight with their new home _____ the sadness they felt at leaving their old friends and neighbors. *(mitigate)*

5. _____

6. The relief funds had _____ the growth of the country's economy after the war. *(foster)*

6. _____

7. Working as an undercover detective allowed Mr. Bryce to employ his investigative skills under the _____ of the law. *(aegis)*

7. _____

8. Lucille knew that the mistakes she had made were _____. *(rectify)*

8. _____

9. Jill's father was not moved by her _____; regardless of what she said, he would not permit her to drive on the icy streets. *(importune)*

9. _____

10. "There's no need to apologize to me," said Harvey, "but you should try to make _____ to Terri." *(amends)*

10. _____

© Great Source DO NOT COPY

READING COMPREHENSION

Each numbered sentence in the following passage contains an italicized vocabulary word. After you read the passage, you will complete an exercise.

"WHO'S AFRAID OF THE BIG, BAD WOLF?": EXPOSING THE MYTH

The belief that wolves are dangerous to people is deeply ingrained in our consciousness. (1) Superstition and folklore have *fostered* the image of the wolf as cruel and vicious. Farmers and ranchers have hated wolves as killers of livestock. Since 1793 the Canadian government has paid a bounty of twenty-five dollars for each adult wolf killed. Even though listed on the endangered-species list, the wolf continues to be hunted as a major enemy.

(2) In recent years scientists have done much to try to *mitigate* the fear of those who regard the wolf as a treacherous creature. (3) Under the *aegis* of the United States and Canadian governments, researchers have discovered that wolves are intelligent, social animals and good parents. For example, the Canadian government, concerned that wolves were destroying helpless herds of caribou and deer, hired Farley Mowat, a naturalist, to investigate the situation. (4) Living among the wolves for two years under conditions *conducive* to close observation, Mowat discovered that wolves are loyal, responsible animals.

The wolf population is divided into packs composed of seven to ten parents, pups, and close relatives. Wolves mate for life. Although a pack may contain more than one family, only one wolf couple per pack mates each year.

Each pack seems to have a very definite social system. The leader is the largest and strongest animal, followed in order of strength by younger and older males, the mate of the leader, other females, and the pups. Each pack also seems to have one member at the lowest end of the social scale. This wolf trails behind the pack and does not participate in gestures of mutual respect and affection, such as tail-wagging. (5) While it may try to make *amends* to the others for some unknown violation, there does not seem to be anything the outcast can do to change its position. The pack functions as a complete unit, however, when driving off strangers or when interacting with neighboring packs.

The wolf pack acts as a family, in that all members accept the responsibility for the education, protection, and feeding of the pups. (6) The pups' relatives supervise while the parents hunt, and they often *mediate* when play becomes too rough. (7) Although wolves attack and maul each other while playing, they are always *conciliatory* at the end of these sessions.

Besides good care of the young, the pack organization also provides greater hunting efficiency. To their surprise, researchers found that wolves seldom attack and kill herd animals. (8) Wolves are not particularly fast, so most healthy deer and caribou can *extricate* themselves from an attack by fleeing. Wolves prey on young, old, or sick animals that are most easily caught and killed. They cleverly rely on food sources that are most readily available in the largest quantity with the least expenditure of energy. Farley Mowat was astounded to discover that the staple diet of the wolves he observed consisted of field mice.

Most people believe that wolves are capable of catching almost anything and that they will slaughter everything that comes within their range. Mowat discovered, however, that wolves never kill for the sake of killing. Once they obtain enough food for their own and the pack's needs, they spend the rest of their time resting, socializing, or playing. (9) Another misconception that Mowat was able to *rectify* was that wolves attack people. Mowat found that the wolves he observed ignored his presence, even when he was close to the dens and pups. The wolves stalked him only out of curiosity, before they had caught his scent. Wolves take full advantage of their ability to command a situation by threatening to attack. Once they can identify the unknown, they back down.

The work done by Mowat and other researchers has also proved that the wolf is vitally important in preserving, rather than destroying, herds of caribou, moose, and deer. However, ingrained prejudices still exist. (10) Environmentalists continue to *importune* government agencies to put a stop to the widespread extermination of the wolf.

READING COMPREHENSION EXERCISE

Each of the following statements corresponds to a numbered sentence in the passage. Each statement contains a blank and is followed by four answer choices. Decide which choice fits best in the blank. The word or phrase that you choose must express roughly the same meaning as the italicized word in the passage. Write the letter of your choice on the answer line.

1. The image of the wolf as cruel and vicious has been _____ by folklore.
   a. protected   **b.** promoted   **c.** created   **d.** described

   1. _____

2. Scientists have done much to _____ people's fears of wolves.
   a. intensify   **b.** explain   **c.** find excuses for   **d.** lessen the severity of

   2. _____

3. Researchers under government _____ have found good traits in wolves.
   a. supervision   **b.** direction   **c.** contracts   **d.** sponsorship

   3. _____

4. Farley Mowat lived with the wolves under conditions _____ close observation.
   a. favorable to   **b.** dangerous for   **c.** inevitable for   **d.** unfavorable to

   4. _____

5. The outcast of the pack tries to _____ the other wolves for some violation.
   a. injure   **b.** attack   **c.** make up to   **d.** get even with

   5. _____

6. Wolf relatives _____ when play among the pups gets rough.
   a. punish   **b.** intervene   **c.** hide   **d.** howl

   6. _____

7. Although they attack each other, wolves are _____ when play ends.
   a. hostile   **b.** soothing   **c.** resentful   **d.** exhausted

   7. _____

8. Healthy animals can easily _____ from a wolf attack.
   a. disengage themselves   **b.** defend themselves   **c.** profit   **d.** die

   8. _____

9. Mowat _____ the misconception that wolves attack people.
   a. built   **b.** advanced   **c.** proved   **d.** corrected

   9. _____

10. Environmentalists _____ government agencies to stop the slaughter of wolves.
    a. insistently press   **b.** often tell   **c.** help   **d.** direct

    10. _____

WRITING ASSIGNMENT

Self-help books are among the most popular and best-selling nonfiction on the market. You have decided to use your expertise in a particular area, such as time management, sports, or cooking, to write such a book. Using at least five of the vocabulary words from this lesson, write a brief summary of your book that you will submit to a publisher. Underline each word that you use.

VOCABULARY ENRICHMENT

In Greek mythology the word *aigis* was originally the name for a goatskin worn by Zeus, the king of the gods. He lent the skin to his favorite daughter, Athena, so often that it became associated with her. In time Athena came to use it as a shield. When she helped Perseus kill Medusa, a monster who turned people to stone, Perseus gave Athena the monster's head. Athena placed it on the shield, so that it turned enemies to stone besides protecting the wearer from harm. Despite its violent history, the word *aegis* is used today in a positive sense of protection or sponsorship.

Activity   Many other English words derive from classical mythology. Look up the following words in a dictionary and write a brief explanation of each etymology. Then write the modern definition of each word.

1. chimerical   2. nemesis   3. protean   4. saturnine   5. mercurial

© Great Source   DO NOT COPY

TEST-TAKING SKILLS
READING COMPREHENSION TEST ITEMS

The reading comprehension section is an important and challenging part of the PSAT and other standardized tests. In a test of reading comprehension, you are asked to read paragraphs and longer selections and to answer questions about them. Since the tests are timed, you must be able to read quickly but carefully. Reading comprehension tests call upon all of your reading skills: knowledge of vocabulary, recall of facts, and the ability to draw conclusions from what you have read. The following strategies will help you when you take a test of reading comprehension.

STRATEGIES

1. *Focus on the main idea.* The main idea of a reading selection is the overall point that the author wishes to communicate. A test question may ask you to select a title for the passage. The best answer choice is the one that expresses the main idea. Alternatively, a test question may ask you to determine the author's purpose in writing the passage. To answer the question, you must determine how the author presented the main idea to the reader.

2. *Note sentences that support the main idea.* Writers support their main ideas with sentences that give reasons and examples. You should note these sentences and mentally arrange them under the main idea that they support. Reading comprehension questions often require you to identify supporting data given in the passage.

3. *Distinguish conclusions from support sentences.* Conclusions are general statements that sum up the ideas presented in prior sentences. Conclusions are signaled by such words and phrases as *thus, therefore,* and *in summary.* Tests frequently ask you to identify a conclusion that has been stated in the reading passage.

4. *Be prepared to make inferences about what you have read.* An inference is an unstated conclusion that can be drawn on the basis of what has been stated. Suppose, for example, that you read the following sentence: "McGee was just getting back to normal after two weeks in the hospital." From the sentence you can draw the inference that McGee recently was ill or suffering from an injury. Test questions frequently require you to draw inferences based on statements in the reading passage.

5. *Read as fast as you can and still retain the meaning.* Read the passage before you answer the questions. Verify each answer by quickly checking the relevant part of the passage. Answer the questions in terms of the passage, not in terms of what you may already know about the subject.

Read the passage carefully and then answer the questions about it. For each question write the letter of your choice on the answer line.

The moon is a satellite orbiting around Earth; the moon's changing position relative to Earth and the sun generates its phases. The lunar cycle or month starts when the moon is in the same direction as the sun when viewed from Earth. When the moon is *new*, it is invisible since we on Earth cannot see the sunlit side. A few days later, the moon has progressed in its orbit to the point where we can see a little sliver, or *crescent*, of the sunlit moon. At this point in the cycle, the moon is still close to the sun in the sky and sets shortly after sunset.

One week after its new-moon phase, the moon is at a right angle to the sun in the sky. Half of the part of the moon that we see from Earth is now sunlit, and half is in darkness. We see a half moon at this *first-quarter* phase, named because the moon is one quarter of the way around its orbit. The first quarter-moon is a prominent feature of the late afternoon sky, since it rises at noon and sets at midnight.

A few days after the first-quarter phase, the moon has moved around in its orbit so that all but a slim crescent, in the part of the moon farthest from the sun, is illuminated. In this *gibbous* phase, the almost complete disk of the moon is quite bright, dominating the southeastern part of the evening sky. A few days after the gibbous phase, the moon has reached the point in its orbit opposite to the sun. The entire sunlit side of the moon now faces Earth. This *full* moon rises in the east at sunset.

During the last two weeks of the lunar cycle, the moon retraces its phases in reverse order—gibbous, last quarter, crescent, and back to a new moon again.

1. The author's purpose in writing the passage was
   (A) to present controversial theory about a phenomenon
   (B) to compare theories about a phenomenon
   (C) to explain and describe a phenomenon
   (D) to persuade the reader to agree with his opinion
   (E) to demonstrate a scientific approach

1. _____

2. The phases of the moon result from the moon's changing position relative to which of the following?
   I. Earth
   II. the sun
   III. the stars
   (A) I only   (B) II only   (C) III only   (D) I and II only   (E) I, II, and III

2. _____

3. The moon is said to be gibbous when it is
   (A) at the first-quarter phase   (B) new   (C) only a crescent   (D) full
   (E) nearly full

3. _____

4. It can be inferred that the moon becomes more visible from Earth as the moon
   (A) moves closer to the sun   (D) moves farther from Earth
   (B) moves farther from the sun   (E) rises in the sky
   (C) moves closer to Earth

4. _____

5. The moon in the first quarter rises at
   (A) noon   (B) night   (C) midnight   (D) sunrise   (E) sunset

5. _____

                                    © Great Source   DO NOT COPY

The roots *-cede-* and *-cess-*, which come from the Latin word *cedere*, meaning "to go" or "to yield," have given us many English words. Similarly, the roots *-grad-* and *-gress-*, which come from the Latin word *gradi*, meaning "to step," have also given us a number of English words. If you *precede* someone in line, you go before that person. An *excessive* amount of energy goes beyond the average. If you complete a task *gradually*, you do it step by step. *Progress* deals with making steps forward in the right direction. In this lesson you will learn other words that refer to going and to taking steps.

WORD LIST

concede
deceased
egress
gradation
gradient
predecessor
regress
secession
transgress
unprecedented

DEFINITIONS

After you have studied the definitions and example for each vocabulary word, write the word on the line to the right.

1. **concede** (kən-sēd′) *trans. verb* **a.** To acknowledge as true or real, often unwillingly. **b.** To give; yield; grant. *intrans. verb* To make a concession; yield. (From the Latin word *concedere*, meaning "to yield")

   Related Word concession *noun*
   Example The speaker *conceded* that the audience had been inattentive.

   1. _____

2. **deceased** (dĭ-sēst′) *adjective* No longer living; dead. *noun* A dead person. (From the Latin *de-*, meaning "away," and *cedere*, meaning "to go")

   Example In horror films characters believed to be *deceased* often come to life again.

   2. _____

3. **egress** (ē′grĕs′) *noun* A path or means of going out; an exit. (From the Latin *ex-*, meaning "out," and *gradi*, meaning "to step")

   Example To encourage people to leave a circus exhibit, P. T. Barnum once posted a sign that read: "See the *egress!*"

   3. _____

4. **gradation** (grā-dā′shən) *noun* **a.** A degree or stage in a series of gradual changes. **b.** A series of such changes; systematic progression. (From the Latin word *gradus*, meaning "step")

   Example The picture was notable for the *gradations* in shading from light to dark.

   4. _____

5. **gradient** (grā'dē-ənt) *noun*   **a.** The degree to which something inclines; slope.
   b. An ascending or descending part; an incline. (From the Latin word *gradus*, meaning "step")

   Example   The *gradient* of the mountain sharply increased after the first mile of climbing.

5. _____

6. **predecessor** (prĕd'ĭ-sĕs'ər) *noun*   Someone or something that comes before another in time, especially in an office or position; forerunner. (From the Latin *prae-*, meaning "before," and *de-*, meaning "away," and *cedere*)

   Example   Helen had difficulty adjusting to the new job because her *predecessor* had been so disorganized.

6. _____

   USAGE NOTE: Compare with *successor*, "one who comes *after* in time," and *intercessor*, "one who pleads on another's behalf" (or goes *between*).

7. **regress** (rĭ-grĕs') *intrans. verb*   To go back; return to a previous condition. (From the Latin *re-*, meaning "back," and *gradi*, meaning "to step")

   Related Words   regression *noun;* **regressive** *adjective*
   Example   When the trainer was not present, the athletes *regressed* to their former bad habits.

7. _____

8. **secession** (sĭ-sĕsh'ən) *noun*   The act of withdrawing formally from membership in an organization, association, or union. (From the Latin *se-*, meaning "apart," and *cedere*)

   Related Word   secede *verb*
   Example   The *secession* of southern states from the Union preceded the Civil War.

8. _____

9. **transgress** (trăns-grĕs') *trans. verb*   **a.** To go beyond or over (a limit or boundary).
   b. To act in violation of, as a law. (From the Latin *trans-*, meaning "across," and *gradi*)

   Related Words   transgression *noun;* **transgressor** *noun*

   Example   Harold *transgressed* safe driving rules by not stopping for a red light.

9. _____

10. **unprecedented** (ŭn'prĕs'ĭ-dĕn'tĭd) *adjective*   Not having occurred before; without precedent; novel.

    Related Word   precedent *noun*
    Example   The political candidate's overwhelming victory was *unprecedented* in the large suburban community.

10. _____

© Great Source   DO NOT COPY

EXERCISE I WRITING CORRECT WORDS

On the answer line, write the word from the vocabulary list that fits each definition.

1. The degree to which something inclines; slope

2. No longer living; dead

3. A formal withdrawal from membership in an organization, association, or union

4. A degree or step in a series of gradual changes

5. Someone or something that comes before another in time

6. A path or means of going out; an exit

7. Not having occurred before; without precedent

8. To go beyond or over (a limit or boundary); to act in violation of

9. To acknowledge as true or real, often unwillingly

10. To go back; return to a previous condition

1. _____

2. _____

3. _____

4. _____

5. _____

6. _____

7. _____

8. _____

9. _____

10. _____

EXERCISE 2 USING WORDS CORRECTLY

Each of the following statements contains an italicized vocabulary word. Decide whether the sentence is true or false, and write *True* or *False* on the answer line.

1. For most teen-agers in this country, going to school is an *unprecedented* activity.

2. The *gradient* of a cliff could make it difficult to climb.

3. It is impossible for a *deceased* person to breathe.

4. A person who eats moderately *transgresses* all sensible diet rules.

5. If you became class president, the student who held the position before you would be your *predecessor*.

6. People who stray from the topic are often said to *egress*.

7. *Regressing* frequently makes progress difficult.

8. Using a thesaurus is a good way to become familiar with the *gradations* of meanings in words that express a given concept.

9. When you *concede* something, you stubbornly hold to your previous position.

10. A *secession* causes association members to become more closely involved with the organization.

1. _____

2. _____

3. _____

4. _____

5. _____

6. _____

7. _____

8. _____

9. _____

10. _____

EXERCISE 3 CHOOSING THE BEST WORD

Decide which vocabulary word or related form best completes the sentence, and write the letter of your choice on the answer line.

1. The subtle _____ from dark to light gave the painting an interesting quality.
   a. transgression   **b.** gradient   **c.** gradation   **d.** egress

1. _____

2. The movie rights for the obscure novel were sold for an _____ twenty million dollars.
   - **a.** deceased
   - **b.** regressive
   - **c.** seceded
   - **d.** unprecedented

2. _____

3. Strict new rules caused a _____ on the part of the outraged club members.
   - **a.** transgression
   - **b.** secession
   - **c.** regression
   - **d.** gradation

3. _____

4. The _____ left several thousand dollars to the library in her will.
   - **a.** concession
   - **b.** predecessor
   - **c.** deceased
   - **d.** egress

4. _____

5. Without a ruler or rules, the civilized people of the ancient city-state _____ to chaotic behavior.
   - **a.** regressed
   - **b.** deceased
   - **c.** seceded
   - **d.** conceded

5. _____

6. The ranger spoke harshly to those who _____ the rules of the national park.
   - **a.** conceded
   - **b.** seceded from
   - **c.** regressed to
   - **d.** transgressed

6. _____

7. During the fishing tournament, Hank _____ that he had not caught as many fish as the other contestants had.
   - **a.** seceded
   - **b.** transgressed
   - **c.** conceded
   - **d.** regressed

7. _____

8. The easiest _____ from the forest is the narrow path along the brook.
   - **a.** secession
   - **b.** gradation
   - **c.** gradient
   - **d.** egress

8. _____

9. President John Quincy Adams was James Monroe's _____.
   - **a.** secession
   - **b.** predecessor
   - **c.** concession
   - **d.** transgressor

9. _____

10. Because the _____ of the river bank was so steep, Elizabeth was afraid to go swimming.
   - **a.** gradient
   - **b.** secession
   - **c.** egress
   - **d.** concession

10. _____

EXERCISE 4 USING DIFFERENT FORMS OF WORDS

Decide which form of the vocabulary word in parentheses best completes the sentence. The form given may be correct. Write the answer on the answer line.

1. The mother was discouraged by her four-year-old's seeming _____. *(regress)*

1. _____

2. The thief was found guilty of many _____. *(transgress)*

2. _____

3. Today it is unlikely that any state would _____ from the union. *(secession)*

3. _____

4. The baby sitter's _____ caused the children to squeal with delight. *(concede)*

4. _____

5. The fall leaves were arranged in _____ of colors from bright yellow to deep red. *(gradation)*

5. _____

6. Many people sent flowers to express their sympathy to the family of the _____. *(deceased)*

6. _____

7. The developer refused to build the homes on the hill with the steep _____. *(gradient)*

7. _____

8. The hibernating animal looked sleepily for the _____ of the cave. *(egress)*

8. _____

9. The new president vowed to correct the errors of his _____. *(predecessor)*

9. _____

10. Charles Lindbergh's first transatlantic flight was an _____ event. *(unprecedented)*

10. _____

READING COMPREHENSION

Each numbered sentence in the following passage contains an italicized vocabulary word. After you read the passage, you will complete an exercise.

SPELUNKING IN COCKLEBIDDY CAVE

(1) Cocklebiddy Cave in southwestern Australia is to spelunkers, or cave explorers, what Mt. Everest is to mountain climbers: an *unprecedented* challenge. Cocklebiddy is believed to be the world's longest submerged cave. Even seasoned spelunkers with scuba-diving experience can be easily overwhelmed by Cocklebiddy's dangerous, forbidding depths.

(2) Like all caves Cocklebiddy possesses its share of steep *gradients* and rocky grottoes. (3) The cave's most distinctive feature, however, is its unique *gradation* of lakes. Many levels of lakes fill the cave's interior. These lakes, housed in air-filled caverns, are situated one above the other.

The structure of the cave could be compared to that of a tall building with many floors of offices. Whereas an office building rises out of the ground, Cocklebiddy Cave reaches the lower depths of the earth. Just as the floors of a building are connected by a staircase, the different levels of Cocklebiddy are joined by means of narrow channels called siphons. These rocky siphons are about the same size as large sewer pipes and are completely filled with water.

To reach any of the lakes, the diver, wearing full scuba gear, must swim through these long siphons.

(4) Spelunkers who attempt to explore Cocklebiddy Cave *concede* that they must be as good at scuba diving as they are at rock or mountain climbing.

(5) Recently, such a group of French men and women investigated areas of the cave that had not been explored by any of their *predecessors*. The goal of the French diving team was to see how deeply they could penetrate the submerged cave.

Members of the team forged ahead until the siphons became too narrow for further exploration. During their record-breaking, forty-seven-hour expedition, members of the group discovered new information about the underground lakes and siphons.

When the French team took their initial plunge into the depths of the cave, they had no idea of what was waiting for them. Nervous and excited, they inflated and set up a rubber raft on the first lake. In the clear water, artificially lit by battery-operated lamps, they observed the entrance to one of the siphons that would take them deeper into the cave. The siphon was so narrow that the divers, connected by a rope at the waist, had to swim single-file through the long channel.

When the divers reached the end of the siphon, they swam into a second underground lake. After surfacing and then resting, they searched for a siphon that would lead them to the next lake and even deeper into Cocklebiddy Cave. This process was repeated until the divers had traveled more than three miles beneath the surface.

The divers faced unpleasant and sometimes alarming conditions. Because of the length of some of the siphons, the divers were forced to spend many hours underwater. Being so far underground, the divers had to endure tremendous water pressure in the siphons. At times they became frightened, lost their way, and groped about aimlessly. (6) This disorientation in the eerie atmosphere caused the divers to *transgress* safety rules for slow resurfacing.

On one occasion panicky divers, after resurfacing, discovered bat

skeletons on the cave's rocky ledges. (7) The bats, *deceased* for many years, disintegrated into powder as soon as the divers accidentally touched them. In their disoriented state, the anxious divers overreacted and began to hallucinate. (8) They temporarily *regressed* to childlike behavior.

(9) Faced with constant danger and physically exhausting conditions, less heroic spelunkers might have considered *seceding* from the diving organization. (10) This courageous French team, however, walked through the *egress* of Cocklebiddy Cave with every member smiling. They felt proud of their achievement, for the scuba dive through six kilometers of siphons had set a new world record.

© Great Source   DO NOT COPY

READING COMPREHENSION EXERCISE

Each of the following statements corresponds to a numbered sentence in the passage. Each statement contains a blank and is followed by four answer choices. Decide which choice fits best in the blank. The word or phrase that you choose must express roughly the same meaning as the italicized word in the passage. Write the letter of your choice on the answer line.

1. To spelunkers, Cocklebiddy Cave is a _____ challenge.
   a. small **b.** novel **c.** surprising **d.** large

   1. _____

2. The cave features steep _____.
   a. caverns **b.** ledges **c.** slopes **d.** levels

   2. _____

3. Its _____ of lakes is unusual.
   a. systematic progression **b.** circle **c.** variety **d.** number

   3. _____

4. Veteran spelunkers _____ that exploring Cocklebiddy Cave requires excellent scuba-diving and rock-climbing skills.
   a. acknowledge **b.** promise **c.** predict **d.** complain

   4. _____

5. None of the _____ of the French team had ventured as far in their exploration of Cocklebiddy.
   a. advisers **b.** forerunners **c.** trainers **d.** sponsors

   5. _____

6. Confusion in the unsettling atmosphere caused the divers to _____ certain diving rules.
   a. forget **b.** ignore **c.** neglect **d.** violate

   6. _____

7. The skeletons of the _____ bats crumbled in the divers' hands.
   a. dried **b.** dead **c.** preserved **d.** frightening

   7. _____

8. A few divers had hallucinations and _____ childlike behavior.
   a. imitated **b.** talked about **c.** mimicked **d.** returned to

   8. _____

9. Less courageous spelunkers might have _____ the group.
   a. withdrawn from **b.** criticized **c.** insulted **d.** stayed with

   9. _____

10. The French team of spelunkers smiled as they walked through the cave's _____.
    a. channel **b.** exit **c.** tunnel **d.** entrance

    10. _____

PRACTICE WITH ANALOGIES

Directions On the answer line, write the letter of the phrase that best completes the analogy.

See page 79 for some strategies to use with analogies.

1. EXTRICATE : DIFFICULTY :: (A) liberate : captivity (B) initiate : loyalty (C) articulate : sincerity (D) separate : finality (E) eradicate : uniformity

   1. _____

2. MEDIATOR : CONCILIATORY :: (A) soldier : brave (B) braggart : modest (C) liar : honest (D) traitor : loyal (E) philanthropist : generous

   2. _____

3. MITIGATE : SEVERE :: (A) reorganize : efficient (B) specify : vague (C) buttress : supportive (D) abandon : uneasy (E) annual : final

   3. _____

4. FOSTER : FRIENDSHIP :: (A) cultivate : garden (B) betray : ally (C) secede : organization (D) withdraw : position (E) remove : obstacle

   4. _____

5. GRADIENT : SLOPE :: (A) plane : incline (B) ocean : depth (C) mountain : summit (D) peak : valley (E) altitude : height

   5. _____

The Roots -cede-, -cess- and -grad-, -gress-   © Great Source DO NOT COPY

"Variety's the very spice of life."
"Consistency is a jewel."

Regardless of which viewpoint you share, you probably devote quite a bit of time to evaluating both the uniformity and distinctiveness of people, places, objects, and situations. Knowing whether something will be predictable or novel allows us to prepare for it. While things that are similar are familiar and comfortable, things that are different offer interest and challenge. As the English proverb reminds us, "It takes all sorts to make a world." The words in this lesson will help you to express the similarities and differences in your experience.

WORD LIST

analogous
antithesis
comparable
deviate
differentiate
disparity
heterogeneous
homogeneous
nuance
tantamount

DEFINITIONS

After you have studied the definitions and example for each vocabulary word, write the word on the line to the right.

1. **analogous** (ə-năl'ə-gəs) *adjective*   **a.** Similar in certain qualities, circumstances, or uses.   **b.** In biology, similar in function but not in origin or structure: *The fins of fish are analogous to the wings of birds.*   (From the Greek word *analogos*, meaning "proportionate")

   Related Word   analogy *noun*
   Example   The eye is *analogous* to the camera.

1. _____
   See *comparable*.

2. **antithesis** (ăn-tĭth'ĭ-sĭs) *noun*   **a.** Direct contrast; opposition.   **b.** In speech and writing, the placement of sharply contrasting ideas in balanced or parallel words, phrases, or grammatical structures, as in the famous Pope quotation "To err is human; to forgive, divine." (From the Greek *anti-*, meaning "against," and tithenai, meaning "to set")

   Related Word   **antithetical** *adjective*
   Example   With his sloppy work habits and inadequate computer skills, Norman was the *antithesis* of a good staff assistant.

2. _____

3. **comparable** (kôm'pər-ə-bəl) *adjective*   **a.** Having like traits; similar; equivalent.   **b.** Worthy or capable of comparison. (From the Latin *com-*, meaning "together," and *par*, meaning "equal")

   Related Word   **comparably** *adverb*
   Example   The three-week, intensive language course was *comparable* to a standard semester-long class.

3. _____
   USAGE NOTE: *Comparable* describes things that are similar. *Analogous* describes similarities in things that are different.

4. **deviate** (dē′vē-āt′) *intrans. verb*   To differ or move away from a specified course or prescribed mode of behavior; diverge. (From the Latin *de-*, meaning "away," and *via*, meaning "road")

> **Related Word**   **deviation** *noun*
> **Example**   When the scientists *deviated* from the standard methods of experimentation, they made an important discovery.

4. _____

5. **differentiate** (dĭf′ə-rĕn′shē-āt′) *trans. verb*   **a.** To serve as the distinction between. **b.** To understand, perceive, or show the differences in or between.   *intrans. verb* **a.** To become different, distinct, or specialized.   **b.** To make distinctions; discriminate. (From the Latin *dis-*, meaning "apart," and *ferre*, meaning "to carry")

> **Related Word**   **differentiation** *noun*
> **Example**   The colorful sails of the lead boat *differentiated* it from the other boats in the race.

5. _____

6. **disparity** (dĭ-spăr′ĭ-tē) *noun*   **a.** The condition or fact of being unequal in age, rank, or degree; difference.   **b.** Lack of similarity; unlikeness. (From the Latin *dis-*, meaning "not," and *par*, meaning "equal")

> **Related Word**   **disparate** *adjective*
> **Example**   The forty-year *disparity* in their ages did not affect the friendship between the two women.

6. _____

7. **heterogeneous** (hĕt′ər-ə-jē′nē-əs, hĕt′ər-ə-jēn′yəs) *adjective*   Consisting of dissimilar elements or parts; miscellaneous; varied. (From the Greek words *heteros*, meaning "other," and *genos*, meaning "kind")

> **Related Words**   **heterogeneity** *noun;* **heterogeneously** *adverb*
> **Example**   Nick takes pride in his *heterogeneous* box collection, which consists of everything from a small jade container to a large stone sarcophagus.

7. _____

8. **homogeneous** (hō′mə-jē′nē-əs, hō′mə-jēn′yəs) *adjective*   **a.** Consisting of elements of a similar or related nature.   **b.** Uniform in structure or composition. (From the Greek words *homos*, meaning "same," and *genos*, meaning "kind")

> **Related Words**   **homogeneity** *noun;* **homogeneously** *adverb*
> **Example**   Coal from this region is remarkably *homogeneous.*

8. _____

9. **nuance** (nōō-äns′, nyōō-äns′, nōō′äns′, nyōō′äns′) *noun*   A subtle or slight degree of difference, as in meaning, color, or tone; a delicate shading; gradation. (From the Latin word *nubes*, meaning "cloud")

> **Example**   Bethany's ability to capture *nuances* of voice and gesture made her a wonderful imitator of famous people.

9. _____

10. **tantamount** (tăn′tə-mount′) *adjective*   Equivalent in significance, effect, or value. (From the Anglo-Norman phrase *tant amunter*, meaning "to amount to as much")

> **Example**   The attack on the territory was *tantamount* to a declaration of war.

10. _____

© Great Source   DO NOT COPY

EXERCISE I WRITING CORRECT WORDS

On the answer line, write the word from the vocabulary list that fits each definition.

1. Similar in certain qualities

2. Difference or inequality in age, rank, or degree

3. Consisting of dissimilar elements or parts; miscellaneous

4. Direct contrast or opposition

5. Consisting of similar or related elements; uniform in structure

6. Having equivalent traits

7. A slight difference in meaning, color, or tone

8. To serve as the distinction between; to understand or show the difference in or between

9. To move away from a specified course; diverge

10. Equivalent in significance, effect, or value

1. _____

2. _____

3. _____

4. _____

5. _____

6. _____

7. _____

8. _____

9. _____

10. _____

EXERCISE 2 USING WORDS CORRECTLY

Each of the following statements contains an italicized vocabulary word. Decide whether the sentence is true or false, and write *True* or *False* on the answer line.

1. A cat, a caterpillar, and a catfish make up a *homogeneous* group of animals.

2. People who are tone-deaf can readily *differentiate* between various pitches in music.

3. The invention of the printing press was *tantamount* to the invention of the mechanical pencil.

4. There is a great *disparity* between the vocabulary of an average three-year-old child and that of an average tenth grader.

5. Most people hope to enjoy the *antithesis* of good health throughout their lives.

6. *Nuances* in a person's facial expression convey differences in emotion to the careful observer.

7. When the prices of two brands of a product are *comparable*, a shopper can make a choice based on quality rather than cost.

8. Trying to do something successfully after you have once failed is *analogous* to getting back on a horse after you have been thrown off.

9. Cake batters are beaten vigorously to make them *heterogeneous*.

10. People who *deviate* from a plan follow it exactly.

1. _____

2. _____

3. _____

4. _____

5. _____

6. _____

7. _____

8. _____

9. _____

10. _____

EXERCISE 3 CHOOSING THE BEST WORD

Decide which vocabulary word or related form best completes the sentence, and write the letter of your choice on the answer line.

1. The idea that birds sing because they are happy results from drawing an incorrect _____ between the behavior of birds and that of humans.

   a. disparity   **b.** antithesis   **c.** nuance   **d.** analogy

1. _____

2. Until the twentieth century, when a gentleman slapped another gentleman's face with a glove, it was _____ to a challenge to duel.
   a. comparable   b. tantamount   c. heterogeneous   d. homogeneous

2. _____

3. Scientists who make the greatest contributions are often those whose views represent a _____ from the conventional thinking of their time.
   a. nuance   b. disparity   c. analogy   d. deviation

3. _____

4. Since most of its residents were descended from Scandinavian settlers, the town was remarkable for its _____.
   a. disparity   b. nuance   c. homogeneity   d. deviation

4. _____

5. Proust's long, intricate sentences are the _____ of Hemingway's clipped, concise style.
   a. analogy   b. disparity   c. antithesis   d. nuance

5. _____

6. The United States has such a(n) _____ population that some people have called it a great "melting pot."
   a. tantamount   b. heterogeneous   c. analogous   d. comparable

6. _____

7. James Whistler was a master at utilizing _____ of gray in his paintings.
   a. nuances   b. disparities   c. differentiations   d. antitheses

7. _____

8. There was such a great _____ in the news reports about the peace conference that readers did not know what to believe.
   a. homogeneity   b. differentiation   c. analogy   d. disparity

8. _____

9. _____ between red and green is impossible for people with certain types of colorblindness.
   a. Differentiation   b. Disparity   c. Nuance   d. Analogy

9. _____

10. Carving cliff dwellings out of the side of the Jemez Mountains was a feat _____ to building the Egyptian pyramids.
    a. heterogeneous   b. comparable   c. homogeneous   d. antithetical

10. _____

EXERCISE 4 USING DIFFERENT FORMS OF WORDS

Decide which form of the vocabulary word in parentheses best completes the sentence. The form given may be correct. Write your answer on the answer line.

1. Recent theories attempt to account for the _____ of neutrons and protons in the nucleus of an atom. (*heterogeneous*)

1. _____

2. The Bulldogs' 30-point lead seemed _____ to victory. (*tantamount*)

2. _____

3. Jim thought that the greatest _____ between the two jobs was in the salary each offered. (*disparity*)

3. _____

4. In her art course, Kay learned to _____ one French Impressionist painter from another. (*differentiate*)

4. _____

5. The two speakers expressed _____ views of the proposed legislation. (*antithesis*)

5. _____

6. The actor's frequent _____ from the topic make him difficult to interview. (*deviate*)

6. _____

7. Alice's lawsuit claimed that her salary increases were not _____ to those of other workers in her office. (*comparable*)

7. _____

8. The meter of poetry is _____ to the rhythm of music. (*analogous*)

8. _____

9. David appreciated jazz for its many _____ of melody and harmony. (*nuance*)

9. _____

10. Lynnette found that the _____ of her classes did not provide the variety she had hoped for. (*homogeneous*)

10. _____

© Great Source   DO NOT COPY

READING COMPREHENSION

Each numbered sentence in the following passage contains an italicized vocabulary word or related form. After you read the passage, you will complete an exercise.

KAYAK COMMUTER

(1) The *homogeneous* appearance of crowds of people on their way to work in large cities might lead one to generalize about the uniformity in the lives and backgrounds of commuters. (2) Certainly, their business suits and briefcases do not help to *differentiate* one urban professional from another. (3) The *disparity* between appearance and reality, however, is nicely illustrated by Micah Marty, a photographer and videotape producer in Chicago. Before Marty showers at his office and exchanges his neoprene rubber wetsuit for a suit and tie, he paddles his kayak six miles across portions of Lake Michigan and the Chicago River. Along with his briefcase, Micah Marty carries a ship-to-shore radio in a waterproof sack, a life vest and helmet, and a collapsible double-bladed paddle.

(4) Marty's kayak is a light-weight, narrow boat that is *comparable* to a canoe but has an enclosed deck and cockpit. Because kayaks ride low in the water, they have a waterproof plastic or nylon flap attached to the cockpit that fits tightly around the kayaker and keeps the inside of the boat dry. The kayaker sits on a seat at the bottom of the craft and presses against the interior braces with hips, legs, and feet in order to balance. While a novice would find the kayak extremely unsteady, the experienced kayaker has learned to lean into turns and brace the paddle against the water currents to maintain stability.

(5) Micah Marty's exciting commute to work is the *antithesis* of the boring trips made by other commuters in cars, buses, or trains. Marty copes daily with the rough water of Lake Michigan. (6) He must constantly evaluate the *nuances* of the lake's shifting currents. A mile from shore in water one hundred feet deep, he must anticipate the sudden three- to nine-foot waves that can easily overturn his boat. If the kayak capsized, he needs to execute an acrobatic maneuver called the "eskimo roll," which involves righting the boat while he is upside down and several feet below the surface.

(7) Spending more than a few moments in water that is near freezing may be *tantamount* to disaster. The sudden drop of body temperature, called hypothermia, can be fatal.

As Marty approaches the shore, he encounters other dangers and inconveniences. Waves pounding off the stone breakwaters are unpredictable and throw the kayak about. To make headway, he must paddle furiously. On some days he is lucky when a powerboat arrives at the mouth of the river at the same time he does. This allows him to ride through the locks.

(8) On other days he must *deviate* from this course because the lock tenders will not open the locks for a craft as small as a kayak. Then he is forced to carry his kayak across a stretch of land before putting it into the river downstream from the locks. The river, too, is dangerous. Treacherous wakes from other boats and strange currents set up by factory waste pipes discharging under water make this part of his trip precarious.

(9) One aspect of Micah Marty's commute to work is *analogous* to the trip made on crowded highways. He has experienced a number of anxious moments on days when the lake and river have been particularly crowded with other boats. Because the kayak rides so low in the water, motorboats and commercial vessels often do not see it until they are almost upon it.

In spite of the dangers and discomforts of his method of traveling to work, Micah Marty enjoys his mode of travel. Dawn and sunset on the lake are particularly beautiful, and he enjoys watching the effects of shifting patterns of light on the Chicago skyline. Having chosen kayaking to replace the long-distance running that ruined his knees, he relishes the challenge and exertion of his two hours a day on the water. (10) Hearing about Micah Marty, one must wonder what a *heterogeneity* of interests, talents, and hobbies hides behind the conventional appearance of the people who commute to work in most large cities.

Each of the following statements corresponds to a numbered sentence in the passage. Each statement contains a blank and is followed by four answer choices. Decide which choice fits best in the blank. The word or phrase that you choose must express roughly the same meaning as the italicized word in the passage. Write the letter of your choice on the answer line.

1. People on their way to work have a(n) _____ appearance.
   a. businesslike   **b.** similar   **c.** attractive   **d.** motivated

   1. _____

2. Business suits and briefcases do not _____ one urban professional and another.
   a. show the differences between   **c.** encourage similarities between
   b. separate   **d.** prohibit friendships between

   2. _____

3. Micah Marty illustrates the _____ between appearance and reality.
   a. comparison   **b.** relationship   **c.** conformity   **d.** difference

   3. _____

4. The kayak is _____ a canoe.
   a. totally different from   **c.** similar to
   b. used instead of   **d.** better than

   4. _____

5. Marty's commute is _____ the trips made by others.
   a. the opposite of   **b.** the same as   **c.** similar to   **d.** unlike

   5. _____

6. He must constantly evaluate the _____ of the lake current.
   a. causes   **c.** complex effects
   b. shades of difference   **d.** extent

   6. _____

7. Spending any time in near-freezing water may be _____ disaster for Micah Marty.
   a. the cause of   **b.** reason to fear   **c.** the beginning of   **d.** equivalent to

   7. _____

8. When the lock tenders will not open the locks, Marty must _____ the easier course.
   a. continue on   **b.** reverse   **c.** diverge from   **d.** go parallel to

   8. _____

9. One aspect of his commute is _____ that made on crowded highways.
   a. similar to   **b.** different from   **c.** opposite to   **d.** harder than

   9. _____

10. One must wonder what a _____ of interests and talents lies behind the conventional appearance of commuters.
    a. lack   **b.** variety   **c.** surprising group   **d.** frequency

    10. _____

One effective way of describing a person is through an unusual comparison. Choose someone you know well, and compare that person's physical and personality characteristics to those of an animal, a plant, a piece of furniture, or a food. In your composition, use at least five of the words from this lesson and underline them.

© Great Source   DO NOT COPY

The concepts of authority and dominion have been at the heart of many philosophical debates throughout the ages. Philosophers have raised such questions as what constitutes legitimate authority, or under what circumstances dominion of one institution or person by another is justifiable. Such questions have on occasion been resolved, as in the case of the United States, for example, where the government derives its authority solely from the consent of the governed. By contrast, in many monarchies of ages past, the rulers governed by a supposed divine right granted to them and their descendants. This lesson introduces ten words related to these concepts of authority and dominion.

WORD LIST

autonomy
despot
feudal
hegemony
hierarchy
prerogative
regime
sovereign
totalitarian
usurp

DEFINITIONS

After you have studied the definitions and example for each vocabulary word, write the word on the line to the right.

1. **autonomy** (ô-tŏn′ə-mē) *noun* Independence; the quality or condition of being self-governing. (From the Greek word *autos*, meaning "self," and *nomos*, meaning "law")

   Related Words autonomous *adjective*; **autonomously** *adverb*
   Example Perhaps the most important difference between elementary and secondary school students is in the greater amount of *autonomy* given to the latter.

   1. _____

2. **despot** (dĕs′pət) *noun* **a.** A ruler having absolute power or authority. **b.** A person who exercises power oppressively; a tyrant. (From the Greek word *despotēs*, meaning "master" or "lord")

   Related Words despotic *adjective*; **despotically** *adverb*; **despotism** *noun*
   Example After Napoleon declared himself Emperor of France in 1804, he ruled as a *despot*, answerable to no one but himself.

   2. _____

3. **feudal** (fyoōd′l) *adjective* Characteristic of a social and economic system of government used in Europe, whereby a person, in return for being granted control of land, owed service and loyalty to a lord.

   Related Word feudalism *noun*
   Example *Feudal* societies were based upon contractual obligations between lords and their vassals.

   3. _____

4. **hegemony** (hĭ-jĕm′ə-nē) *noun* **a.** Dominion or control, particularly of one country over others. **b.** Dominant influence or authority. (From the Greek word *hēgemonia*, meaning "leadership")

   Example In the sixteenth century, Spain sought *hegemony* over all of the New World.

   4. _____

5. **hierarchy** (hī′ə-rär′kē, hīrär′kē) *noun*   An order of persons or entities classified according to authority, rank, or importance. (From the Greek words *hieros,* meaning "sacred," and *arkhos,* meaning "leader")

   Related Words **hierarch** *noun;* **hierarchical** *adjective;* **hierarchically** *adverb*
   Example   An earl ranks above a lord in the *hierarchy* of British aristocracy.

   5. _____
   MEMORY CUE: In a hierarchy one person or thing is *higher* than another.

6. **prerogative** (prĭ-rŏg′ə-tĭv) *noun*   A right or privilege, particularly a hereditary or official one, held by a person or group. (From the Latin *prae-,* meaning "before," and *rogare,* meaning "to ask")

   Example   The President has the *prerogative* of vetoing bills passed by Congress.

   6. _____

7. **regime** (rā-zhēm′, rĭ-zhēm′) *noun*   A government or any other administrative organ in power.

   Example   Many *regimes* in South America have been unstable.

   7. _____

8. **sovereign** (sŏv′ər-ĭn, sŏv′rĭn) *noun*   The chief of state, usually in a monarchy. *adjective* **a.** Self-governing; independent. **b.** Having the highest rank or supreme power.

   Related Word   **sovereignty** *noun*
   Example   Tsar Nikolai II was the last *sovereign* of Russia.

   8. _____

9. **totalitarian** (tō-tăl′ĭ-târ′ē-ən) *adjective*   Referring to a government that exercises control over all aspects of life.

   Related Word   **totalitarianism** *noun*
   Example   Newspapers and books were heavily censored in the *totalitarian* state.

   9. _____
   MEMORY CUE: In a *totalitarian* state, the government has *total* control.

10. **usurp** (yoo-sûrp′, yoo-zûrp′) *trans. verb*   To seize and retain the rights, power, property, or position of another without legal authority. (From the Latin word *usurpare,* meaning "to seize for use")

    Related Words **usurpation** *noun;* **usurper** *noun*
    Example   The barbarian hordes swept through Rome in the fifth century to *usurp* the territory of the Roman citizenry.

    10. _____

© Great Source DO NOT COPY

EXERCISE 1 MATCHING WORDS AND DEFINITIONS

Match the definition in Column B with the word in Column A. Write the letter of the correct definition on the answer line.

Column A

1. regime
2. feudal
3. autonomy
4. prerogative
5. hegemony
6. totalitarian
7. hierarchy
8. usurp
9. despot
10. sovereign

Column B

a. independence; self-government

b. characteristic of the medieval European social system

c. a ruler having total authority

d. characterized by one person or party having absolute power to the exclusion of any opposition

e. an order of persons classified by rank

f. a government in power

g. a chief of state in a monarchy

h. a hereditary or official right or privilege

i. dominion of one country over another

j. to seize and retain without legal authority

1. _____
2. _____
3. _____
4. _____
5. _____
6. _____
7. _____
8. _____
9. _____
10. _____

EXERCISE 2 USING WORDS CORRECTLY

Decide whether the italicized vocabulary word has been used correctly in the sentence. On the answer line, write *Correct* for correct use and *Incorrect* for incorrect use.

1. The military leader behaved like a *despot,* working his platoon hard from dawn until dusk.

2. The *sovereign* paid homage to his king.

3. European *hegemony* in Africa and Asia has greatly decreased in the last fifty years.

4. A fad or fashion that is extremely popular with teen-agers is *totalitarian.*

5. An infantry unit of two or more battalions is also called a *regime.*

6. Joshua took Byron's book, but Mr. Buxtehude made him *usurp* it back.

7. Class structure was important in *feudal* society.

8. There is a *hierarchy* in a military unit that allows sergeants to exercise authority over privates and corporals.

9. It is the principal's *prerogative* to visit classrooms at any time.

10. "The best thing about living in my own apartment is the *autonomy* that I have," said Jane.

1. _____
2. _____
3. _____
4. _____
5. _____
6. _____
7. _____
8. _____
9. _____
10. _____

EXERCISE 3 IDENTIFYING SYNONYMS

Decide which word or phrase has the meaning that is closest to that of the capitalized vocabulary word. Write the letter of your choice on the answer line.

1. HIERARCHY:
   a. dictator
   b. an order by rank
   c. government official
   d. list of authorities

1. _____

2. FEUDAL:
   a. medieval   b. hopeless   c. modern   d. authoritative

2. _____

3. DESPOT:
   a. constitutional monarch   c. enemy
   b. legislature   d. absolute ruler

3. _____

4. TOTALITARIAN:
   a. complete   b. democratic   c. frivolous   d. dictatorial

4. _____

5. PREROGATIVE:
   a. privilege   b. responsibility   c. gift   d. obligation

5. _____

6. SOVEREIGN:
   a. monarch   b. subject   c. associate   d. outlaw

6. _____

7. USURP:
   a. release provisionally   c. take by divine right
   b. pay back systematically   d. seize illegally

7. _____

8. AUTONOMY:
   a. law   b. independence   c. subjugation   d. democracy

8. _____

9. REGIME:
   a. electoral poll   c. government in power
   b. military unit   d. government in exile

9. _____

10. HEGEMONY:
    a. dominion   b. subjugation   c. independence   d. preference

10. _____

EXERCISE 4 USING DIFFERENT FORMS OF WORDS

Decide which form of the vocabulary word in parentheses best completes the sentence. The form given may be correct. Write your answer on the answer line.

1. After World War II, the Soviet Union extended its _____ over many of the nations of Eastern Europe. *(hegemony)*

1. _____

2. _____ in Europe began to break down after the Hundred Years' War. *(feudal)*

2. _____

3. One consequence of a revolution is the dissolution of stable _____ social structures. *(hierarchy)*

3. _____

4. Communism and fascism are two examples of twentieth-century _____. *(totalitarian)*

4. _____

5. A nation independent of any external power has _____. *(sovereign)*

5. _____

6. The member states of the United Nations are, with few exceptions, _____. *(autonomy)*

6. _____

7. The _____ ruler came to power and jailed all his political adversaries. *(despot)*

7. _____

8. The brutal _____ of Hitler resulted in the deaths of millions of people. *(regime)*

8. _____

9. One of the _____ of airline employees is free or reduced-rate air travel. *(prerogative)*

9. _____

10. Baron de Courcy returned to the castle to find that a _____ had taken his position and gained the king's favor. *(usurp)*

10. _____

© Great Source   DO NOT COPY

READING COMPREHENSION

Each numbered sentence in the following passage contains an italicized vocabulary word or related form. After you read the passage, you will complete an exercise.

UTOPIA

In 1516 Sir Thomas More published a book entitled *On the Highest State of the Republic and On the New Island of Utopia.* No one had ever heard of such an island. Was it some outpost tucked away in a remote corner of Europe? **(1)** Was it a constitutional republic guided by a democratic *regime?* In fact, it was an ideal land that existed only in the pages of More's book.

Though the word *utopia,* derived from the Greek words *ou,* meaning "not," and *topos,* meaning "place," was created only in the sixteenth century, the concept of the perfect state predates More by at least two thousand years. Plato, who lived during the fourth century B.C., wrote a philosophical dialogue called *The Republic,* which examines the factors needed to create a good society and a perfect state. Accordingly, Plato's republic is a kind of utopia.

(2) The Platonic utopia is organized into a three-part *hierarchy:* the guardians, or ruling class; the auxiliary class; and the laborers. **(3)** The rulers, who are trained as philosophers, have *hegemony* over the rest of the citizens, and all of the political power. **(4)** Nevertheless, this same rul-

ing class has little *autonomy* and is forbidden to own property and even to marry and raise families. **(5)** This prevents them from exercising the *feudal* power that was later to be the basis of so much abuse in medieval Europe.

(6) Because of this rigid, aristocratic social structure, some philosophers, such as Karl Popper, have found the ideal Platonic state to be *totalitarian.* Others, however, have found it to be the system that is best able to take advantage of the abilities and limitations of each individual.

Like Plato and More, many other thinkers and writers, such as Dante, Edward Bellamy, and H. G. Wells, have written about utopian communities. For the last two or three centuries, however, certain religious groups and political visionaries have attempted to create such communities. From the Dutch Mennonite community established in Delaware in 1663 to the various communities that arose throughout the country in the 1960s and 1970s, utopian experiments have been part of the social history of the United States. **(7)** Ever since the revolution against the British *sovereign,* Americans have been particularly

open to the expression of freedom typical of most utopian communities. **(8)** They have always tended to regard such social experimentation as the legitimate *prerogative* of any citizen of a free country.

Despite the large number of utopian societies founded in the United States in the nineteenth century, few of them lasted into the twentieth. **(9)** One persistent problem was that many of the leaders of these communities, although not *despots,* had such strong personalities that when they died, their communities more or less died with them. There was no one sufficiently authoritative to take over the leadership. **(10)** Another widespread problem affecting utopian communities was the tendency for disgruntled members either to break away and form their own rival communities or to *usurp* the power of the authorities and attempt to refashion their communities according to their own thinking. These altogether human failings, which so often resulted in the downfall of these ideal communities, lead one to consider the possibility that Plato, More, and others were wise to confine their utopias to writing.

READING COMPREHENSION EXERCISE

Each of the following statements corresponds to a numbered sentence in the passage. Each statement contains a blank and is followed by four answer choices. Decide which choice fits best in the blank. The word or phrase that you choose must express roughly the same meaning as the italicized word in the passage. Write the letter of your choice on the answer line.

1. Was Utopia guided by a democratic _____?
   a. party   **b.** president   **c.** government   **d.** constitution

   1. _____

2. Plato's utopia has a three-part _____.
   a. order or authority   **b.** legislature   **c.** laboring class   **d.** ruling class

   2. _____

3. In Plato's republic the guardians have _____.

   a. it made   **b.** dominion   **c.** certain obligations **d.** independence

3. _____

4. The guardians also have little _____.

   a. to do   **b.** to restrain them **c.** money   **d.** independence

4. _____

5. This prevents them from exercising the _____ power which was later to be the basis of so much abuse in medieval Europe.

   a. system of checks and balances   **c.** system of democratic rule

   b. system of corruption   **d.** system of land control

5. _____

6. Some philosophers have found Plato's republic to be _____.

   a. complete in every way

   b. lacking in law courts

   c. utopian

   d. characterized by power being in the hands of one party exclusively

6. _____

7. Ever since the colonists revolted against the British _____, Americans have been champions of utopian freedom.

   a. commonwealth **b.** king   **c.** prime minister **d.** nation

7. _____

8. Americans have regarded social experiments as the _____ of free citizens.

   a. downfall   **b.** right   **c.** obligation   **d.** danger

8. _____

9. Utopian leaders were not _____.

   a. kings   **b.** cruel   **c.** strong   **d.** tyrants

9. _____

10. Disgruntled members sometimes tried to _____ the power of the authorities.

   a. share   **b.** campaign for **c.** block the use of **d.** seize illegally

10. _____

WRITING ASSIGNMENT

For a discussion in a history class, prepare a report comparing and contrasting two different forms of government. Show, for example, the similarities and differences between constitutional monarchy and state socialism. Point out the weaknesses and strengths of the two forms you choose; use at least five words from this lesson, underlining each one.

VOCABULARY ENRICHMENT

The word *despot* did not always have the negative connotations that it usually has today. Etymologically, the word in Greek denotes "lord or master of a household." In the Byzantine Empire, which lasted for a thousand years from the fifth to the fifteenth centuries, it was used when addressing the emperor, the patriarch, and all bishops. Today, in fact, *despot* is still the common form of address for an Eastern Orthodox bishop.

   In the last days of the empire, the term was used by minor rulers in outlying provinces, and it is in this form that the word first became known in Western languages. The word acquired its negative connotation, however, through revolutionaries in France who, at the time of the French Revolution, used the term frequently to describe their adversaries. Throughout the nineteenth and twentieth centuries, *despot* has more frequently meant a tyrant or oppressor than a powerful, exalted ruler.

Activity When words are adopted into one language from another, they frequently change meaning. The following four words were commonly used in Byzantine Greek, and they remain in use in English today. Using a dictionary, write a definition for the current meaning of each word in English, and give the meaning of the Greek source word or words from which it is derived.

1. basil   2. ecumenical   3. iconoclast   4. tessera

© Great Source DO NOT COPY

READING SKILLS

CONTEXT CLUES: EXAMPLES AND APPOSITIVES

A sentence containing an unfamiliar word can also contain information that helps you define the word. The words providing this information are called **context clues**. Two of the most useful types of context clues are examples and appositives.

An example is something that is representative of a group. There are three types of example context clues: list clues, summary clues, and "for example" clues.

1. *Example clues: lists.* Sometimes an unfamiliar word is part of a list of known words. These list clues can help you determine the general meaning of the unfamiliar word. The following sentence contains a list clue.

    The tour group visited London, Paris, *Budapest,* and *Belgrade.*

    The first two names, *London* and *Paris,* tell you that *Budapest* and *Belgrade* are probably also the names of large European cities.

2. *Example clues: summaries.* In a summary clue, the items in the list help define the word that summarizes the list. The following sentence has a summary clue.

    The *ruminants* that we will study are sheep, camels, and antelope.

    The items in the list tell you that the word *ruminant* must mean a type of animal. Specifically, a ruminant is a hoofed, even-toed mammal that chews a cud.

3. *Example clues: "for example."* A part of a sentence that includes the phrase *for example* or *for instance* may suggest the meaning of an unfamiliar word. The following sentence contains such a clue.

    He seemed to be a *phlegmatic* sort of person who was, for example, never bothered by rude bus drivers or store clerks.

    The part of the sentence beginning with *for example* suggests an easy-going person. A dictionary definition of *phlegmatic* is "having or indicating a calm, sluggish temperament."

An **appositive** is a noun or a noun phrase that is placed beside another noun and explains or identifies it. Appositives are often excellent clues to the meaning of an unfamiliar word. In the following sentences, the italicized appositives explain the words in boldface type.

    The hills of the region consist of **moraine,** *rock and soil deposited by a glacier.*

    An **iman,** *a recognized leader or religious teacher,* is an important person in an Islamic community.

Word meanings that you determine from context clues are not always precise. Whenever possible, check your definitions in the dictionary.

Step 1: Using context clues, write your own definition of the italicized word in each of the following sentences. *Step 2:* Write the appropriate dictionary definition of the word. *Step 3:* Write a sentence of your own in which you use the word according to the dictionary definition.

1. The fishing boats returned with a catch of salmon, tuna, and *menhaden*.

    Your Definition _____

    Dictionary Definition _____

    Sentence _____

2. The nation's *dire* circumstances—for example, drought and famine—prompted offers of assistance from around the world.

    Your Definition _____

    Dictionary Definition _____

    Sentence _____

3. Because the curtains were torn, the paint was peeling, and the stairs needed repair, the house looked *dilapidated*.

    Your Definition _____

    Dictionary Definition _____

    Sentence _____

4. At the Renaissance Fair, each performer wore a *jerkin*, a kind of sleeveless jacket.

    Your Definition _____

    Dictionary Definition _____

    Sentence _____

5. The *facile* street artist was, for example, able to juggle six balls at once.

    Your Definition _____

    Dictionary Definition _____

    Sentence _____

6. *Paradoxes*, true but seemingly contradictory statements, fascinated the ancient Greeks.

    Your Definition _____

    Dictionary Definition _____

    Sentence _____

7. We saw red and white pines, maples, and *larches* on our walk.

    Your Definition _____

    Dictionary Definition _____

    Sentence _____

8. The city engineer was accused of *nepotism* after he put his wife on the payroll and found a place for a friend and two relatives in the sanitation department.

    Your Definition _____

    Dictionary Definition _____

    Sentence _____

The Latin root -*sent*-and its alternative form -*sens*- mean "feeling," and the Greek root -*path*- means "feeling" and "suffering." Both roots are the basis of many English words that describe emotional experiences. If, for example, you see the *pathos* of a situation, you experience feelings of pity, sympathy, tenderness, or sorrow. If you are a *sensitive* person, you are aware of and responsive to the attitudes or feelings of others. If you *resent* someone, you feel angry or bitter toward that person. The words in this lesson, all of which are derived from the roots -*sent*- and -*path*-, will enable you to write with greater understanding about feelings and suffering.

WORD LIST

apathy
assent
empathy
pathetic
pathology
presentiment
sensational
sensibility
sententious
sentiment

DEFINITIONS

After you have studied the definitions and example for each vocabulary word, write the word on the line to the right.

1. **apathy** (ăp′ə-thē) *noun*   **a.** Lack of feeling or emotion; impassiveness.   **b.** Lack of interest in things generally found exciting, interesting, or moving; indifference. (From the Greek *a-*, meaning "without," and *pathos*, meaning "feeling")

   Related Word   apathetic *adjective*
   Example   Public *apathy* resulted in a low voter turnout at the election.

   1. _____

2. **assent** (ə-sĕnt′) *noun*   Acceptance, as of a proposal or statement; compliance. *intrans. verb*   To agree to something, especially after thoughtful consideration. (From the Latin *ad-*, meaning "toward," and *sentire*, meaning "to feel")

   Example   The architect needed her client's *assent* before making expensive structural modifications.

   2. _____

3. **empathy** (ĕm′pə-thē) *noun*   **a.** Understanding, concerned identification with another's situation or feelings.   **b.** The attribution of one's own feelings to an object. (From the Greek *en-*, meaning "in," and *pathos*)

   Related Words   empathetic *adjective;* **emphasize** *verb*
   Example   The woman who had permanently injured her leg as a child had *empathy* for those with physical handicaps.

   3. _____

4. **pathetic** (pə-thĕt′ĭk) *adjective*   **a.** Expressing or arousing pity, sympathy, or tenderness; sad.   **b.** Distressing and inadequate: *pathetic effort at humor.* (From the Greek word *pathos*)

   Related Words   pathetically *adverb;* **pathos** *noun*
   Example   The weak and *pathetic* cries for help finally attracted the attention of a pedestrian.

   4. _____

© Great Source   DO NOT COPY

5. **pathology** (pă-thŏl'ə-jē) *noun*   **a.** The scientific and medical study of a disease, its causes, its processes, and its effects.   **b.** The physical changes in the body and its functioning as a result of a disease or disorder. (From the Greek word *pathos*)

   Related Words   **pathological** *adjective;* **pathologist** *noun*
   Example   Medical researchers are studying the *pathology* of cystic fibrosis.

5. _____

6. **presentiment** (prĭ-zĕn'tə-mənt) *noun*   A sense of something about to occur; premonition; foreboding. (From the Latin *prae-*, meaning "before," and *sentire*)

   Example   Grandmother awoke the morning of the accident with a *presentiment* of danger.

6. _____

7. **sensational** (sĕn-sā'shə-nəl) *adjective*   **a.** Arousing great interest or excitement.   **b.** Designed to shock or thrill spectators or readers.   **c.** Outstanding; spectacular. (From the Latin word *sentire*)

   Related Words   **sensation** *noun;* **sensationalism** *noun;* **sensationally** *adverb*
   Example   Helen hasn't stopped talking about the outfielder's *sensational* catch in last night's game.

7. _____

8. **sensibility** (sĕn'sə-bĭl'ĭ-tē) *noun*   **a.** The ability to feel, sense, or perceive; mental or emotional responsiveness toward something.   **b.** Refined awareness and appreciation in matters of feeling and perception: *the sensibility of an artist.* (From the Latin word *sentire*)

   Related Words   **sensible** *adjective:* **sensibly** *adverb*
   Example   His loud clothing and bizarre hair style offended his grandparents' *sensibilities.*

8. _____

   USAGE NOTE: *Sensible* has a range of meanings, from "perceptible by the senses or by the mind," to "acting with, or showing, good sense."

9. **sententious** (sĕn-tĕn'-shəs) *adjective*   **a.** Inclined to give advice in a self-righteous way.   **b.** Inclined to wise sayings; abounding in proverbs.   **c.** Brief and pointed in meaning or expression; saying much in a few words. (From the Latin word *sententiosus,* meaning "full of meaning")

   Related Words   **sententiously** *adverb;* **sententiousness** *noun*
   Example   Larry's *sententious* speech was filled with useless advice.

9. _____

10. **sentiment** (sĕn'tə-mənt) *noun*   **a.** A thought, view, or attitude based more on feeling than on reason.   **b.** A general cast of mind regarding something.   **c.** Tender, romantic, or nostalgic feeling. (From the Latin word *sentire*)

    Related Words   **sentimental** *adjective;* **sentimentally** *adverb*
    Example   The referendum will indicate increased public *sentiment* for better roads.

10. _____

EXERCISE 1 WRITING CORRECT WORDS

On the answer line, write the word from the vocabulary list that fits each definition.

1. Expressing or arousing pity, sympathy, or tenderness; distressing and inadequate

2. A sense of something about to occur; foreboding

3. The ability to feel, sense, or perceive; refined appreciation in matters of feeling

4. Lack of feeling, emotion, or interest

5. Concerned identification with another's situation or feelings

6. Arousing interest, excitement, or shock; spectacular

7. Acceptance of a proposal or statement; to agree

8. A thought, view, or attitude based on feeling rather than reason; tender, romantic, or nostalgic feeling

9. The scientific and medical study of a disease.

10. Inclined to give advice self-righteously; brief and pointed in meaning

1. _____
2. _____
3. _____
4. _____
5. _____
6. _____
7. _____
8. _____
9. _____
10. _____

EXERCISE 2 USING WORDS CORRECTLY

Decide whether the italicized vocabulary word has been used correctly in the sentence. On the answer line, write *Correct* for correct use and *Incorrect* for incorrect use.

1. Someone interested in *pathology* would need to learn map and compass skills.

2. The board *assented* to the proposal by defeating it in a vote of nine to three.

3. His *apathy* toward the chorus became clear when he failed to attend practice regularly.

4. Most readers are bored by *sensational* articles in magazines.

5. A person with a *presentiment* may have a vague sense of approaching misfortune.

6. A *sententious* speaker tends to stutter.

7. The immigrant told a *pathetic* tale of hardship.

8. Rhoda's *sentiments* are always with the underdog.

9. Never having had a pet, Beth felt no *empathy* for Lucas, whose dog was very sick.

10. A colorblind artist has an unusual *sensibility* to the shades and tones of color.

1. _____
2. _____
3. _____
4. _____
5. _____
6. _____
7. _____
8. _____
9. _____
10. _____

EXERCISE 3 CHOOSING THE BEST WORD

Decide which vocabulary word or related form best expresses the meaning of the italicized word or phrase in the sentence. On the answer line, write the letter of the correct choice.

1. The *thrilling* discovery of a chest of gold coins in the wreckage of the pirate ship made the front page of most newspapers.
   a. pathetic   **b.** sensational   **c.** apathetic   **d.** sensible

1. _____

© Great Source   DO NOT COPY   The Roots *-sent-* and *-path-*

2. The audience expressed *agreement* by applauding enthusiastically.   2. _____
   a. empathy   **b.** sensation   **c.** assent   **d.** sensibility

3. "I can't believe that this sleek animal was once a starving, *pitiful* kitten," Dr.   3. _____
   Giordano told Brad.
   a. pathetic   **b.** sensational   **c.** pathological   **d.** sententious

4. As part of a combined program in health and science, students are studying the   4. _____
   causes, processes, and effects of diseases.
   a. sensibility   **b.** pathology   **c.** sensations   **d.** presentiment

5. "The decline in voter registration indicates *lack of interest* among the citizens of this   5. _____
   county," the politician announced.
   a. sensibility   **b.** empathy   **c.** pathology   **d.** apathy

6. Carolyn is an extraordinary leader who generates *feelings* of good will and   6. _____
   cooperation among her committee members.
   a. sententiousness   **b.** sensibilities   **c.** sentiments   **d.** assents

7. I find Jasper's *tendency to give self-righteous advice* offensive.   7. _____
   a. sententiousness   **b.** pathology   **c.** empathy   **d.** presentiment

8. Having had a *premonition* of disaster, Lacey decided to spend the day quietly in   8. _____
   her room.
   a. pathology   **b.** presentiment   **c.** apathy   **d.** sentiment

9. The bank manager had *understanding and concern* for Mr. Fairchild's financial   9. _____
   situation, but there was nothing he could do.
   a. apathy   **b.** sentiment   **c.** empathy   **d.** sensibility

10. The art teacher sought to increase her students' *emotional responsiveness* to the   10. _____
    beauty of nature.
    a. sensibility   **b.** empathy   **c.** presentiment   **d.** assent

EXERCISE 4 USING DIFFERENT FORMS OF WORDS

Decide which form of the vocabulary word in parentheses best completes the sentence.
The form given may be correct. Write your answer on the answer line.

1. After testing the tissue samples, the _____ called the surgeon awaiting the results   1. _____
   in the operating room. *(pathology)*

2. For a week Su Ling's father _____ with her grief over the loss of her turtle.   2. _____
   (empathy)

3. Jacob likes _____ ballads almost as much as he likes classical music. *(sentiment)*   3. _____

4. Hillary sobbed _____ as her parents waved good-by. *(pathetic)*   4. _____

5. Rosalind spoke _____ about the attitudes and practices that lead to success.   5. _____
   (sententious)

6. Jay took advantage of Mr. Bruzie's good mood to get his _____. *(assent)*   6. _____

7. The _____ of the gossip column attracted many curious readers. *(sensational)*   7. _____

8. Roger would not allow his _____ friends to dissuade him from participating in the   8. _____
   festival. *(apathy)*

9. No one doubted Mrs. Nellis's _____ of disaster. *(presentiment)*   9. _____

10. Musicians are fortunate to have a special type of _____. *(sensibility)*   10. _____

      © Great Source   DO NOT COPY

READING COMPREHENSION

Each numbered sentence in the following passage contains an italicized vocabulary word or related form. After you read the passage, you will complete an exercise.

FLORENCE NIGHTINGALE: LADY OF THE LAMP

Florence Nightingale is best remembered as the dedicated English woman who turned nursing from menial employment requiring no special skills or training into a career worthy of professional status. What may not be as well known, however, are her pioneering efforts in many other areas of health care.

Florence was born in 1820, the second daughter of a wealthy English family. Although she had a classical education under the direction of her father, she was brought up to be a lady of leisure. (1) The *sentiments* of Victorian England required a woman of her social class to make a brilliant marriage. (2) A life filled with little more than parties offended Florence's *sensibilities,* however. Energetic and intelligent, she resisted marriage.

At the age of seventeen, Florence felt that she had been called to a life of service. As a child she had been devoted to helping others. (3) With *empathy* and kindness she cared for people on her father's estate. While her parents did not object to her attempts to alleviate suffering in family members, animals, or neighbors, they were horrified when Florence talked of making nursing a career. (4) Giving *sententious* reasons for their opposition, they forbade her to work in hospitals, which, at that time, were dirty and disreputable institutions. Florence, in despair, studied nursing as best she could from books. (5) She learned *pathology* and also became an expert on hospitals.

(6) Realizing that her parents would never *assent* to her plans, Florence Nightingale finally ignored their disapproval and broke free of her family. During 1850 and 1851, she underwent intensive nurses' training in Germany and France. She also visited many European hospitals and learned how they were run.

In 1853 Nightingale became superintendent of a small private hospital in London. (7) Dismayed by the *pathetic* conditions she found there, she introduced the latest nursing techniques and imposed strict routines on the nurses. (8) The *sensational* reforms that she effected attracted much praise.

In 1854 reports of heavy English and French losses against the Russians in the Crimean War were released. (9) Florence Nightingale had a *presentiment* that her services would be needed. Her feelings were proved accurate when the Secretary of War asked her to direct a team of nurses at a base hospital near Constantinople, Turkey. (10) Within a week she discovered that the high death rate was due, in part, to *apathetic* and uncoordinated medical treatment. In less than six months, she reduced the hospital death rate from 42 percent to only 2 percent. As she walked through the dark wards, bringing comfort and hope to the injured and sick, she became known as the Lady of the Lamp or the Angel of the Crimea.

When Nightingale was awarded a large sum of money honoring her work in the Crimean War, she used the money to found the Nightingale Training School for Nurses in 1860, which became the model for similar schools throughout the world. As part of the school, she also established a public health center with teams of district, or visiting, nurses.

Ultimately, Florence Nightingale was responsible for reforms in sanitation, nutrition, public health, general nursing, and hospital construction and management. The founder of modern nursing died in 1910.

READING COMPREHENSION EXERCISE

Each of the following statements corresponds to a numbered sentence in the passage. Each statement contains a blank and is followed by four answer choices. Decide which choice fits best in the blank. The word or phrase that you choose must express roughly the same meaning as the italicized word in the passage. Write the letter of your choice on the answer line.

1. According to Victorian _____, women of the privileged class were supposed to make brilliant marriages.

    a. biases   **b.** views   **c.** historians   **d.** letters

1. _____

2. Florence's _____ was offended by conventional social life.
   a. intelligence   **b.** personality   **c.** emotional responsiveness   **d.** behavior

2. _____

3. She cared for people with kindness and _____.
   a. concern   **b.** skill   **c.** pleasure   **d.** dedication

3. _____

4. Her parents gave _____ reasons for their opposition to nursing.
   a. emotional   **b.** definite   **c.** self-righteous   **d.** shallow

4. _____

5. By reading, Florence learned _____.
   a. science   **c.** healing techniques
   b. medical care   **d.** the causes and development of disease

5. _____

6. Florence realized that her parents would never _____ her plans.
   a. question   **b.** agree to   **c.** understand   **d.** disrupt

6. _____

7. Nightingale was dismayed by the _____ conditions she found at the hospital.
   a. pitiful   **b.** inappropriate   **c.** decent   **d.** insulting

7. _____

8. Her _____ reforms attracted much praise.
   a. honorable   **b.** outstanding   **c.** generous   **d.** responsible

8. _____

9. Nightingale had a(n) _____ that her services would be needed in the Crimean War.
   a. dream   **b.** impression   **c.** indication   **d.** premonition

9. _____

10. She discovered that the high death rate was partially due to _____ medical treatment.
    a. unskilled   **b.** quality   **c.** indifferent   **d.** substantial

10. _____

PRACTICE WITH ANALOGIES

See page 79 for some strategies to use with analogies.

Directions   Write the letter of the phrase that best completes the analogy.

1. EXECUTIVE : HIERARCHY :: (A) edge : knife
   (B) shore : lake   (C) step : ladder   (D) agenda : meeting
   (E) summit : mountain

1. _____

2. USURP : POWER :: (A) hijack : airplane   (B) copy : document
   (C) advertise : product   (D) overcome : obstacle   (E) conceal : surprise

2. _____

3. APATHETIC : EMOTION :: (A) ridiculous : laughter
   (B) informal : style   (C) aimless : purpose   (D) fascinating : interest
   (E) analogous : parallel

3. _____

4. HOMOGENEOUS : VARIATION :: (A) flexible : change
   (B) rational : logic   (C) dependent : assistance
   (D) inert : motion   (E) contagious : illness

4. _____

5. PATHETIC : PITY :: (A) contemptible : scorn
   (B) ridiculous : fear   (C) threatening : amusement
   (D) enviable : trust   (E) embarrassment : silly

5. _____

6. DEVIATE : PATH :: (A) create : idea   (B) veer : course
   (C) solve : problem   (D) face : mistake   (E) ban : book

6. _____

7. NUANCE : SUBTLE :: (A) movie : profitable
   (B) quotation : memorable   (C) rumor : harmful
   (D) whisper : honest   (E) skit : brief

7. _____

8. PATHOLOGY : DISEASE :: (A) geology : sky   (B) zoology : plants
   (C) cosmology : make-up   (D) psychology : behavior
   (E) ideology : ocean

8. _____

© Great Source   DO NOT COPY

Crime and wrongdoing have troubled every society from past to present. While highway robbery and piracy were commonplace among the ancient Romans, today hijacking and the capture of hostages happen all too frequently. In response to crime and wrongdoing, each society has devised various methods of prevention and control. For example, in the United States, acts of wrongdoing are punishable under a complex system of laws, organized according to the nature and severity of the crime. This lesson features words that refer to crime and wrongdoing.

WORD LIST

culpable
exonerate
extort
illicit
incorrigible
misdemeanor
purloin
ruffian
unscrupulous
vile

DEFINITIONS

After you have studied the definitions and example for each vocabulary word, write the word on the line to the right.

1. **culpable** (kŭl′pə-bel) *adjective*   Responsible for wrong or error; blameworthy; deserving censure. (From the Latin word *culpa,* meaning "fault")

   Related Word   **culpability** *noun*
   Example   The president of a company may be *culpable* for the wrongdoings of his subordinates.

   1. _____

2. **exonerate** (ĭg-zŏn′ə-rāt′) *trans. verb*   To free from a charge; declare blameless. (From the Latin *ex-,* meaning "off," and *onus,* meaning "burden")

   Related Word   **exoneration** *noun*
   Example   The defendant was *exonerated* from the charge of armed robbery when the jury delivered a favorable verdict.

   2. _____

3. **extort** (ĭk-stôrt′) *trans. verb*   To obtain by threats or other coercive means; exact; wring. (From the Latin *ex-,* meaning "out," and *torquere,* meaning "to twist")

   Related Word   **extortion** *noun*
   Example   The detective tried to *extort* a confession from the suspect.

   3. _____

4. **illicit** (ĭ-lĭs′ĭt) *adjective*   Not permitted by custom or law; illegal. (From the Latin *in-,* meaning "not," and *licitus,* meaning "lawful")

   Related Words   **illicitly** *adverb;* **illicitness** *noun*
   Example   Because of the bank president's alleged *illicit* activities, he was arrested and charged with embezzlement.

   4. _____
   USAGE NOTE: Don't confuse *illicit* with *elicit,* which means "to draw forth a response."

5. **incorrigible** (ĭn-kôr′ĭ-jə-bəl, ĭn-kŏr′ĭ-jə-bəl) *adjective*   Incapable of being corrected or reformed.   *noun*   A person who cannot be reformed. (From the Latin *in-*, meaning "not," and *corrigere,* meaning "to correct")

5. _____

    Related Words   **incorrigibility** *noun;* **incorrigibly** *adverb*
    Example   "Your *incorrigible* dishonesty astounds me," the judge told the veteran shoplifter.

6. **misdemeanor** (mĭs′dĭ-mē′nər) *noun*   **a.** An offense of less seriousness than a felony.   **b.** Misbehavior.

6. _____

    Example   Lorraine was guilty of a *misdemeanor* when she made an illegal left turn onto Elm Street.

7. **purloin** (pər-loin′, pûr′-loin′) *trans. verb*   To steal.   *intrans. verb*   To commit theft.

7. _____

    Related Word   **purloiner** *noun*
    Example   The thief *purloined* the jewelry and the television set from the apartment.

8. **ruffian** (rŭf′ē-ən, rŭf′yən) *noun*   A tough or rowdy person.   *adjective*   Tough or rowdy.

8. _____

    Example   The customers were frightened by the *ruffians* who stood outside the restaurant.

9. **unscrupulous** (ŭn-skroo′pyə-ləs) *adjective*   Without scruples or principles; not honorable.

9. _____

    Related Words   **unscrupulously** *adverb;* **unscrupulousness** *noun*
    Example   The *unscrupulous* clerk did not give customers all the change to which they were entitled.

10. **vile** (vīl) *adjective*   **a.** Unpleasant; disgusting.   **b.** Miserable; wretched. **c.** Morally low or base. (From the Latin word *vilis,* meaning "cheap, poor, or worthless")

10. _____

    Related Words   **vilely** *adverb;* **vileness** *noun*
    Example   "If Lane Stewart had not acted in such a *vile* manner toward his friends and family, he might still be alive today," the detective commented.

© Great Source   DO NOT COPY

EXERCISE 1 COMPLETING DEFINITIONS

On the answer line, write the word from the vocabulary list that best completes each definition.

1. An offense that is less serious than a felony is a _____.

2. Something not permitted by custom or law is _____.

3. A dishonorable person who is without principles is _____.

4. To _____ is to free from a charge or to declare blameless.

5. Someone who is tough or rowdy is a _____.

6. Someone who steals is said to _____ other people's property.

7. If someone is responsible for error or is blameworthy, that person is _____.

8. Someone whose actions are unpleasant or disgusting is behaving in a _____ way.

9. To obtain by threats or other coercive means is to _____.

10. Someone who is incapable of being corrected or reformed is _____.

1. _____

2. _____

3. _____

4. _____

5. _____

6. _____

7. _____

8. _____

9. _____

10. _____

EXERCISE 2 USING WORDS CORRECTLY

Decide whether the italicized vocabulary word has been used correctly in the sentence. On the answer line, write *Correct* for correct use and *Incorrect* for incorrect use.

1. The vice principal was on the lookout for two *ruffians* who liked to pick fights on the school playground.

2. Only a professional thief would have dared to *purloin* the priceless painting from such a well-guarded gallery.

3. "Oh, Bobby Lee, you're *incorrigible*," his aunt scolded. "When will you mend your ways?"

4. Susan gave *illicit* instructions that no one was to touch her guitar while she was away.

5. Mother thought that the pink slippers were the most *culpable* pair she had ever tried on.

6. The ease with which Mr. Hyde lies and cheats shows that he is an *unscrupulous* person.

7. Desmond received a sentence of life imprisonment for his *misdemeanor*.

8. Andrea's generosity to charity was a good example of her *vile* personality in action.

9. The petty criminal tried to *extort* money from the shopkeeper in return for protecting his business.

10. With a maximum ten-year prison sentence, Terence was *exonerated* from the charge of robbery.

1. _____

2. _____

3. _____

4. _____

5. _____

6. _____

7. _____

8. _____

9. _____

10. _____

EXERCISE 3 IDENTIFYING SYNONYMS AND ANTONYMS

Decide which word or phrase has the meaning that is the same as (a synonym) or opposite to (an antonym) that of the capitalized vocabulary word. Write the letter of your choice on the answer line.

1. MISDEMEANOR (synonym):
   a. behavior   b. misbehavior   c. problem   d. gratitude

2. INCORRIGIBLE (antonym):
   a. reformable   b. stubborn   c. forgiving   d. hopeless

3. EXTORT (synonym):
   a. cheat   b. exact   c. remember   d. contribute

4. CULPABLE (antonym):
   a. burdened   b. guilty   c. innocent   d. relaxed

5. RUFFIAN (synonym):
   a. intellectual   b. student   c. good citizen   d. rowdy

6. PURLOIN (synonym):
   a. protect   b. purchase   c. cook   d. steal

7. UNSCRUPULOUS (antonym):
   a. honest   b. unsavory   c. domesticated   d. rampant

8. EXONERATE (antonym):
   a. bother greatly   b. procrastinate   c. eliminate trust   d. find guilty

9. ILLICIT (antonym):
   a. precise   b. cherished   c. legal   d. borrowed

10. VILE (synonym):
    a. poisonous   b. changeable   c. unpleasant   d. cabinet

1. _____

2. _____

3. _____

4. _____

5. _____

6. _____

7. _____

8. _____

9. _____

10. _____

EXERCISE 4 USING DIFFERENT FORMS OF WORDS

Decide which form of the vocabulary word in parentheses best completes the sentence. The form given may be correct. Write your answer on the answer line.

1. The _____ of those plotting to overthrow the government was undeniable. (*culpable*)

2. At the trial the young woman's testimony resulted in the defendant's immediate _____. (*exonerate*)

3. The convicted bigamist was also held on charges of _____. (*extort*)

4. The new employee was quickly disillusioned by the _____ of the company's business dealings. (*illicit*)

5. The only person I know who is _____ blunt is Alfred Hunter. (*incorrigible*)

6. The _____ of the main character in the movie was difficult to tolerate. (*vile*)

7. Ryan moved on from committing _____ to perpetrating felonies. (*misdemeanor*)

8. "Sticky-Fingers" Flanagan is a well-known _____. (*purloin*)

9. Although Mr. James looked like a _____, the children could tell that he was really a gentle person. (*ruffian*)

10. The real-estate agent _____ misrepresented the swampland and sold it to an unsuspecting customer. (*unscrupulous*)

1. _____

2. _____

3. _____

4. _____

5. _____

6. _____

7. _____

8. _____

9. _____

10. _____

© Great Source   DO NOT COPY

READING COMPREHENSION

Each numbered sentence in the following passage contains an italicized vocabulary word or related form. After you read the passage, you will complete an exercise.

THE BOSTON TEA PARTY

History is full of stories about honest people who, when consistently treated in an unfair manner, have felt that they had no alternative other than to break the law. (1) Many of these stories have ended with the lawbreakers deserving and receiving full *exoneration.* (2) For example, during the years before the American Revolution, much unrest existed among the colonists, and *misdemeanors* were routinely perpetrated against the British. (3) The Boston Tea Party was one of the most famous of these *illicit* acts, an act for which society has heartily forgiven the "criminals."

(4) In 1773 the people of Massachusetts were enraged by what they considered to be the *unscrupulous* behavior of the British. The British Parliament had passed a new act that allowed the East India Trading Company to send tea directly to the colonies, where British agents could then sell and collect taxes on the tea. Colonial merchants were threatened by this new ruling. (5) They felt that the British were trying to *extort* money from the colonists, and that the landing of the English ships with tea would be an attack on American liberties. (6) They were determined to stop the British in what they considered to be the latest in a long series of *vile* actions.

After the British ships carrying cargoes of tea arrived in the Boston harbor, the colonists called a town meeting and passed a resolution urging Governor Thomas Hutchinson of Massachusetts to order the ships to return to England. (7) When Hutchinson refused their request, the colonists considered his behavior *culpable.* They then decided to take matters into their own hands.

(8) In that celebrated act of resistance on December 16, 1773, a band of patriots, who might have been mistaken for *ruffians,* raided the British ships that were docked in Boston Harbor. (9) Late at night, these *incorrigible* Bostonians, who disguised themselves as Indians, crept aboard the British ships. (10) They then *purloined* large quantities of tea and threw it into the bay.

This insulting raid upon the British ships stirred up bad feelings between the American colonists and the British government. The king of England and the British Parliament decided that they could not let such acts of violence go unpunished. Consequently, they imposed even harsher taxes and restrictions. The colonists became increasingly rebellious, and more and more British laws were broken, culminating in the American Revolution.

READING COMPREHENSION EXERCISE

Each of the following statements corresponds to a numbered sentence in the passage. Each statement contains a blank and is followed by four answer choices. Decide which choice fits best in the blank. The word or phrase that you choose must express roughly the same meaning as the italicized word in the passage. Write the letter of your choice on the answer line.

1. Many protesters have later been declared _____.
   a. blameworthy   b. blameless   c. guilty   d. incapable

   1. _____

2. The colonists committed many _____ against the British.
   a. major crimes   b. major assaults   c. minor crimes   d. petty thefts

   2. _____

3. The best known of these _____ acts was the Boston Tea Party.
   a. unfair   b. understandable   c. intolerable   d. illegal

   3. _____

4. The colonists felt that the British acted in a(n) _____ manner.
   a. dishonorable   b. irresponsible   c. pitiful   d. uncivilized

   4. _____

© Great Source   DO NOT COPY

5. The colonists claimed that the British were trying to _____ money unfairly.
   a. repay   **b.** handle   **c.** exact   **d.** impose

5. _____

6. They wanted to stop the British from committing any more _____ actions.
   a. dangerous   **b.** spontaneous   **c.** delayed   **d.** hateful

6. _____

7. The colonists considered Governor Hutchinson's behavior to be _____.
   a. foolish   **b.** blameworthy   **c.** intelligent   **d.** destructive

7. _____

8. To retaliate against the British, a band of patriots, who might have been mistaken for _____, raided the English ships.
   a. rowdies   **b.** colonists   **c.** angry citizens   **d.** aristrocrats

8. _____

9. The group that raided the British ships was _____.
   a. unable to be seen   **c.** incapable of being reformed
   b. unable to be stopped   **d.** irresponsible

9. _____

10. The patriots _____ the tea and threw it into the bay.
    a. stole   **b.** damaged   **c.** examined   **d.** traded

10. _____

WRITING ASSIGNMENT

Imagine yourself as a court reporter who is looking for an interesting case to write about for a local newspaper. Make up a case that might intrigue your readers and recount it in several paragraphs. Explain the most important details—who, what, where, when, and how. Use five vocabulary words from this lesson and underline each one.

VOCABULARY ENRICHMENT

The word *unscrupulous* comes from the English prefix *un-*, meaning "not," and the Latin word *scrupulus*, meaning "little stone." *Unscrupulous* has a curious history that can be traced to Roman times. A little stone, or *scrupulus*, might find its way into someone's sandal and cause the person discomfort when walking. There would be a feeling of uneasiness, perhaps even of worry, resulting from the pressure of the stone. At times the word *scrupulus* was used for describing uneasiness or even mental trouble. English borrowed the word *scrupulous* in the metaphorical sense from Latin and created its antonym, *unscrupulous*.

Scrupulous individuals hesitate out of doubt or uneasiness over what is right or proper. They are careful and discreet, worrying about the correct course of action. Unscrupulous people, on the other hand, are not. They have few principles and do not worry about whether their behavior is right or wrong. Thus, the word *unscrupulous* has traveled a long way from its original connection with a little stone that caused discomfort.

Activity Using your dictionary, look up the following words and write their definitions and their Latin roots. Then write an explanation of the connection between each root and its definition.

1. dilapidated   2. lapidary   3. calculator   4. miscalculation   5. gem

© Great Source   DO NOT COPY

LESSON 21 GOOD HUMOR

Laughter is an experience common to all people and, yet, a strange one. Why should it be that we respond with spasmodic gasping to what we find amusing? Whatever the reason, laughter and good humor under appropriate circumstances are neither foolish nor weird but can even be healthful and therapeutic. In this lesson you will learn words that relate to humor.

WORD LIST

banter
caricature
droll
facetious
flippant
hilarity
ludicrous
mirth
whimsical
witticism

DEFINITIONS

After you have studied the definitions and example for each vocabulary word, write the word on the line to the right.

1. **banter** (băn′tər) *noun* Good-humored, playful conversation. *intrans. verb* To converse in a teasing or playful manner.

   Example The *banter* between the two comics appearing at the Rivoli is hysterically funny.

   1. _____

2. **caricature** (kăr′ĭ-kə-chŏor′) *noun* A representation, usually pictorial, which exaggerates or distorts the subject's features to produce a comic or ridiculous effect. *trans. verb* To depict someone in such a way.

   Related Word caricaturist *noun*
   Example Closk's book is more a *caricature* than a biography of the President.

   2. _____

3. **droll** (drōl) *adjective* Amusingly odd or comical. (From the French word *drole*, meaning "amusing")

   Related Words drollery *noun;* drolly *adverb*
   Example The storyteller delighted the children with the *droll* tale about the Nutcracker and the Mouse king.

   3. _____

4. **facetious** (fə-sē′shəs) *adjective* **a.** Playfully humorous. **b.** Jesting, often in an inappropriate or offensive way. (From the Latin word *facetus*, meaning "witty")

   Related Words facetiously *adverb;* facetiousness *noun*
   Example The *facetious* comments Mr. Webster made in class about my comedy routine were funnier than the skit itself.

   4. _____
   See *whimsical.*

5. **flippant** (flĭp′ənt) *adjective*   Marked by a disrespectful frivolity or indifference; rudely witty.

   Related Words   flippancy *noun;* **flippantly** *adverb*
   Example   Mrs. Díaz scolded Hernando for his *flippant* remarks.

5. _____

6. **hilarity** (hĭ-lăr′ĭ-tē, hī-lâr′ĭ-tē) *noun*   Loud and lively merriment; boisterousness. (From the Greek word *hilaros,* meaning "joyous" or "cheerful")

   Related Word   **hilarious** *adjective*
   Example   There was much *hilarity* and celebration at my parents' twenty-fifth anniversary party.

6. _____
   See *mirth.*

7. **ludicrous** (loo′dĭ-krəs) *adjective*   Laughable because of an obvious absurdity or ridiculousness. (From the Latin word *ludere,* meaning "to play")

   Related Words   **ludicrously** *adverb;* **ludicrousness** *noun*
   Example   The opera star sounded *ludicrous* singing "You Ain't Nothin' but a Hound Dog."

7. _____

8. **mirth** (mûrth) *noun*   Gladness or lightheartedness, especially when expressed by laughter; gaiety, merriment.

   Related Word   **mirthful** *adjective*
   Example   When Tracy, Randy, and I get together for an evening, I know I have a couple of hours of *mirth* and merriment to look forward to.

8. _____
   USAGE NOTE: *Hilarity* implies boisterousness and an unrestrained expression of merriment, whereas *mirth* merely implies an easy, relaxed feeling of enjoyment.

9. **whimsical** (hwĭm′zĭ-kəl) *adjective*   **a.** Playful or fanciful; imaginatively humorous. **b.** Characterized by unpredictability.

   Related Words   **whimsically** *adverb;* **whimsy** *noun*
   Example   This *whimsical* writer has a special gift for creating fantastic fairy tales for children.

9. _____
   USAGE NOTE: *Facetious* and *whimsical* both involve playfulness and humor, but facetiousness can have a sharp edge.

10. **witticism** (wĭt′ĭ-sĭz′əm) *noun*   A witty or clever remark or saying.

   Related Word   **witty** *adjective*
   Example   Referring to the need for loyalty to the cause of American independence, Benjamin Franklin coined the *witticism* "We must all hang together, or assuredly we shall all hang separately."

10. _____

© Great Source   DO NOT COPY

EXERCISE 1 WRITING CORRECT WORDS

On the answer line, write the word from the vocabulary list that best fits
each definition.

1. A distorted representation that produces a comic or ludicrous effect

2. Rudely witty

3. A clever remark

4. Gaiety or merriment; gladness or lightheartedness

5. Good-humored, playful conversation

6. Boisterous merriment

7. Amusingly odd or comical

8. Playful, fanciful; characterized by unpredictability

9. Laughable because of an obvious absurdity

10. Playfully humorous; jesting

1. _____

2. _____

3. _____

4. _____

5. _____

6. _____

7. _____

8. _____

9. _____

10. _____

EXERCISE 2 USING WORDS CORRECTLY

Decide whether the italicized vocabulary word has been used correctly in the sentence.
On the answer line, write *Correct* for correct use and *Incorrect* for incorrect use.

1. The *banter* of the star athletes in the television interview was serious and profound.

2. Our teacher was pleased when Mark answered her question with a *flippant* remark.

3. To write a *whimsical* story, one must limit the content to facts.

4. The French poet Nerval was a *droll* character who walked around Paris with his
pet lobster on a leash.

5. The other players thought Janet *ludicrous* because she brought her hockey stick to
soccer practice.

6. The comedian made a *facetious* remark about the political candidate.

7. The speaker began his talk with a *witticism*, a scholarly analysis of the causes of
inflation.

8. There is usually great *hilarity* during a chemistry test.

9. Can you name the principal *caricatures* in *The Scarlet Letter?*

10. Max and Tidbit expressed their *mirth* by laughing joyously.

1. _____

2. _____

3. _____

4. _____

5. _____

6. _____

7. _____

8. _____

9. _____

10. _____

EXERCISE 3 CHOOSING THE BEST DEFINITION

For each italicized vocabulary word in the following sentences, write the letter of the
best definition on the answer line.

1. Wearing a winter coat when it is ninety-eight degrees is *ludicrous*.
   a. playful   b. ridiculous   c. clever   d. disrespectful

2. In the *whimsical* world of *The Wind in the Willows* by the English author Kenneth
Grahame, the animal characters act like human beings.
   a. unimaginative   b. childish   c. crude   d. fanciful

1. _____

2. _____

3. Barry unwisely made a *facetious* remark about his parents' new car.
   a. harmlessly imaginative   c. inappropriately humorous
   b. playful   d. subtly witty

3. _____

4. The *banter* between Sue and David during school amuses all the other students immensely.
   a. playful conversation   c. disrespectful remark
   b. snorting chuckle   d. ridiculous comment

4. _____

5. Filled with *mirth*, the peasants of medieval Flanders sang and danced in the streets of Antwerp.
   a. disrespect   b. sadness   c. humor   d. merriment

5. _____

6. Audiences still find humor in the *witticisms* in Cole Porter's sophisticated lyrics.
   a. mockeries   b. imagination   c. clever remarks   d. arch disrespect

6. _____

7. Our *droll* class president keeps a huge, green Madagascar parrot on his shoulder when he studies.
   a. amusingly odd   b. offensively clever   c. scary   d. insufferably boring

7. _____

8. After the team won the state championships, there was a great deal of *hilarity* in the locker room.
   a. boisterousness   b. mockery   c. rudeness   d. imagination

8. _____

9. The best part of the movie was Vicki Mendoza's *caricature* of a 1950s teenager.
   a. interpretation   c. serious portrayal
   b. comical exaggeration   d. playing the part

9. _____

10. Because of George's *flippant* answers, the interviewer decided that he should not be hired.
    a. amusing   b. playful   c. fanciful   d. impertinent

10. _____

EXERCISE 4 USING DIFFERENT FORMS OF WORDS

Decide which form of the vocabulary word in parentheses best completes the sentence. The form given may be correct. Write your answer on the answer line.

1. Abby shocked her mother by answering her very reasonable question about school _____. *(flippant)*

1. _____

2. Tommy Soong got a job as a _____ because he is such a talented artist. *(caricature)*

2. _____

3. The show was so _____ that we kept repeating the jokes to our friends for weeks. *(hilarity)*

3. _____

4. All children are _____ on the first day of summer vacation. *(mirth)*

4. _____

5. Shakespeare is often very _____ in his comedies. *(witticism)*

5. _____

6. The _____ of the man who could talk, walk, and write backwards surprised the passers-by. *(droll)*

6. _____

7. The poet described the lion _____ as "the fearsome ferocious fur-ball of the forest." *(whimsical)*

7. _____

8. We laughed wildly because of the _____ of his disguise. *(ludicrous)*

8. _____

9. Oriana was not amused when Sarah told her _____ that her lost wallet could probably be found where she last left it. *(facetious)*

9. _____

10. Lynn thought that it was fun _____ with the elderly woman during the long bus ride to Wilkes-Barre. *(banter)*

10. _____

© Great Source   DO NOT COPY

READING COMPREHENSION

Each numbered sentence in the following passage contains an italicized vocabulary word. After you read the passage, you will complete an exercise.

A CLASSICAL COMIC AND HIS COMICAL CLASSICS

(1) Which ancient playwright inspired the *hilarity* in *A Funny Thing Happened on the Way to the Forum*, a hit Broadway play that was subsequently made into a popular movie? (2) Which author, known for his *witticisms* and clever dialogue, influenced many other famous comic dramatists, including William Shakespeare, Molière and Giraudoux? The answer to both these questions is Plautus (c. 254–184 B.C.), the brilliant Roman comic dramatist. (3) During the religious festivals at which Roman drama was performed, Plautus' plays were well attended because audiences were sure to enjoy the complicated plots and humorous *banter.*

(4) Although Plautus wrote more than twenty comedies, the characters in each of the plays are usually *caricatures* of the various types of people common at that time. (5) There is usually a *whimsical* young man from a respectable family, and he leads a rather carefree and wild life. He is often in debt and almost always falls in love with a beautiful but unsuitable girl. (6) His *droll* father, whose old fashioned ideas make audiences snicker, does not approve of his son's behavior. (7) Ever present is the clever but *flippant* slave who leads the youth into and out of trouble. (8) Amidst some *ludicrous* circumstances involving haunted houses or mistaken identities or shipwrecks or long-lost children, everything, of course, turns out just right. The young man settles down and weds his beloved, who turns out to be a refined and respectable young lady from a fine family. (9) The father forgives his son, and the crafty slave escapes punishment, although he continues to make *facetious* remarks to the audience.

The slapstick humor and absurd situations of Plautus' comedies made Romans chortle with delight. (10) No matter what their mood when they entered, the audience would always exit full of *mirth*, having had a rollicking good time.

© Great Source   DO NOT COPY

Each of the following statements corresponds to a numbered sentence in the passage. Each statement contains a blank and is followed by four answer choices. Decide which choice fits best in the blank. The word or phrase that you choose must express roughly the same meaning as the italicized word in the passage. Write the letter of your choice on the answer line.

1. Which ancient dramatist inspired the _____ in a Broadway play and a hit movie?
   a. serious theme
   b. crude jokes
   c. lively merriment
   d. silly gags

1. _____

2. Which author was known for his _____ and influenced many other successful playwrights for centuries to come?
   a. precise dialogue
   b. clever remarks
   c. funny characters
   d. intricate plots

2. _____

3. Audiences knew that they would enjoy the complicated plots and humorous _____ .
   a. chatter
   b. whispers
   c. dramatic speeches
   d. playful conversation

3. _____

4. The characters are usually _____ of common types of people.
   a. exaggerated, comical representations
   b. sketches
   c. monstrously deformed portrayals
   d. great examples

4. _____

5. One of the characters is a _____ young man who leads a happy-go-lucky existence.
   a. silly
   b. serious
   c. fanciful
   d. practical

5. _____

6. The _____ father has old-fashioned ideas that make the audience snicker.
   a. gruff
   b. kindly
   c. comical
   d. strict

6. _____

7. The slave is clever but _____ .
   a. cunning
   b. odd
   c. crafty
   d. disrespectful

7. _____

8. Some _____ situations and settings occur, such as haunted houses and mistaken identities.
   a. absurd
   b. weird
   c. dangerous
   d. threatening

8. _____

9. In the end the slave is forgiven, but he keeps making _____ remarks to the audience.
   a. jesting
   b. disturbing
   c. some
   d. informative

9. _____

10. Audiences always left the theater feeling _____ .
    a. pleasant
    b. lighthearted
    c. content
    d. silly

10. _____

WRITING ASSIGNMENT

Imagine that you are a playwright who has written a successful Broadway comedy and who now wishes to sell a film or television script of the same play to a Hollywood studio. Using five words from the lesson, write a letter to a prospective producer explaining why you believe your Broadway comedy will make a successful movie. Be sure to include examples of the most comical situations in your play in case the producer has not had a chance to see it. Underline each vocabulary word that you use.

© Great Source   DO NOT COPY

READING SKILLS

CONTEXT CLUES: CONTRAST

In this lesson you will consider context clues of contrast. A sentence that contains an unfamiliar word may also include a word or phrase that is opposite in meaning to the unfamiliar word. Such a word or phrase is a context clue of contrast (sometimes called opposition). There are three main kinds: antonyms, the word *not* or *no*, and connecting words that signal contrast. The following strategies will help you use these context clues to define unfamiliar words.

STRATEGIES

1. *Look for an antonym of the unfamiliar word.* In an antonym clue, the structure of the sentence tells you that one word is opposite in meaning to another.

    Sasha was *itinerant* for three years and *settled* during the rest of his life.

    Both *itinerant* and *settled* are adjectives modifying *Sasha.* The opposite of *settled* is *moving.* The dictionary definition of *itinerant* is "traveling from place to place."

    When you look for antonyms of an unfamiliar word, pay particular attention to possible antonyms with negative prefixes, such as *non-, un-, dis-,* and sometimes *in-.*

2. *Look for words preceded by* not *and* no. *Not* and *no* can signal a word whose meaning is opposite to that of another word in the sentence. Such words as *no one, nobody,* and *nothing* can also provide this clue.

    The agent's manner suggested *duplicity,* not *straightforwardness.*

    The word *not* and the sentence structure tell you that *straightforwardness* contrasts with *duplicity.* The dictionary defines *duplicity* as "deliberate deceptiveness in behavior or speech."

3. *Look for connecting words and phrases that indicate a contrast.* Such words can be in the same sentence or in different sentences. Connecting words and phrases that indicate a contrast include *although, but, however, nevertheless, yet, on the other hand, unless, despite, or,* and *rather than.* In the following sentences, *although* and *however* are signals that the word *polite* contrasts in meaning with *boorish.*

    Although Tina was *polite,* her brother was *boorish.*
    Tina was *polite.* Her brother, however, was *boorish.*

    The clues tell you that *boorish* probably means "not polite." The dictionary definition is "resembling a boor; crude, rude, and offensive."

EXERCISE GETTING MEANING FROM CONTRAST CLUES

Step 1: Using context clues, write your own definition of the italicized word in each of the following sentences. *Step 2:* Write the appropriate dictionary definition of the word. *Step 3:* Write a sentence of your own in which you use the word according to the dictionary definition.

1. In a good mood Kay is soft-spoken, and in a bad mood she is *caustic.*

   Your Definition _____

   Dictionary Definition _____

   Sentence _____

2. Although his relatives were wealthy, he was *destitute.*

   Your Definition _____

   Dictionary Definition _____

   Sentence _____

3. Despite the *gravity* of her illness, Ruth made a full recovery.

   Your Definition _____

   Dictionary Definition _____

   Sentence _____

4. Her first rule of leadership was to be firm and decisive rather than *equivocal.*

   Your Definition _____

   Dictionary Definition _____

   Sentence _____

5. No one could say that the official was humble, for his actions were often *presumptuous.*

   Your Definition _____

   Dictionary Definition _____

   Sentence _____

6. We could tell from the look on the children's faces that their story was not *fabricated* but true.

   Your Definition _____

   Dictionary Definition _____

   Sentence _____

7. Usually composed, Alicia became *distraught* when she realized that she might have prevented the accident.

   Your Definition _____

   Dictionary Definition _____

   Sentence _____

8. Most people had to pay for the tote bag; however, those who made a donation to charity received it *gratis.*

   Your Definition _____

   Dictionary Definition _____

   Sentence _____

© Great Source   DO NOT COPY

The vocabulary of English is large, rich, and varied. It includes many pairs of words that are easily confused because they are similar in sound or spelling, although they have different or even opposite meanings. Four such pairs are discussed in this lesson: *adverse* and *averse*, *emigrate* and *immigrate*, *ingenious* and *ingenuous*, and *persecute* and *prosecute*. The pair *figuratively* and *literally* do not look or sound alike, but their meanings are often confused. *Literally* is sometimes used as if it meant the same thing as *figuratively*, although it means the opposite.

WORD LIST

adverse
averse
emigrate
figuratively
immigrate
ingenious
ingenuous
literally
persecute
prosecute

DEFINITIONS

After you have studied the definitions and example for each vocabulary word, write the word on the line to the right.

1. **adverse** (ăd-vûrs′, ăd′vûrs′) *adjective* **a.** Unfavorable to one's interest or welfare: *adverse circumstances*. **b.** Contrary or opposing in intention or effect; hostile: *adverse criticism*. (From the Latin *ad-*, meaning "toward," and *vertere*, meaning "to turn")

   Related Words **adversely** *adverb;* **adversity** *noun*
   Example   After listening to their *adverse* remarks, I became very discouraged about continuing with the project.

1. _____
USAGE NOTE: Be sure to distinguish *adverse* from *averse.*

2. **averse** (ə-vûrs′) *adjective* Having a strong feeling of dislike or reluctance. (From the Latin *ab-*, meaning "away from," and *vertere*, meaning "to turn")

   Related Words **aversely** *adverb;* **aversion** *noun*
   Example   Cindy was usually *averse* to criticizing her friends, but she could not let Joey's insulting behavior toward the new student go unnoticed.

2. _____

3. **emigrate** (ĕm′ĭ-grāt′) *intrans. verb* To leave one country or region in order to settle in another. (From the Latin *ex-*, meaning "out," and *migrare*, meaning "to move")

   Related Words **emigrant** *noun;* **emigration** *noun*
   Example   During the American Revolution, many Tories *emigrated* from the United States and settled in Canada.

3. _____
USAGE NOTE: Note that people *emigrate from* or *immigrate to* a country.

4. **figuratively** (fĭg′yər-ə-tĭv-lē) *adverb* In a manner marked by metaphorical language or figures of speech.

   Related Word **figurative** *adjective*
   Example   I was speaking only *figuratively* when I said that my uncle was so lucky that everything he touched turned to gold.

4. _____

5. **immigrate** (ĭm'ĭ-grāt') *intrans. verb*   To enter and settle in a country or region that is not one's native land. (From the Latin *in-*, meaning "in," and *migrare*, meaning "to move")

> **Related Words**   **immigrant** *noun;* **immigration** *noun*
> **Example**   For thousands of years, people have *immigrated* to new areas, escaping harsh rulers or seeking better living conditions.

5. _____
MEMORY CUE: *Immigrants* come *into* a country.

6. **ingenious** (ĭn-jēn'yəs) *adjective*   **a.** Having or showing creative or inventive skill: *an ingenious silversmith.*   **b.** Original or imaginative in design or execution: *an ingenious gadget.* (From the Latin word *ingenium*, meaning "inborn talent")

> **Related Words**   **ingeniously** *adverb;* **ingeniousness** *noun*
> **Example**   The poet Ogden Nash was an *ingenious* versifier, and he invented many clever and amusing rhymes.

6. _____
USAGE NOTE: Be sure to distinguish *ingenious* from *ingenuous.*

7. **ingenuous** (ĭn-jĕn'yŏo-əs) *adjective*   Showing or having simplicity, openness, and honesty, in a childlike way. (From the Latin word *ingenuus*, meaning "honest" or "freeborn")

> **Related Words**   **ingenuously** *adverb;* **ingenuousness** *noun*
> **Example**   Sue was still *ingenuous* enough to believe that talent and hard work alone would inevitably lead to success.

7. _____
MEMORY CUE: An *ingenuous* person is *genuine* in a way.

8. **literally** (lĭt'ər-ə-lē) *adverb*   **a.** According to the actual meaning of a word or phrase.   **b.** According to the facts; without exaggeration or metaphor: *He literally could not add two and two.*   **c.** Word for word: *literally translated.* (From the Latin word *littera*, meaning "letter")

> **Related Words**   **literal** *adjective;* **literalness** *noun*
> **Example**   Lester took every statement so *literally* that he could not enjoy a joke.

8. _____
USAGE NOTE: *Literally* is not correctly used as a synonym of *figuratively.*

9. **persecute** (pûr'sĭ-kyŏot') *trans. verb*   **a.** To ill-treat persistently and grievously.   **b.** To annoy continually; pester. (From the Latin *per-*, an intensive prefix, and *sequi*, meaning "to follow")

> **Related Word**   **persecution** *noun*
> **Example**   Although many groups came to the New World seeking freedom of belief, some were quick to *persecute* members of their communities who did not agree with their opinions.

9. _____
USAGE NOTE: Be sure to distinguish *persecute* from *prosecute.*

10. **prosecute** (prŏs'ĭ-kyŏot') *trans. verb*   To bring a legal action against in order to convict of a violation of a law. (From the Latin *pro-*, meaning "forward," and *sequi*, meaning "to follow")

> **Related Words**   **prosecution** *noun;* **prosecutor** *noun*
> **Example**   The farmer *prosecuted* three hunters for trespassing.

10. _____

© Great Source   DO NOT COPY

EXERCISE 1 WRITING CORRECT WORDS

On the answer line, write the word from the vocabulary list that best fits
each definition.

1. To leave one's country permanently for another

2. Having a strong feeling of dislike

3. Having inventive skill

4. In a manner marked by figures of speech

5. Unfavorable to one's interest or welfare

6. To bring a legal action against

7. To enter and settle in a country not one's own

8. Showing childlike simplicity, honesty, and openness

9. To ill-treat persistently

10. According to the actual meaning of a word or phrase

1. _____

2. _____

3. _____

4. _____

5. _____

6. _____

7. _____

8. _____

9. _____

10. _____

EXERCISE 2 USING WORDS CORRECTLY

Decide whether the italicized vocabulary word has been used correctly in the sentence.
On the answer line, write *Correct* for correct use and *Incorrect* for incorrect use.

1. Nicky's piano teacher *emigrated* from Albania when she was a girl.

2. In spite of their *ingenuous* and quite elaborate plans for a getaway, the bank
robbers were still caught red-handed.

3. My uncle is so *averse* to exercise that he feels imposed upon if he has to walk more
than a few yards from his car to the front door.

4. That spider was *literally* ten feet long.

5. Many Australians *immigrated* from England in the nineteenth century.

6. The children *prosecuted* the baby sitter by throwing temper tantrums and
incessantly asking for treats.

7. The women of the town where my grandmother grew up were famous for their
ingenious quilt designs.

8. Human beings are adaptable enough to survive in very *adverse* environments.

9. Many Renaissance poems *figuratively* describe women as having lips of coral, skin
of ivory, and hair of golden wire.

10. In Greek mythology Orestes was *persecuted* by the Furies for killing his mother.

1. _____

2. _____

3. _____

4. _____

5. _____

6. _____

7. _____

8. _____

9. _____

10. _____

EXERCISE 3 IDENTIFYING SYNONYMS AND ANTONYMS

Decide which word or phrase has the meaning that is the same as (a synonym) or
opposite to (an antonym) that of the capitalized vocabulary word. Write the letter of
your choice on the answer line.

1. PERSECUTE (antonym):
   a. treat well   b. sue   c. acquit   d. hurt

1. _____

2. **EMIGRATE** (synonym):
   a. arrive   c. settle
   b. be forced out   d. permanently leave one's country

2. _____

3. **INGENIOUS** (antonym):
   a. knowing   b. unimaginative   c. childish   d. inventive

3. _____

4. **LITERALLY** (synonym):
   a. alphabetically   b. almost   c. actually   d. metaphorically

4. _____

5. **IMMIGRATE** (antonym):
   a. leave one's country   c. be uprooted
   b. settle in a country not one's own   d. visit

5. _____

6. **PROSECUTE** (synonym):
   a. bring legal action against   c. annoy continually
   b. accuse   d. convict

6. _____

7. **ADVERSE** (antonym):
   a. hostile   b. reluctant   c. willing   d. favorable

7. _____

8. **FIGURATIVELY** (synonym):
   a. according to the facts   c. mathematically
   b. metaphorically   d. geometrically

8. _____

9. **INGENUOUS** (antonym):
   a. specific   b. real   c. sophisticated   d. open

9. _____

10. **AVERSE** (antonym):
   a. loath   b. willing   c. straightforward   d. contrary

10. _____

EXERCISE 4 USING DIFFERENT FORMS OF WORDS

Decide which form of the vocabulary word in parentheses best completes the sentence. The form given may be correct. Write your answer on the answer line.

1. The defendant had been previously _____ on a number of charges but had never been found guilty. (*prosecute*)

1. _____

2. Many once-vivid _____ expressions have become lifeless clichés. (*figuratively*)

2. _____

3. The Great Potato Famine in Ireland during the mid-nineteenth century resulted in the _____ of thousands of people from that country. (*emigrate*)

3. _____

4. Rube Goldberg was famous for his drawings of _____ complex machinery for performing simple tasks. (*ingenious*)

4. _____

5. Every now and then my aunt will overcome her _____ to rural life and visit us on our farm. (*averse*)

5. _____

6. Some _____ to the United States returned to their native countries without having fulfilled their dreams and ambitions. (*immigrate*)

6. _____

7. A _____ translation of the French word for potato is "apple of earth." (*literally*)

7. _____

8. The recent change in graduation requirements has affected many students _____. (*adverse*)

8. _____

9. His _____ behavior and appearance concealed the cunning and treachery of a natural con man. (*ingenuous*)

9. _____

10. Pat was bright but lazy, and she often felt _____ by her teachers and parents. (*persecute*)

10. _____

© Great Source   DO NOT COPY

READING COMPREHENSION

Each numbered sentence in the following passage contains an italicized vocabulary word or related form. After you read the passage, you will complete an exercise.

THE GOLDEN AGE OF IMMIGRATION

The movement of people from one region to another has been going on for thousands of years. People have moved as individuals or in groups for social, economic, political, and religious reasons. Seen from this wider perspective, the settlement of the United States both before and after the American Revolution is hardly unusual. (1) The large numbers of people involved, however, as well as their varied backgrounds, make the story of European *immigration* to the United States one of the most important examples of human migration in history.

(2) People *emigrate* from their homelands for many reasons, but they usually do so freely. (3) Other kinds of resettlement, such as those brought about by colonization, deportation, or enslavement, are wholly or partly forced upon persons or groups *averse* to making such a wrenching change in their lives. In addition to voluntary migration, forced relocation brought people to the United States, especially before the Revolution. It was during the nineteenth and early twentieth centuries that great masses of voluntary immigrants arrived.

The European immigrants of the nineteenth century can be divided into two groups. (4) One group includes those who left Europe primarily to escape *adverse* conditions in their own countries. The population of Europe was increasing to such an extent that younger people could not expect to maintain their accustomed living standards. Technological advances were destroying jobs in many traditional crafts and industries. (5) Religious minorities were often *persecuted,* and entire congregations resettled in the vast continent of North America. The greatest number, however, emigrated because of the Potato Famine of 1845–1849. (6) As a result of this tragedy, half a million people in Ireland alone *literally* starved to death, and over a million of the survivors fled.

The immigrants of the first group were well aware of the attractions of the United States as a new home, but for many these were secondary. The second group, however, actively sought the advantages of a new world. They were not always under great pressure to leave Europe. Instead, they sought to improve the social and economic status that they enjoyed in their homelands. (7) Some believed—and not just *figuratively*—that the streets of the United States were "paved with gold." (8) Such an *ingenuous* belief could not possibly survive the actual conditions of American life. As a result, some immigrants returned home disillusioned and disappointed. Others with more realistic expectations remained and prospered. They took advantage of opportunities to apply their skills in new industries and technologies. A chronic shortage of labor and an underpopulated continent made it easy for almost any newcomer to find a place in the growing nation.

The late nineteenth and early twentieth century in America was a period of widespread social unrest caused by increased population, rapid industrial development, and an unstable economy. Many citizens, established descendants of earlier immigrants, blamed the troubles on the more recently arrived groups, and, as a result, attitudes toward immigration became negative and then hostile. (9) The malcontents and troublemakers were *prosecuted,* and, beginning in 1882, steps were taken to restrict the entry of new immigrants. (10) In the 1920s *ingenious* but false theories of ethnic superiority and inferiority were used to justify excluding most prospective immigrants, and by the 1930s the golden age was over.

Each of the following statements corresponds to a numbered sentence in the passage. Each statement contains a blank and is followed by four answer choices. Decide which choice fits best in the blank. The word or phrase that you choose must express roughly the same meaning as the italicized word in the passage. Write the letter of your choice on the answer line.

1. The Europeans' _____ the United States is historically important.
   a. exploration of
   b. civilization of
   c. arrival and settlement in
   d. colonization of

   1. _____

2. People _____ their native countries for many reasons.
   a. permanently leave   b. love   c. respond to   d. travel around in

   2. _____

3. Persons who are forced to leave their homelands are usually _____ to do so.
   a. happy   b. reluctant   c. persuaded   d. embarrassed

   3. _____

4. One group of European emigrants sought to escape _____ conditions.
   a. squalid   b. economic   c. backward   d. unfavorable

   4. _____

5. Religious minorities were often _____.
   a. subject to legal action   c. forced to leave   b. persistently ill-treated   d. resettled

   5. _____

6. In Ireland half a million people _____ starved to death during the Potato Famine.
   a. in a manner of speaking   c. in fact
   b. were rumored to have   d. unavoidably

   6. _____

7. Some immigrants believed that the streets of America were not just _____ "paved with gold."
   a. metaphorically   b. ornately   c. cleverly   d. extravagantly

   7. _____

8. Such a(n) _____ belief could not survive reality.
   a. imaginative   b. hypocritical   c. unintelligent   d. childishly simple

   8. _____

9. Those who caused social unrest were _____ for violating the law.
   a. oppressed   b. subjected to legal action   c. punished   d. restricted

   9. _____

10. Policies restricting immigration were justified by _____ theories.
    a. scientific   b. popular   c. imaginative   d. political

    10. _____

PRACTICE WITH ANALOGIES

Directions   On the answer line, write the letter of the phrase that bests completes the analogy.

See page 79 for some strategies to use with analogies.

1. CULPABLE : BLAME :: (A) merciful : raise   (B) noteworthy : attention
   (C) unscrupulous : attention   (D) pitiless : praise   (E) admirable : judgment

   1. _____

2. MISDEMEANOR : OFFENSE :: (A) scandal : disgrace   (B) tiff : quarrel
   (C) blotch : stain   (D) asset : liability   (E) wail : cry

   2. _____

3. UNSCRUPULOUS : MORALITY :: (A) dejected : hopeful
   (B) specific : clarity   (C) renowned : fame   (D) flippant : respect
   (E) ruthless : cruelty

   3. _____

4. RUFFIAN : ROWDY :: (A) ruler : deposed   (B) braggart : guilty
   (C) laggard : hostile   (D) loafer : energetic   (E) miscreant : evil

   4. _____

5. LITIGATOR : PROSECUTES :: (A) surgeon : operates   (B) witness : instructs
   (C) teacher : confuses   (D) judge : misinforms   (E) writer : suffers

   5. _____

© Great Source   DO NOT COPY

There are many kinds of wealth. Some are tangible, such as cold, hard, jangling coins made of gold, silver, or other metals. Some have intrinsic value, such as cattle and land. Some are intangible, such as the increase in value of a stock or commodity that is in great demand. Just as there are many kinds of wealth, there are many degrees of poverty. In this lesson you will learn a few of the words used to refer to wealth, those who have it, and those who do not.

WORD LIST

austerity
depreciate
equity
frugal
indigent
munificent
pecuniary
recession
remunerate
solvent

DEFINITIONS

After you have studied the definitions and example for each vocabulary word, write the word on the line to the right.

1. **austerity** (ô-stĕr′ĭ-tē) *noun*   **a.** Strict economy, especially that imposed by force. **b.** Severity or sternness of appearance or disposition.   **c.** Severity or strictness of discipline, especially moral discipline.   **d.** The state of being bare of ornamentation or decoration. (From the Greek word *austeros,* meaning "harsh")

   Related Words **austere** *adjective;* **austerely** *adverb*
   Example   For two years the *austerity* we were required to practice was unrelieved by even the smallest treat.

   1. _____

2. **depreciate** (dĭ-prē′shē-āt′) *intrans. verb*   To decrease in value.   *trans. verb* **a.** To cause to decrease in price or value.   **b.** To undervalue; belittle. (From the Latin *de-,* meaning "down," and *pretium,* meaning "price")

   Related Words **depreciable** *adjective;* **depreciation** *noun*
   Example   Our investments *depreciated* so quickly that we were forced to sell at a loss.

   2. _____
   USAGE NOTE: Compare with *deprecate,* which means "to express disapproval of" as well as "to belittle." An antonym of *depreciate* is *appreciate,* "to increase in value."

3. **equity** (ĕk′wĭ-tē) *noun*   **a.** The value of a property after subtracting the liabilities that can be claimed against it; net value.   **b.** The state of quality of being just, impartial, and fair.   **c.** Something that is just, impartial, or fair. (From the Latin word *aequus,* meaning "even" or "fair")

   Related Words **equitable** *adjective;* **equitably** *adverb*
   Example   It is possible to get a loan based on the *equity* in one's house.

   3. _____
   USAGE NOTE: Note that *equity* (fairness) does not mean the same thing as *equality* (sameness).

4. **frugal** (froo′gəl) *adjective*   **a.** Avoiding the unnecessary expenditure of money; thrifty: *a frugal housekeeper.*   **b.** Costing little; inexpensive: *a frugal meal.* (From the Latin word *frux*, meaning "fruit" or "value")

   Related Words   frugality *noun;* **frugally** *adverb*
   Example   Even though she is a wealthy woman who owns her own business, Ms. Clayton still keeps the *frugal* habits she adopted when she was poor.

5. **indigent** (ĭn′dĭ-jənt) *adjective*   Lacking money or resources to provide adequately the necessities of life; needy; impoverished. (From the Latin *indu-*, meaning "in," and *egere*, meaning "to lack" or "to need")

   Related Words   indigence *noun;* **indigently** *adverb*
   Example   When the refugees arrived, they were *indigent,* but through hard work they soon prospered.

6. **munificent** (myoo-nĭf′ĭ-sənt) *adjective*   **a.** Very generous in giving: *a munificent donor.*   **b.** Marked by or showing great generosity: *a munificent contribution.* (From the Latin words *munus*, meaning "gift," and *facere*, meaning "to make")

   Related Words   munificence *noun;* **munificently** *adverb*
   Example   One alumna's *munificent* donation made it possible for the college to build a new library.

7. **pecuniary** (pĭ-kyoo′nē-ĕr′ē) *adjective*   Consisting of or having to do with money: *pecuniary motives.* (From the Latin word *pecunia*, meaning "wealth")

   Example   The injured workers sued the company to recover their *pecuniary* losses, as well as to get compensation for mental and physical suffering.

8. **recession** (rĭ-sĕsh′ən) *noun*   **a.** A moderate and brief decline in economic activity.   **b.** The act of withdrawing or going back.

   Related Word   recessive *adjective*
   Example   During the last *recession,* the number of people without jobs increased by nearly a million.

9. **remunerate** (rĭ-myoo′nə-rāt′) *trans. verb*   **a.** To pay compensation for goods, services, or losses: *remunerated their efforts.*   **b.** To pay compensation to for goods, services, or losses: *remunerated them for their time.* (From the Latin *re-*, meaning "back," and *munus*, meaning "gift")

   Related Words   remuneration *noun;* **remunerative** *adjective*
   Example   Although he was working as a volunteer, Darrel nevertheless expected to be *remunerated* in some way.

10. **solvent** (sŏl′vənt, sôl′vənt) *adjective*   **a.** Capable of meeting all financial obligations, such as the payment of debts.   **b.** Capable of dissolving another substance.   *noun*   A liquid capable of dissolving another substance. (From the Latin word *solvere*, meaning "to loosen," "to dissolve," or "to pay")

    Related Word   solvency *noun*
    Example   Because the business is no longer *solvent,* the store will close next week.

4. _____

5. _____

USAGE NOTE: Don't confuse *indigent* with *indignant,* "filled with anger aroused by something unjust, mean, or unworthy."

6. _____

7. _____

8. _____

9. _____

10. _____

© Great Source   DO NOT COPY

EXERCISE 1 MATCHING WORDS AND DEFINITIONS

Match the definition in Column B with the word in Column A. Write the letter of the correct definition on the answer line.

Column A   **Column B**

1. depreciate   a. impoverished; needy   1. _____

2. pecuniary   b. net value; fairness   2. _____

3. austerity   c. able to meet financial obligations   3. _____

4. recession   d. to decrease in value   4. _____

5. frugal   e. to pay compensation   5. _____

6. indigent   f. thrifty   6. _____

7. equity   g. having to do with money   7. _____

8. remunerate   h. a moderate decline in economic activity   8. _____

9. munificent   i. strict economy   9. _____

10. solvent   j. generous in giving   10. _____

EXERCISE 2 USING WORDS CORRECTLY

Decide whether the italicized vocabulary word has been used correctly in the sentence. On the answer line, write *Correct* for correct use and *Incorrect* for incorrect use.

1. Because she lived during some very hard times, my grandmother learned to be *frugal*.   1. _____

2. I sincerely *depreciate* all the help that Coach Turner has given me to get ready for this race.   2. _____

3. Sara was *indigent* when her brother teased her about her freckles.   3. _____

4. Everyone prospered during the *recession*.   4. _____

5. An expert has a right to be *remunerated* for professional advice.   5. _____

6. The increasing cost of raw materials made it more and more difficult for the makers of crafts to remain *solvent*.   6. _____

7. Clayton drove down Main Street in a *munificent* new station wagon.   7. _____

8. Judge Nelson strongly believed in the *equity* of all persons before the law.   8. _____

9. As the war dragged on, the need for civilian *austerity* increased.   9. _____

10. The teacher looked at me with a *pecuniary* look on her face.   10. _____

EXERCISE 3 CHOOSING THE BEST WORD

Decide which vocabulary word or related form best expresses the meaning of the italicized word or phrase in the sentence. On the answer line, write the letter of the correct choice.

1. Even though the family lived a life of *strict economy*, the children always had enough good food to eat and clean clothes to wear.   1. _____
   a. recession   b. equity   c. austerity   d. depreciation

© Great Source DO NOT COPY

2. Charlotte knew that she had to be *thrifty* if she was going to save enough money to go on a vacation.
   a. indigent   b. frugal   c. munificent   d. solvent

   2. _____

3. Horatio Alger wrote about *impoverished and needy* people who worked hard and became very successful.
   a. indigent   b. pecuniary   c. solvent   d. austere

   3. _____

4. This make of car will not undergo *a decrease in value* as quickly as the other one will.
   a. remuneration   b. depreciation   c. solvency   d. recession

   4. _____

5. Last year's *moderate decline in the economy* was followed by a period of great economic growth.
   a. equity   b. austerity   c. depreciation   d. recession

   5. _____

6. The profits from the car wash were distributed among the classes according to strict *fairness*.
   a. remuneration   b. munificence   c. equity   d. frugality

   6. _____

7. Our company gave a *very generous* donation to the hospital.
   a. munificent   b. pecuniary   c. equitable   d. frugal

   7. _____

8. Mrs. Littleton used to run a nursery school, but when the school was no longer *able to meet its financial obligations,* she had to close it down.
   a. frugal   b. pecuniary   c. remunerative   d. solvent

   8. _____

9. Mr. Aziz never discussed his *monetary* affairs with anyone.
   a. munificent   b. pecuniary   c. solvent   d. austere

   9. _____

10. It was difficult to think of a suitable *compensation* for Dr. Lopez's help in the emergency, since she would not accept any money.
    a. depreciation   b. equity   c. remuneration   d. munificence

    10. _____

EXERCISE 4   USING DIFFERENT FORMS OF WORDS

Decide which form of the vocabulary word in parentheses best completes the sentence. The form given may be correct. Write your answer on the answer line.

1. Those critical of the administration's economic policies are predicting a _____ in the coming year. *(recession)*

   1. _____

2. The Mortons regret the _____ of their early married life and wish that they had enjoyed themselves more while they were young. *(frugal)*

   2. _____

3. Kristin calculated the _____ of her car at a yearly rate of 20 percent. *(recession)*

   3. _____

4. The clinic went from _____ to bankruptcy in just a few months. *(solvent)*

   4. _____

5. The prospector hoped that finding gold would enable him to exchange _____ for a life of comfort and ease. *(indigent)*

   5. _____

6. Their _____ childhood spent in a remote country village left them totally unprepared to make their way as adults in a large city. *(austerity)*

   6. _____

7. The duke was famous for his public _____ and private miserliness. *(munificent)*

   7. _____

8. Andrea's poor judgment has gotten her into many difficulties, especially _____ ones. *(pecuniary)*

   8. _____

9. The special consultants were _____ at a rate that many people considered excessive. *(remunerate)*

   9. _____

10. I did not want special favors or privileges, but simple _____. *(equity)*

    10. _____

© Great Source   DO NOT COPY

READING COMPREHENSION

Each numbered sentence in the following passage contains an italicized vocabulary word or related form. After you read the passage, you will complete an exercise.

THE GREAT DEPRESSION

The Great Depression that occurred between World War I and World War II was not unprecedented in modern times. For a long time, the United States and Europe had suffered the unpredictable alternation of good times and bad times. (1) A period of prosperity was followed by a *recession,* which in turn gave way to another period of prosperity. The Great Depression was unusual mainly for its persistence. In the United States, it lasted more than a decade.

(2) Simply put, the economic problem underlying the period of *austerity* called The Great Depression was, ironically, an over-supply of goods. There were more things for sale—food, raw materials, manufactured products—than people, individually and collectively, could buy. Competition forced producers to lower their prices below the cost of production. There were two possible remedies for this situation. The supply of goods could be reduced, if not by consumption then by outright destruction. Alterna-

tively, the cost of production could be reduced below the selling price. (3) Guided primarily by *pecuniary* considerations, producers tried both methods of increasing their profits. Farmers, for example, did not harvest their crops, and ranchers did not send their cattle to market. Other producers tried to reduce their costs by firing workers or lowering wages.

Both courses of action had tragic results. Food did not get to hungry people, and millions of workers lost their jobs. Many could no longer afford to buy even the necessities of life. (4) As once-prosperous people became *indigent,* they were able to buy less and less. This caused prices and profits to fall even more. A cycle was begun that no one was able to stop. (5) By 1932, eighteen million people were receiving relief payments that, although criticized for their supposed *munificence,* were scarcely enough in many cases to ward off utter destitution.

Ruin came to many individuals as a consequence of the economic system, not because of their own

imprudence. (6) For example, banks that appeared *solvent* had to close, because they could not sell their investments for what they were actually worth. This meant that the banks could not raise enough money to meet their depositors' demands. (7) The value of other assets likewise *depreciated.* (8) *Equity* in real estate disappeared as market values fell below the amount of outstanding mortgages, and people lost their homes. (9) Those who had been *frugal* all their lives saw their savings and investments wiped out. (10) Even those who still had *remunerative* work had no sense of security about the future.

The Great Depression was brought to an end not by innovative and compassionate social programs, but by World War II, which literally consumed the surplus resources of the whole world. Both of these terrible events—economic collapse and total war—have left a legacy of problems that even today we have not begun to solve.

READING COMPREHENSION EXERCISE

Each of the following statements corresponds to a numbered sentence in the passage. Each statement contains a blank and is followed by four answer choices. Decide which choice fits best in the blank. The word or phrase that you choose must express roughly the same meaning as the italicized word in the passage. Write the letter of your choice on the answer line.

1. A period of prosperity was followed by a(n) _____.
   a. decline in economic activity
   b. war
   c. period of good times
   d. imbalance of supply and demand

   1. _____

2. The Great Depression was a period of _____.
   a. generosity   b. fairness   c. declining values   d. strict economy

   2. _____

© Great Source   DO NOT COPY

3. Producers were motivated by _____ considerations.
   a. compassionate   **b.** selfish   **c.** monetary   **d.** unusual

3. _____

4. People who were once prosperous became _____.
   a. angry   **b.** poor   **c.** unemployed   **d.** hungry

4. _____

5. Relief payments were criticized for unnecessary _____.
   a. generosity   **b.** stinginess   **c.** complexity   **d.** frequency

5. _____

6. Banks that appeared _____ had to close for lack of funds.
   a. stable   **c.** capable of meeting their financial obligations
   b. to be losing money   **d.** innovative

6. _____

7. Other assets also _____.
   a. disappeared   **c.** became unpopular
   b. decreased in value   **d.** were criticized

7. _____

8. The _____ real estate disappeared.
   a. supply and demand of   **c.** equal distribution of
   b. investors in   **d.** net value of

8. _____

9. Those who had been _____ all their lives also lost their savings.
   a. foolish   **b.** rich   **c.** thrifty   **d.** needy

9. _____

10. Those with _____ work were insecure about the future.
    a. interesting   **b.** steady   **c.** boring   **d.** paid

10. _____

WRITING ASSIGNMENT

Money is one of the things that people feel most strongly about, and what they do with it is very revealing of their characters. Imagine that an anonymous benefactor wants to give you a million dollars. The only condition attached to the gift is that you tell your benefactor how you plan to use the money. Using at least five of the words from this lesson and underlining each that you use, write a paragraph explaining your plan.

VOCABULARY ENRICHMENT

Early in this lesson, you learned that the word *frugal* comes from the Latin word *frux,* meaning "fruit." Associated with *frux* are the Latin words *frui,* "to enjoy," and *fructus,* which can mean "enjoyment," "produce," or "results." These associated meanings have given English the words *fruition,* "desired outcome," and *fructify,* "to make fruitful."

Activity   Other English words are similarly derived from Greek or Latin words for kinds of food and drink. Look up the following five words in a dictionary. Write the Greek or Latin word from which each one is derived. Then, in a sentence, explain how the meaning of the English word is related to the Greek or Latin word.

1. bucolic 2. companion 3. galaxy 4. pommel 5. salary

© Great Source   DO NOT COPY

The conquest of England by the Norman French in 1066 brought great changes to the English language. Thousands of French words became part of the English vocabulary, and numerous modifications occurred in pronunciation, verb forms, and pronouns. In the area of law and government, for example, the French contributed such words as *court, justice, parliament, council,* and *tax.* Such military terms as *battle, siege, armor,* and *fortress* also entered the language.

The borrowing of French words continues today. We have become accustomed to seeing French words in advertisements and to using them in connection with food, the arts, history, fashion, conversation and writing, and people. The vocabulary words in this lesson will familiarize you with some of these words that have added color and sophistication to our language.

WORD LIST

adroit
blasé
cliché
clientele
entrepreneur
forte
gauche
naive
nonchalant
rendezvous

DEFINITIONS

After you have studied the definitions and example for each vocabulary word, write the word on the line to the right.

1. **adroit** (ə-droit′) *adjective*   **a.** Having or showing skill, cleverness, or resourcefulness in handling difficult situations.   **b.** Skillful in the use of the hands or body; dexterous. (From the French phrase *à droit,* meaning "to the right")

    Related Words   adroitly *adverb;* adroitness *noun*
    Example   Nadine is an *adroit* discussion leader who always encourages participation.

1. _____

ETYMOLOGY NOTE:
Adroit and *gauche* (p. 154) reflect ancient beliefs that right-handed people were superior to left-handed people. *Dexterous* also translates literally as "skillful, on the right side."

2. **blasé** (blä-zā′) *adjective*   **a.** Very sophisticated; worldly.   **b.** Uninterested, unexcited, or bored as a result of excessive indulgence or enjoyment. (From the French word *blaser,* meaning "to blunt" or "to overindulge")

    Example   Having traveled the world, the Garrisons are quite *blasé* about fine hotels and restaurants.

2. _____

3. **cliché** (klē-shā′) *noun*   **a.** A trite or overused expression or idea, such as "time flies."   **b.** Something overly familiar and commonplace. (From the French word *clicher,* meaning "to stereotype")

    Related Word   clichéd, *adjective*
    Example   The cliché "few and far between" is familiar to most of us.

3. _____

4. **clientele** (klī′ən-těl′, klē′-ən-těl′) *noun*   A body of customers or patrons. (From the French word *clientèle*, meaning "clients")

4. _____

   Example   The store catered exclusively to a *clientele* of children.

5. **entrepreneur** (ŏn′trə-prə-nûr′) *noun*   A person who organizes, operates, and assumes the risk of a business venture. (From the French word *entreprendre*, meaning "to undertake")

5. _____

   Related Word   **entrepreneurial** *adjective*
   Example   After completing college, Mark hopes to become an *entrepreneur* of computer software.

6. **forte** (fôrt, fôr′tā′) *noun*   Something in which a person excels; a strong point. (From the French word *fort*, meaning "strong")

6. _____

   Example   Jean's *forte* has always been math.

7. **gauche** (gōsh) *adjective*   Lacking social experience or grace; awkward; rude; tactless. (From the French word *gauche*, meaning "left hand" or "awkward")

7. _____

   Related Words   **gauchely** *adverb;* **gaucheness** *noun*
   Example   Quentin's *gauche* remark about the food offended both the guests and his hostess.

8. **naive** (nä-ēv′) *adjective*   **a.** Marked by unaffected simplicity; unsophisticated; artless.   **b.** Showing a lack of experience or judgment. (From the French word *naïve*, meaning "artless")

8. _____

   Related Words   **naively** *adverb;* **naiveté** *noun*
   Example   The tourists were *naive* about shopping and bargaining in the Turkish bazaars.

9. **nonchalant** (nŏn′shə-länt′) *adjective*   **a.** Cool, carefree, and casually unconcerned, or seeming so.   **b.** Without enthusiasm; indifferent. (From the French *non-*, meaning "not," and *chaloir*, meaning "to be concerned")

9. _____

   Related Words   **nonchalance** *noun;* **nonchalantly** *adverb*
   Example   Bank tellers seem *nonchalant* about the large sums of money they handle.

10. **rendezvous** (rän′dā-vōō′) *noun*   **a.** An appointment or engagement to meet at a fixed place or time.   **b.** A meeting or gathering place.   *intrans. verb*   To meet at a specified time and place. (From the French phrase *rendez-vous*, meaning "present yourselves")

10. _____

   Example   Mrs. Panati and her cousin arranged a three-o'clock *rendezvous* at the corner of Pleasant and Monument Streets.

© Great Source   DO NOT COPY

EXERCISE 1 WRITING CORRECT WORDS

On the answer line, write the word from the vocabulary list that fits each definition.

1. A trite or overused expression or idea

2. Something a person does extremely well; a strong point

3. Unsophisticated; lacking experience or judgment

4. Casually unconcerned; indifferent

5. Very sophisticated; bored as a result of excessive indulgence or enjoyment

6. A prearranged meeting; a gathering place

7. A body of customers or patrons

8. Lacking social grace; tactless

9. Showing cleverness or resourcefulness in handling difficult situations; dexterous

10. A person who organizes, operates, and assumes the risk of a business venture

1. _____

2. _____

3. _____

4. _____

5. _____

6. _____

7. _____

8. _____

9. _____

10. _____

EXERCISE 2 USING WORDS CORRECTLY

Each of the following statements contains an italicized vocabulary word. Decide whether the sentence is true or false, and write *True* or *False* on the answer line.

1. Stockbrokers are usually *naive* about the ways in which money can be invested.

2. Mr. Hart is an *entrepreneur* because he manages a store in which he has invested all his savings.

3. A word that is no longer used is known as a *cliché*.

4. A *gauche* remark is likely to be applauded by polite people.

5. A wide variety of people make up the *clientele* of a law firm.

6. The *forte* of a quarterback is most likely passing.

7. A first-time visitor to San Francisco would be *blasé* about the Golden Gate Bridge.

8. A *nonchalant* teammate would play with great enthusiasm and determination.

9. A *rendezvous* may take place publicly or privately.

10. An *adroit* gymnast would be clumsy.

1. _____

2. _____

3. _____

4. _____

5. _____

6. _____

7. _____

8. _____

9. _____

10. _____

EXERCISE 3 CHOOSING THE BEST DEFINITION

For each italicized vocabulary word in the following sentences, write the letter of the best definition on the answer line.

1. To somersault from one swing to another, a trapeze artist must be courageous as well as *adroit*.
   a. secure   b. precise   c. skillful   d. strong

2. Slurping soup and smacking his lips with delight, Dennis was enjoying his meal too much to pay attention to his *gauche* table manners.
   a. indifferent   b. simple   c. noisy   d. rude

1. _____

2. _____

3. The *naive* scuba divers failed to turn on their air tanks before getting into the water.

   a. anxious   **b.** distracted   **c.** inexperienced   **d.** veteran

3. _____ DO NOT COPY

4. The owners of the art gallery invited their loyal *clientele* to the opening of the controversial photography show.

   a. customers   **b.** investors   **c.** assistants   **d.** artists

4. _____

5. The movers seemed *nonchalant* as they carried the Giacometti sculpture into the building.

   a. patient   **b.** unconcerned   **c.** gratified   **d.** motivated

5. _____

6. Russell's *forte* is writing humorous verse.

   a. strong point   **b.** primary concern   **c.** favorite pastime **d.** downfall

6. _____

7. The helpless, pitiful child is almost a *cliché* in Victorian novels.

   a. familiar adage   **c.** rarity

   b. commonplace character   **d.** theme

7. _____

8. The *entrepreneurs* lost their capital when their investment in windmills failed.

   a. members of the audience   **c.** entertainers

   b. patrons   **d.** organizers of the business venture

8. _____

9. Dr. Lieu Ping Lee issued a bulletin announcing the noon *rendezvous* of the lunar module and the command ship.

   a. meeting   **b.** testing   **c.** orbit   **d.** arrival

9. _____

10. She was so *blasé* about winning first prize that she didn't bother to pick up her trophy.

   a. unsophisticated **b.** moralistic   **c.** bored   **d.** emotional

10. _____

EXERCISE 4 USING DIFFERENT FORMS OF WORDS

Decide which form of the vocabulary word in parentheses best completes the sentence. The form given may be correct. Write your answer on the answer line.

1. The Native American _____ created a beautiful necklace of silver and turquoise. (*adroit*)

1. _____

2. Only a very _____ person would lick his fingers at a formal dinner party. (*gauche*)

2. _____

3. The hockey player _____ skated onto the ice for tryouts. (*nonchalant*)

3. _____

4. Mrs. Rico has profited from her latest _____ venture. (*entrepreneur*)

4. _____

5. Louise lost some of her _____ about the simplicity of life on a farm. (*naive*)

5. _____

6. After classes the art students _____ at the cafe. (*rendezvous*)

6. _____

7. The audience was amazed by the _____ of the magician. (*adroit*)

7. _____

8. The tourists _____ bought expensive souvenirs at the airport. (*naive*)

8. _____

9. Josh refused to believe that too many _____ similes and metaphors would ruin his description. (*cliché*)

9. _____

10. After Julian tore out the uneven hems of his trousers, he admitted that his _____ was not sewing. (*forte*)

10. _____

© Great Source   DO NOT COPY

READING COMPREHENSION

Each numbered sentence in the following passage contains an italicized vocabulary word or related form. After you read the passage, you will complete an exercise.

CREATORS OF STYLE

(1) You have probably heard the *cliché* "dressed to kill." (2) This expression refers to someone who is well dressed in the latest fashions and who has *adroitly* chosen appropriate accessories. (3) Appearing to be sophisticated and *nonchalant,* the person knows that he or she is attired in just the right way. (4) In order to wear what is fashionable for a *rendezvous,* a sporting event, or a dinner party, the "dressed to kill" individual pays close attention to the season's latest styles.

Who sets these trends and determines what we will purchase and wear each season? Some people believe that fashion is the product of brainwashing a receptive public. (5) They see the adoption of new styles as the result of a plot by greedy designers and *entrepreneurs* to require customers to purchase new wardrobes each year. (6) It is not true, however, that the public is so *naive* as to wear anything that fashion dictates.

For example, the introduction of the maxi-skirt in 1969 was a fashion failure. The long skirts impeded movement. They made women look older and heavier at a time when youthfulness, slimness, and energy were considered all-important.

The process of creating new styles and making the public aware of them begins many months in advance of each season. (7) Twice a year each fashion designer displays his or her *forte* in a collection, hoping to set international trends. (8) In January for spring and summer clothes and in May for fall and winter apparel, American and European designers begin to influence their vital *clientele,* the department-store and boutique buyers, as well as the press. (9) They produce major fashion shows in New York, Paris, London, and Milan that attract even the most *blasé* followers of fashion.

After the fashion industry has introduced its current collections,

fashion editors release pictures and articles about the new clothing. Advertising and sales promotions are used to inform the public, and inexpensive copies and adaptations of high fashion are made. Once the fashion message of new shapes, fabrics, and colors is launched, it is up to customers to accept or reject the current trends.

If a proposed style arouses only temporary enthusiasm, it is dismissed as a fad. If, on the other hand, the innovation is irresistible to many people, a new fashion is established. Shoppers choose clothing that is practical and appropriate, that makes them look attractive, and that helps them to gain the acceptance of others. (10) The average person, unwilling to be *gauchely* dressed, adds to his or her wardrobe and in this way profoundly but subtly affects the styles of the season.

READING COMPREHENSION EXERCISE

Each of the following statements corresponds to a numbered sentence in the passage. Each statement contains a blank and is followed by four answer choices. Decide which choice fits best in the blank. The word or phrase that you choose must express roughly the same meaning as the italicized word in the passage. Write the letter of your choice on the answer line.

1. "Dressed to kill" is a(n) _____.
   a. exaggeration
   b. favorite proverb
   c. overused expression
   d. famous quotation

   1. _____

2. The phrase refers to a person who is well-dressed and who has _____ chosen appropriate accessories.
   a. politely   b. creatively   c. intelligently   d. skillfully

   2. _____

3. A well-dressed person appears _____, knowing that he or she is appropriately attired.
   a. casually unconcerned
   b. hopelessly confused
   c. self-confident
   d. wealthy

3. _____

4. People pay attention to the latest styles so that they are fashionably dressed for _____ or a sporting event.
   a. work
   b. a casual situation
   c. an appointment
   d. a formal occasion

4. _____

5. To other people new styles are the result of a plot by greedy designers and _____.
   a. business manager-investors
   b. manufacturers and salespeople
   c. the media
   d. the public

5. _____

6. It is not true that the public is so _____ as to wear anything that fashion dictates.
   a. influential
   b. inexperienced
   c. sophisticated
   d. suspicious

6. _____

7. Each fashion designer displays his or her _____ twice a year.
   a. new collection
   b. old ideas
   c. strong point
   d. failure

7. _____

8. In January and May designers influence their vital _____, the store buyers.
   a. advertisers
   b. supporters
   c. suppliers
   d. customers

8. _____

9. Even the most _____ followers of fashion are attracted by fashion shows.
   a. uninformed
   b. sophisticated
   c. dedicated
   d. ambitious

9. _____

10. The average person is unwilling to be _____ dressed.
    a. awkwardly
    b. specially
    c. artistically
    d. colorfully

10. _____

WRITING ASSIGNMENT

A new French restaurant has just opened, and you, as your community newspaper's food columnist, have been asked to review it. Write a critique of the restaurant, including your evaluation of the decor, the range of selections offered on the menu, and the way in which the food is prepared. Use at least five of the vocabulary words from this lesson in your review, and underline each of them.

VOCABULARY ENRICHMENT

The word *cliché* comes from the technical vocabulary once used by printers and means literally "cast in metal from a mold." A *cliché* was a solid metal plate for printing, also known as a *stereotype*. The plate was made from a mold of a raised printing surface and was unalterable once cast. This metal plate would be inked and then repeatedly pressed on paper to create pages of print. A *cliché,* as we employ it today, usually refers to an expression that is used over and over until it becomes boring. Thus, it reminds us of the plate that was once used again and again to create identical pages of print.

Activity Look up the following words in your dictionary and write their derivations and those definitions that have to do with printing and bookmaking. Then, for each word, include an explanation of the connection between its origin and its present meaning.

1. ink 2. hieroglyphics 3. volume 4. folio 5. type

READING SKILLS

THE PREFIX *AD-*

A **prefix** is a letter or group of letters that is added to the beginning of a root to change its meaning. (A **root** is the part of a word that contains its basic meaning. A root can also be a complete word.) The prefix *ad-* is usually added to roots that come from Latin words; *ad-* has one basic meaning.

Prefix Meaning	Root Word	Word	Word Definition
to, toward	*vocare*, "to call"	advocate	one who argues for a cause
	figere, "to fasten"	affix	to attach

Note that when *ad-* is added to a root beginning with a consonant, the *d* may be dropped and the consonant doubled. Thus, *ad-* has numerous variant forms.

Use the following procedure to determine the meaning of words that begin with *ad-* or with some other prefix.

PROCEDURE

1. *Substitute the prefix and root definitions for the prefix and root.* The verb *adduce* is formed from the prefix *ad-* and the Latin root *-duc-*, from the common root word *ducere*. The prefix means "to" or "toward" and the root means "to lead."

2. *Think of a possible definition of the entire word.* Combining the prefix and root meanings given above results in "to lead to."

3. *If the word appears in a sentence, use the context to help you develop the possible definition.* Suppose that you have read the sentence "The speaker adduced several instances of violation of the safety code." The word *adduced* seems to refer to the use of examples to illustrate a point—perhaps in order to *lead* the audience *to* the same conclusion.

4. *Check your definition of the word in the dictionary.* Word analysis and using the context will give you an approximate definition of an unfamiliar word. For a more precise meaning, check the dictionary. A dictionary definition of *adduce* is "to cite as an example of means of proof."

EXERCISE USING THE PREFIX *AD-*

Each sentence below contains an italicized word beginning with the prefix *ad-* or one of its variant forms. The root word and its meaning appear in parentheses after each sentence. *Step 1:* Taking the context into consideration, write your own definition of the word. *Step 2:* Write the dictionary definition of the word. *Step 3:* Write a sentence of your own in which you use the word correctly.

1. The museum guard *admonished* the child for touching the painting. (Root word: *monere*, "to warn")

   Your Definition _____

   Dictionary Definition _____

   Sentence _____

2. When the novel was published under a pen name, no one *attributed* it to the well-known writer Doris Lessing. (Root word: *tribuere*, "to allot")

Your Definition _____

Dictionary Definition _____

Sentence _____

3. My parents had to have the house *appraised* before they sold it. (Root word: *pretium*, "price")

Your Definition _____

Dictionary Definition _____

Sentence _____

4. Hamlet *adjured* his friends not to reveal what they had witnessed. (Root word: *jurare*, "to swear")

Your Definition _____

Dictionary Definition _____

Sentence _____

5. The company finally *appeased* the union members by improving their pension benefits. (Root word: *pax*, "peace")

Your Definition _____

Dictionary Definition _____

Sentence _____

6. Díaz was a lifelong *adherent* of the Farmers' Party. (Root word: *haerere*, "to stick")

Your Definition _____

Dictionary Definition _____

Sentence _____

7. The government took measures to *alleviate* poverty in the countryside. (Root word: *levis*, "light")

Your Definition _____

Dictionary Definition _____

Sentence _____

8. The vast distance between Saturn and Earth *attenuated* the signal from the spacecraft. (Root word: *tenuis*, "thin")

Your Definition _____

Dictionary Definition _____

Sentence _____

© Great Source   DO NOT COPY

The process of sleep holds a continuing fascination for most people. What happens to our bodies and minds while we sleep? How much sleep do we need, and how much damage is done if we do not get it? Why do we dream, and how significant are our dreams? Although the topic of laziness is not considered as seriously as that of sleep, it does raise some interesting questions. Is laziness helpful or harmful? Can daydreaming, sometimes considered an aspect of laziness, actually provide an opportunity for personal introspection and thoughtful decision-making? In this lesson you will study ten words that apply to the much-discussed states of sleepiness and laziness.

WORD LIST
dilatory
languid
lethargy
quiescent
repose
sloth
somnambulate
somnolence
soporific
stupor

DEFINITIONS

After you have studied the definitions and example for each vocabulary word, write the word on the line to the right.

1. **dilatory** (dĭl'ə-tôr'ē) *adjective* **a.** Characterized by procrastination. **b.** Tending or intended to cause delay. (From the Latin word *dilator*, meaning "delayer")

   Related Word dilatoriness *noun*
   Example Marlene was *dilatory* in answering a letter she had received three weeks before.

1. _____
MEMORY CUE: *If you're dilatory, you* dīlā *(delay).*

2. **languid** (lăng'gwĭd) *adjective* **a.** Lazily slow or relaxed. **b.** Lacking spirit or energy; weak. **c.** Causing a feeling of laziness.

   Related Words languidly *adverb;* **languish** *verb;* **languor** *noun*
   Example Sitting in the hot sun made Marcella feel *languid*.

2. _____

3. **lethargy** (lĕth'ər-jē) *noun* **a.** Drowsy or sluggish indifference; apathy. **b.** An unconscious state resembling deep sleep.

   Related Words lethargic *adjective;* **lethargically** *adverb*
   Example Not able to find anything to be interested in, Henry yawned and concluded that he was in an advanced state of *lethargy*.

3. _____

4. **quiescent** (kwē-ĕs'ənt, kwī-ĕs'ənt) *adjective* In a condition of inactivity or rest. (From the Latin word *quiescere*, meaning "to be quiet")

   Related Words quiescence *noun;* **quiescently** *adverb*
   Example The prince begged the sorcerer to break the spell and release the lifeless town from its *quiescent* state.

4. _____

5. **repose** (rĭ-pōz′) *noun* **a.** The act or condition of resting; relaxation. **b.** Peace of mind; composure. **c.** Calmness; tranquillity. *intrans. verb* To lie at rest. (From the Latin *re-*, meaning "back," and *ponere*, meaning "to place")

   Example After a few hours of *repose*, Brad was ready to play tennis and go swimming.

   5. _____

6. **sloth** (slôth, slōth, slŏth) *noun* **a.** Laziness; indolence. **b.** Any of various slow-moving arboreal mammals of tropical America. (From the Middle English word *slowth*, meaning "laziness")

   Related Word **slothful** *adjective*
   Example "*Sloth* should be eliminated from your daily routine," the coach told her players.

   6. _____

7. **somnambulate** (sŏm-năm′byə-lāt′) *intrans. verb* To walk while asleep. (From the Latin words *somnus*, meaning "sleep," and *ambulare*, meaning "to walk")

   Related Words **somnambulant** *adjective;* **somnambulism** *noun*
   Example In the horror movie, the heroine was afraid to fall asleep at night for fear she would *somnambulate*.

   7. _____

8. **somnolence** (sŏm′nə-ləns) *noun* Drowsiness; sleepiness. (From the Latin word *somnus*, meaning "sleep")

   Related Words **somnolent** *adjective;* **somnolently** *adverb*
   Example Unexpected *somnolence* was the result of the hiker's long climb.

   8. _____

9. **soporific** (sŏp′ə-rĭf′ĭk, sō′pə-rĭf′ĭk) *adjective* **a.** Causing or tending to cause sleep. **b.** Drowsy. *noun* A sleep-inducing drug. (From the Latin words *sopor*, meaning "sleep," and *facere*, meaning "to make")

   Example Reading a dull book before retiring had a *soporific* effect on Roberta.

   9. _____

10. **stupor** (stoo′pər, styoo′pər) *noun* A condition of reduced sensibility or consciousness; daze. (From the Latin word *stupere*, meaning "to be stunned")

    Related Word **stuporous** *adjective*
    Example Kevin was in a *stupor* for several hours after the automobile accident.

    10. _____

© Great Source DO NOT COPY

EXERCISE 1 COMPLETING DEFINITIONS

On the answer line, write the word from the vocabulary list that best completes each definition.

1. To walk in one's sleep is to _____.

2. Drowsiness or sleepiness is _____.

3. To be lazily slow or relaxed is to be _____.

4. To be sluggishly indifferent or apathetic is to be in a state of _____.

5. A condition of reduced sensibility or consciousness is a _____.

6. Something that induces sleep is _____.

7. Laziness or indolence is _____.

8. The act or condition of resting is _____.

9. Someone who procrastinates or delays is _____.

10. An inactive or restful state is a _____ condition.

1. _____

2. _____

3. _____

4. _____

5. _____

6. _____

7. _____

8. _____

9. _____

10. _____

EXERCISE 2 USING WORDS CORRECTLY

Decide whether the italicized vocabulary word has been used correctly in the sentence. On the answer line, write *Correct* for correct use and *Incorrect* for incorrect use.

1. Barry was in such a state of *lethargy* that he spent the morning painting the garage.

2. Cynthia is *dilatory* in her payment of all debts and always takes care of her bills promptly.

3. At first, breaking a leg forces someone into a *quiescent* position.

4. An hour of *repose* restored Lydia's tranquillity.

5. "Your poor grades result from *sloth*, not inability," complained Dad.

6. The child completed difficult math problems while he *somnambulated*.

7. The clown's cartwheels, flips, and funny antics caused the children's *somnolence*.

8. The audience grew increasingly bored during the *soporific* lecture.

9. The child expressed his excitement with *languid* words to his mother.

10. Stunned by his pet's unexpected death, the child sat in a *stupor*.

1. _____

2. _____

3. _____

4. _____

5. _____

6. _____

7. _____

8. _____

9. _____

10. _____

EXERCISE 3 CHOOSING THE BEST WORD

Decide which vocabulary word or related form best expresses the meaning of the italicized word or phrase in the sentence. On the answer line, write the letter of the correct choice.

1. While Miriam watched television, her mother suggested that she was *delaying* the completion of her homework.
   a. somnambulant in   **b.** stuporous in   **c.** somnolent in   **d.** dilatory in

1. _____

2. In *The Pilgrim's Progress,* a seventeenth-century allegory by John Bunyan, Christian meets three men, Simple, *Laziness,* and Presumption, along the road to the Celestial City.
   a. Lethargy   **b.** Sloth   **c.** Repose   **d.** Stupor

  2. _____

3. A heavy meal has a *sleep-inducing* effect on the human body.
   a. lethargic   **b.** dilatory   **c.** soporific   **d.** languid

  3. _____

4. Shakespeare's *Macbeth* contains a famous scene in which a *sleep-walking* Lady Macbeth tries to wash the imaginary bloodstains of her victims from her hands.
   a. lethargic   **b.** languid   **c.** somnambulant   **d.** slothful

  4. _____

5. In a famous line from one of his operettas, W. S. Gilbert suggests that "when you're lying awake with a dismal headache . . . *quiet rest* may be taboo'd by anxiety."
   a. repose   **b.** lethargy   **c.** sloth   **d.** stupor

  5. _____

6. Overcome with *drowsiness,* the baby fell asleep in his high chair.
   a. somnambulism   **b.** stupor   **c.** somnolence   **d.** dilatory

  6. _____

7. The dog gave its owner a *lazily slow* look and then went back to sleep.
   a. languid   **b.** soporific   **c.** stuporous   **d.** dilatory

  7. _____

8. The track team dropout watched *apathetically* as the winner of the race was crowned.
   a. languidly   **b.** lethargically   **c.** somnolently   **d.** quiescently

  8. _____

9. After the hurricane swept through the area, the small town was, once again, mercifully *inactive.*
   a. slothful   **b.** dilatory   **c.** stuporous   **d.** quiescent

  9. _____

10. Jane was jolted out of her *daze* by the teacher's voice.
    a. somnolence   **b.** sloth   **c.** stupor   **d.** repose

 10. _____

EXERCISE 4   USING DIFFERENT FORMS OF WORDS

Decide which form of the vocabulary word in parentheses best completes the sentence. The form given may be correct. Write your answer on the answer line.

1. From the remote mountain cabin, Lydia wrote long letters in which she complained of her self-imposed _____. *(quiescent)*

  1. _____

2. The warm glass of milk had a _____ effect on Emily. *(soporific)*

  2. _____

3. Bob's _____ was noted and criticized by his employer. *(dilatory)*

  3. _____

4. After a few minutes of _____, the cat was alert again and ready to explore her surroundings. *(repose)*

  4. _____

5. Andrew _____ completed his daily chores. *(lethargy)*

  5. _____

6. Helen's _____ attitude toward homework caused her grades to fall. *(sloth)*

  6. _____

7. The assumption that someone who exhibits _____ behavior will never get hurt is false. *(somnambulate)*

  7. _____

8. After falling from her bike, Jill was in a _____ condition and did not remember where she was. *(stupor)*

  8. _____

9. Jonathan's _____ "Hello" told us that the telephone had awakened him. *(somnolence)*

  9. _____

10. The hikers sat _____ by the mountain lake after their long climb. *(languid)*

 10. _____

© Great Source   DO NOT COPY

READING COMPREHENSION

Each numbered sentence in the following passage contains an italicized vocabulary word or related form. After you read the passage, you will complete an exercise.

THE LONG SLEEP

During winters in cold climates one is often struck by the barren environment. (1) The trees are without leaves; the flowers have shriveled and died; and with the exception of an occasional squirrel that has been *dilatory* in preparing for the winter, there is not a living creature in sight. On the surface all appears lifeless, but if one could look below the frozen earth or water, one would see hundreds of hibernating creatures that are waiting for spring to come.

Unlike human beings, hibernating animals do not have to endure freezing temperatures and other difficult winter conditions while waiting for spring. (2) They can simply enter into a lengthy *repose* or, as the Indians used to say, begin the "long sleep." (3) In some cases this *quiescence* is barely distinguishable from death.

(4) Some of the winter hibernators, like the bear, fall into a deep *stupor* in early winter and do not awaken until spring. Other animals, such as the squirrel and the chipmunk, sleep for shorter periods of time. (5) They then appear to *somnambulate* long enough to munch a few stored edibles before returning to sleep again.

Why do hibernating animals go into such a long repose? By slowing down the heartbeat, the breathing rate, and all other bodily functions, the animal is protected from the harsh winter. Scarcity of food in the winter months is another important reason. (6) Since not much food is needed to keep the body functioning in a *somnolent* state, the stored body fat produces enough heat to keep the animal warm all winter.

(7) What are the *soporific* elements that cause animals to hibernate? In addition to cold weather and unavailability of food, the condition of fewer daylight hours influences animals to enter the "long sleep." Another factor is severely warm weather. (8) In the summer some creatures become *slothful* with the summer heat. (9) Then they crawl *lethargically* into a cool, damp place. (10) Their *languid* condition soon becomes hibernation, and they sleep away part of the hot months. Two of the summer sleepers are frogs and toads.

Just as human beings heat homes in the winter and air-condition them in the summer, animals have their own built-in temperature controls to enable them to survive in comfort in spite of temperature extremes.

© Great Source   DO NOT COPY

Each of the following statements corresponds to a numbered sentence in the passage. Each statement contains a blank and is followed by four answer choices. Decide which choice fits best in the blank. The word or phrase that you choose must express roughly the same meaning as the italicized word in the passage. Write the letter of your choice on the answer line.

1. Animals are occasionally _____ in making their winter preparations.
   a. interrupted   **b.** disorganized   **c.** too far ahead   **d.** late

1. _____

2. Hibernating animals enter into a long _____.
   a. dark cave   **c.** condition of activity
   b. state of resting   **d.** period of shedding

2. _____

3. This _____ resembles death.
   a. condition of reduced activity   **c.** state of activity
   b. type of sleepwalking   **d.** troubled sleep

3. _____

4. The winter hibernators' _____ lasts for several months.
   a. increased activity   **c.** condition of reduced consciousness
   b. apathetic indifference   **d.** nervous energy

4. _____

5. Some animals appear to _____ when in search of food.
   a. attack   **b.** sleepwalk   **c.** get frustrated   **d.** work in teams

5. _____

6. Little food is needed to keep the body functioning in a(n) _____ state.
   a. unusual   **b.** active   **c.** starved   **d.** drowsy

6. _____

7. What _____ elements cause animals to hibernate?
   a. sleep-inducing   **b.** dramatic   **c.** key   **d.** constructive

7. _____

8. Warm weather makes some animals _____.
   a. thirsty   **b.** lazy   **c.** hungry   **d.** overheated

8. _____

9. _____, they crawl into a cool, damp place.
   a. Quickly   **c.** Carefully
   b. Enthusiastically   **d.** Sluggishly indifferent

9. _____

10. Their _____ condition soon turns into hibernation.
   a. starved   **b.** unusual   **c.** spiritless   **d.** active

10. _____

Directions   On the answer line, write the vocabulary word or a form of it that completes each analogy.

See page 79 for some strategies to use with analogies.

1. DETERIORATE : QUALITY :: _____ : value *(Lesson 23)*

1. _____

2. FRUGAL : THRIFTY :: _____ : generous *(Lesson 23)*

2. _____

3. TROPHY : VICTORY :: _____ : labor *(Lesson 23)*

3. _____

4. EMPTY : CONTENT :: _____ : money *(Lesson 23)*

4. _____

5. BARREN : FERTILITY :: _____ : originality *(Lesson 24)*

5. _____

6. NONCHALANT : CONCERN :: _____ : sophistication *(Lesson 24)*

6. _____

7. EGOIST : SELFISH :: procrastinator : _____ *(Lesson 25)*

7. _____

8. INTREPID : FEAR :: _____ : energy *(Lesson 25)*

8. _____

© Great Source DO NOT COPY

Although most people lead fairly moderate lives, some slip occasionally from the moderate course and indulge in periodic episodes of behavior that might seem excessive. For example, have you ever

> spent the entire day reading a book for pleasure?
> had three desserts with dinner?
> gone to the movies four times in one weekend?

If practiced infrequently, the above activities should not be criticized. Such activities are harmful only when they have become a habit. Deviating from the moderate course can sometimes yield benefits. The words in this lesson should help you to understand the different degrees of excessive behavior.

WORD LIST

aggrandize
exorbitance
grandiose
hyperbole
intemperate
obsess
opulence
profligate
satiate
superfluous

DEFINITIONS

After you have studied the definitions and example for each vocabulary word, write the word on the line to the right.

1. **aggrandize** (ə-grăn′dīz′, ăg′rən-dīz′) *trans. verb* **a.** To make (something) seem greater; exaggerate. **b.** To make greater in power or influence. **c.** To increase the scope of; enlarge; extend. (From the Latin *ad-*, meaning "to," and *grandis*, meaning "large")

   Related Word **aggrandizement** *noun*
   Example To *aggrandize* his position in society, Rupert claimed that he was related to one of the wealthiest families in Timberline County.

   1. _____

2. **exorbitance** (ĭg-zôr′bĭ-təns) *noun* The condition of exceeding reasonable or proper limits; excessiveness; extravagance. (From the Latin words *ex*, meaning "out of," and *orbita*, meaning "path" or "orbit")

   Related Words **exorbitant** *adjective;* **exorbitantly** *adverb*
   Example At the Après Midi Restaurant, the quality of the food did not justify the *exorbitance* of the prices.

   2. _____

3. **grandiose** (grăn′dē-ōs′, grăn′dē-ōs′) *adjective* **a.** Characterized by pretended or affected grandeur; pompous. **b.** Characterized by greatness of scope or intent; grand. (From the Latin word *grandis*, meaning "large")

   Related Word **grandiosely** *adverb*
   Example The wealthy business executive instructed the architect to design a *grandiose* mansion that would resemble a European palace.

   3. _____

© Great Source   DO NOT COPY

4. **hyperbole** (hī-pûr′bə-lē) *noun*   An exaggerated statement often used as a figure of speech. (From the Greek words *hyper*, meaning "beyond," and *ballein*, meaning "to throw")

4. _____

Related Word   **hyperbolic** *adjective*
Example   The expression "I've told you a million times" is an example of *hyperbole*.

5. **intemperate** (ĭn-tĕm′pər-ĭt, ĭn-tĕm′prĭt) *adjective*   Not temperate or moderate.

5. _____

Related Words   **intemperance** *noun;* **intemperately** *adverb*
Example   When it came to Chinese food, Marla had an *intemperate* appetite and ordered everything from soup to litchi nuts.

6. **obsess** (əb-sĕs′, ŏb-sĕs′) *trans. verb*   To preoccupy the mind excessively.

6. _____

Related Words   **obsession** *noun;* **obsessive** *adjective;* **obsessively** *adverb*
Example   Farley was so *obsessed* with the adventure movie that he went to see it eleven times.

7. **opulence** (ŏp′yə-ləns) *noun*   **a.** The state of having or displaying great wealth and luxury.   **b.** A state of abundance.

7. _____

Related Words   **opulent** *adjective;* **opulently** *adverb*
Example   The *opulence* of the store's display windows impressed its customers.

8. **profligate** (prŏf′lĭ-gĭt, prŏf′lĭ-gāt′) *adjective*   **a.** Recklessly wasteful or extravagant.   **b.** Completely given over to self-indulgence. (From the Latin word *profligare*, meaning "to ruin")

8. _____

Example   Morris, a dedicated spendthrift, depleted his large inheritance in a *profligate* manner.

9. **satiate** (sā′shē-āt′) *trans. verb*   **a.** To gratify to excess.   **b.** To satisfy fully. (From the Latin word *satis*, meaning "enough")

9. _____

Related Word   **satiation** *noun*
Example   The enormous picnic lunch *satiated* even the keenest appetites.

10. **superfluous** (sŏŏ-pûr′flŏŏ-əs) *adjective*   Beyond what is required or sufficient; extra. (From the Latin *super-*, meaning "over," and *fluere*, meaning "to flow")

10. _____

Related Words   **superfluously** *adverb;* **superfluousness** *noun*
Example   Skillful writers prune the *superfluous* words from their first drafts.

© Great Source   DO NOT COPY

EXERCISE 1 WRITING CORRECT WORDS

On the answer line, write the word from the vocabulary list that best fits each definition.

1. Not temperate or moderate

2. To preoccupy the mind excessively

3. To gratify to excess; satisfy fully

4. Recklessly wasteful or extravagant; self-indulgent

5. Characterized by affected grandeur or greatness of scope

6. Beyond what is required or sufficient

7. The state of having or displaying great wealth and luxury

8. An exaggerated statement often used as a figure of speech

9. To make (something) seem greater; make greater in power

10. The condition of exceeding reasonable or proper limits; extravagance

1. _____

2. _____

3. _____

4. _____

5. _____

6. _____

7. _____

8. _____

9. _____

10. _____

EXERCISE 2 USING WORDS CORRECTLY

Each of the following questions contains an italicized vocabulary word. Choose the correct answer to the question, and write *Yes* or *No* on the answer line.

1. If your were *obsessed* with baseball, would you seldom think about it?

2. Is the expression "I could sleep for a week" an example of *hyperbole?*

3. Would a *profligate* person be inclined to invest his or her earnings wisely?

4. Is buying an expensive yacht and a costly sports car in one day an example of *exorbitance?*

5. Could someone's hunger be *satiated* by eating one string bean?

6. Would it be considered *intemperate* to drink two gallons of milk a day?

7. Could a simple hut be called a *grandiose* structure?

8. To *aggrandize* an estate, would someone add to his or her property?

9. Are textbooks, paper, and pens *superfluous* objects to a student?

10. Would a gold statue be considered a sign of *opulence?*

1. _____

2. _____

3. _____

4. _____

5. _____

6. _____

7. _____

8. _____

9. _____

10. _____

EXERCISE 3 IDENTIFYING SYNONYMS AND ANTONYMS

Decide which word or phrase has the meaning that is the same as (a synonym) or opposite to (an antonym) that of the capitalized vocabulary word. Write the letter of your choice on the answer line.

1. HYPERBOLE (antonym):
   a. exaggerated statement
   b. lengthy speech
   c. understatement
   d. rhetorical statement

1. _____

© Great Source DO NOT COPY

2. OBSESS (synonym):
   a. preoccupy   **b.** confuse   **c.** exhaust   **d.** amaze

2. _____

3. AGGRANDIZE (antonym):
   a. gain   **b.** repeat   **c.** continue   **d.** lessen

3. _____

4. PROFLIGATE (antonym):
   a. sufficient   **b.** thrifty   **c.** generous   **d.** extravagant

4. _____

5. GRANDIOSE (synonym):
   a. timeless   **b.** average   **c.** pompous   **d.** ordinary

5. _____

6. SUPERFLUOUS (antonym):
   a. challenging   **b.** satisfactory   **c.** plenty   **d.** essential

6. _____

7. EXORBITANCE (synonym):
   a. extravagance   **b.** visibility   **c.** sufficiency   **d.** credibility

7. _____

8. OPULENCE (antonym):
   a. wealth   **b.** poverty   **c.** affluence   **d.** prominence

8. _____

9. INTEMPERATE (antonym):
   a. indulgent   **b.** generous   **c.** moderate   **d.** humble

9. _____

10. SATIATE (synonym):
   a. gratify   **b.** crowd   **c.** skimp   **d.** attack

10. _____

EXERCISE 4 USING DIFFERENT FORMS OF WORDS

Decide which form of the vocabulary word in parentheses best completes the sentence. The form given may be correct. Write your answer on the answer line.

1. The _____ restaurant patron declined the waiter's offer of dessert. *(satiate)*

1. _____

2. Visiting the amusement park was an _____ with Pete's younger brother. *(obsess)*

2. _____

3. The statement "This book weighs a ton" is an example of _____. *(hyperbole)*

3. _____

4. At the lavish smorgasbord, Julia ate _____. *(intemperate)*

4. _____

5. The _____ interior of the mansion impressed the visitors. *(opulence)*

5. _____

6. In _____ one property, Julian caused his other business interests to suffer. *(aggrandize)*

6. _____

7. The salesperson's _____ offer was met with suspicion by prospective customers. *(grandiose)*

7. _____

8. The credit manager distrusted _____ spenders. *(profligate)*

8. _____

9. The store's _____ prices discouraged customers. *(exorbitance)*

9. _____

10. Anna's tendency to make _____ remarks irritated her friends. *(superfluous)*

10. _____

© Great Source   DO NOT COPY

READING COMPREHENSION

Each numbered sentence in the following passage contains an italicized vocabulary word or related form. After you read the passage, you will complete an exercise.

HOLLYWOOD: THE DREAM FACTORY

Although going to the movies has always been a popular pastime with the American public, certain periods of history, such as the 1930s and 1940s, attracted particularly impressive numbers of devoted fans. (1) For those fans frequent movie-going did not lead to *satiation* with celluloid images; instead, seeing one movie seemed to lead to seeing still another. (2) Why was the public so *obsessed* with movies during this time, and how did filmmakers satisfy these seemingly insatiable needs?

During the thirties and forties, movies were one of the least expensive forms of entertainment. The public flocked to the theaters to escape, if only momentarily, coping with the depression economy of the thirties and, later, the wartime concerns of the forties. (3) The movie-going public seemed determined to flee a dreary reality and to pursue, instead, an *opulent* dream world, where attractive characters tap-danced and sang their way through life.

Filmmakers were happy to satisfy the public's needs. (4) Consequently, *grandiose* sets were constructed for the popular Hollywood extravaganzas. (5) In elaborate musicals beautiful women, dressed in *exorbitantly* expensive costumes, sang and danced in endless chorus lines in front of sets that routinely featured cascading fountains, shimmering mirrors, and flashing lights. In addition, history was re-created in epic movies that spared no expense to please viewers. Whole civilizations came to life again on specially built Hollywood sets that dazzled and absorbed viewers in the movie theater.

Fans were not always content to idealize the characters on screen; they also wanted perfection off-screen. The adoring public easily forgot that movie stars were also human beings. (6) Studio publicists had the difficult task of *aggrandizing* film stars' images by creating fictionalized backgrounds for them. To complete the fantasy, the public wanted to believe that movie stars were similar to the characters they played. In real life, however, the stars didn't always cooperate. (7) Sometimes *profligate* actors and actresses were forced to reform after being threatened with nonrenewal of studio contracts. (8) Often a movie star's *intemperate* behavior was carefully hidden from the adoring public. (9) In studio publicity releases, *hyperbolic* statements touted the stars' virtues and accomplishments. The studios kept the names and faces of their stars constantly in print in order to feed the public's illusions.

Many movie stars actually lived the way their fans wanted them to. Like royalty they married one another and moved into ornate mansions that rivaled palaces. When an actress arrived for a movie premiere, her adoring fans expected to see her draped in expensive furs and glittering with abundant jewels. She must be on the arm of a dashing male star who wore a tuxedo and a charming smile for the occasion.

As the economy grew more prosperous during the 1940s and then the 1950s, television became popular and movie audiences dwindled alarmingly. Even though low-budget television productions could not duplicate the grand motion picture epics, the public readily accepted entertainment on a lesser scale. People now seemed ready to cope with more reality in their film scripts and in their film stars. (10) The tinseled fantasies of Hollywood had become *superfluous*.

© Great Source   DO NOT COPY

Each of the following statements corresponds to a numbered sentence in the passage. Each statement contains a blank and is followed by four answer choices. Decide which choice fits best in the blank. The word or phrase that you choose must express roughly the same meaning as the italicized word in the passage. Write the letter of your choice on the answer line.

1. The craving of some movie fans for celluloid images was not _____.
   a. well understood
   b. gratified to excess
   c. harmful
   d. reasonable

   1. _____

2. Why were people so _____ movies during this time?
   a. thrilled with
   b. impressed with
   c. critical of
   d. preoccupied with

   2. _____

3. Moviegoers chased after a(n) _____ dream world.
   a. luxurious
   b. attractive
   c. unrealistic
   d. glittering

   3. _____

4. Studios built _____ sets for the movie spectaculars.
   a. towering
   b. indoor
   c. large-scale
   d. attractive

   4. _____

5. In the Hollywood musicals, beautiful women were dressed in _____ expensive costumes.
   a. excessively
   b. fashionably
   c. ridiculously
   d. moderately

   5. _____

6. Publicists were asked to _____ movie stars' images.
   a. write about
   b. dissect
   c. exaggerate
   d. criticize

   6. _____

7. Possible nonrenewal of contracts forced _____ stars to reform.
   a. headstrong
   b. self-indulgent
   c. glamorous
   d. successful

   7. _____

8. A star's _____ behavior was often hidden from the public.
   a. conceited
   b. awkward
   c. careless
   d. immoderate

   8. _____

9. _____ statements appeared in studio press releases.
   a. Exaggerated
   b. True
   c. Irresponsible
   d. False

   9. _____

10. The dream world of Hollywood had become _____.
    a. magnificent
    b. unnecessary
    c. abundant
    d. important

    10. _____

Imagine yourself as a reviewer of restaurants for your community newspaper. Your current assignment takes you to a restaurant that does everything to excess—from the food to the interior decoration. Write a review of several paragraphs in which you give your reactions to the food, setting, and service. In the review use five words from this lesson and underline each one.

Word History: satiate

Latin: *satis*=enough

To *satiate* means "to gratify to excess" and comes from the Latin words *satis,* "enough." Let's consider some other English words based on the Latin root *satis* that convey the idea of "enough." For example, if you feel *dissatisfied,* you have not had "enough"; an *insatiable* appetite is one that never has "enough"; a *satisfactory* performance is "enough" to get by. You will certainly gain a sense of *satisfaction* by knowing "enough" about *satis* and its numerous derivatives.

© Great Source DO NOT COPY

J ust as people experience love and friendship, they also experience hostility and anger. Everyone has favorites among persons, things, and activities, and almost everyone dislikes someone or something. Even people with the calmest temperaments occasionally become angry. The words in this lesson will help you to understand better these important and useful concepts.

WORD LIST

affinity
animosity
antipathy
ardent
contemptible
disdain
enamored
estrange
penchant
repugnance

DEFINITIONS

After you have studied the definitions and example for each vocabulary word, write the word on the line to the right.

1. **affinity** (ə-fĭn′ĭ-tē) *noun*   **a.** A natural attraction; liking.   **b.** Similarity based on relationship or causal connection: *an affinity between two languages.*   **c.** Chemical or physical attraction: *a dye with an affinity for certain fibers.* (From the Latin word *affinis,* meaning "related by marriage")

    Example   Some people seem to have an *affinity* for learning languages.

    1. _____

2. **animosity** (ăn′ə-mŏs′ĭ-tē) *noun*   Active hatred; a hostile attitude. (From the Latin word *animus,* meaning "spirit" or "anger")

    Example   The disagreement between the candidates developed into *animosity* as the election drew near.

    2. _____
    See *antipathy.*

3. **antipathy** (ăn-tĭp′ə-thē) *noun*   A strong feeling of dislike, distaste, or opposition. (From the Greek *anti-,* meaning "against," and *pathos,* meaning "feeling")

    Related Word   **antipathetic** *adjective*
    Example   He grew up in a community that expressed a great *antipathy* toward new ideas.

    3. _____
    USAGE NOTE: *Antipathy* is not as strong a word as *animosity. Antipathy* indicates a more passive dislike and avoidance.

4. **ardent** (är′dnt) *adjective*   **a.** Marked by or showing warmth of emotion or desire; passionate: *an ardent suitor.*   **b.** Marked by enthusiasm or eagerness: *ardent pursuit of knowledge.* (From the Latin word *ardere,* meaning "to burn")

    Related Words **ardently** *adverb:* **ardor** *noun*
    Example   Mrs. O'Dea was an *ardent* believer in the benefits of exercise and swam two miles every day.

    4. _____

5. **contemptible** (kən-tĕmp′tə-bəl) *adjective*   Deserving to be regarded with a feeling of dislike and disrespect. (From the Latin word *contemnere,* meaning "to despise")

   Related Words   contempt *noun;* **contemptibly** *adverb*
   Example   The athletic coaches thought physical weakness *contemptible.*

5. _____

6. **disdain** (dĭs-dān′) *trans. verb*   To consider or reject as unworthy; treat as inferior; scorn.   *noun*   A feeling of dislike and disrespect; scorn. (From the Latin *de-,* meaning "not," and *dignus,* meaning "worthy")

   Related Words   disdainful *adjective;* **disdainfully** *adverb*
   Example   Harry *disdained* to be my friend because I was two years younger than he was.

6. _____

7. **enamored** (ĭ-năm′ərd) *adjective*   Inspired with love; charmed; captivated. (From the Latin *in-,* meaning "in," and *amor,* meaning "love")

   Example   Owen, *enamored* of all things Welsh, spent a summer in Wales learning the language.

7. _____

8. **estrange** (ĭ-strānj′) *trans. verb*   To destroy the affection or friendliness of; to make hostile or unsympathetic; alienate. (From the Latin word *extraneus,* meaning "strange")

   Related Word   estrangement *noun*
   Example   A silly misunderstanding almost permanently *estranged* the two friends.

8. _____

9. **penchant** (pĕn′chənt) *noun*   A definite and habitual liking; inclination. (From the French word *pencher,* meaning "to incline")

   Example   Grandmother had a *penchant* for taking long walks in the rain.

9. _____

10. **repugnance** (rĭ-pŭg′nəns) *noun*   A feeling of strong dislike or distaste. (From the Latin *re-,* meaning "against," and *pugnare,* meaning "to fight")

   Related Words   repugnant *adjective;* **repugnantly** *adverb*
   Example   Alana was filled with *repugnance* at the thought of dissecting a frog.

10. _____

© Great Source   DO NOT COPY

EXERCISE 1 MATCHING WORDS AND DEFINITIONS

Match the definition in Column B with the word in Column A. Write the letter of the correct definition on the answer line.

Column A	Column B	
1. antipathy	a. to destroy the affection of	1. _____
2. contemptible	b. marked by warmth of emotion	2. _____
3. estrange	c. inspired with love; charmed	3. _____
4. animosity	d. active hatred	4. _____
5. repugnance	e. a strong feeling of dislike or opposition	5. _____
6. enamored	f. to consider or reject as unworthy	6. _____
7. affinity	g. a feeling of strong dislike	7. _____
8. ardent	h. deserving to be regarded with disrespect	8. _____
9. penchant	i. a natural attraction; liking	9. _____
10. disdain	j. a definite, habitual liking	10. _____

EXERCISE 2 USING WORDS CORRECTLY

Decide whether the italicized vocabulary word has been used correctly in the sentence. On the answer line, write *Correct* for correct use and *Incorrect* for incorrect use.

1. Because Ben was filled with *repugnance,* he thanked his friend warmly.   1. _____

2. If you're looking for a pet, go to the *animosity* shelter on Sumac Lane.   2. _____

3. Jason *estranged* the shirt that he got for his birthday because it was too small.   3. _____

4. Most cats have a natural *antipathy* toward dogs.   4. _____

5. Where did you get that beautiful *penchant* hanging around your neck?   5. _____

6. Patricia succeeds in school because of her *ardent* desire to learn.   6. _____

7. Let Suki be the club treasurer; she has an *affinity* for mathematical details.   7. _____

8. Martha *disdained* her sister and considered her a good friend.   8. _____

9. Mr. Gordon considered the rowdy behavior of his students to be *contemptible.*   9. _____

10. Andy has become *enamored* of the bright colors and swirling shapes in the paintings of Vincent van Gogh.   10. _____

EXERCISE 3 CHOOSING THE BEST DEFINITION

For each italicized vocabulary word or related form in the following sentences, write the letter of the best definition on the answer line.

1. Margo finds large noisy parties *repugnant.*   1. _____
   a. fun   b. distasteful   c. boring   d. tiring

2. Benedict Arnold swore that he had done nothing to merit his country's *disdain*.
   a. blessing **b.** faith **c.** sorrow **d.** scorn

2. _____

3. Sir Galahad spent his life in *ardent* quest of the Holy Grail.
   a. greedy **b.** sporadic **c.** misguided **d.** passionate

3. _____

4. I thought Dora showed a *contemptible* lack of conviction about such a serious matter.
   a. despicable **b.** admirable **c.** thoughtful **d.** typical

4. _____

5. The tourists were *enamored* of the classical splendor of Athens.
   a. upset **b.** bored **c.** fascinated **d.** bewildered

5. _____

6. Kent is trying to overcome his *antipathy* toward math.
   a. neglect **b.** dislike **c.** mistrust **d.** excessive love

6. _____

7. The bookcase, lamp, and carvings in Lila's room are evidence of her *penchant* for woodworking.
   a. inclination **b.** hatred **c.** heritage **d.** blueprint

7. _____

8. The atmosphere at family gatherings has been very strained since my aunt became *estranged* from my grandparents.
   a. alienated **b.** independent **c.** removed **d.** distant

8. _____

9. Although they both ran for class president, Phil bore Dolores no *animosity* after she had won.
   a. ridicule **b.** gratitude **c.** congratulations **d.** ill will

9. _____

10. Teresa learned in chemistry that alkali metals, such as sodium, have a strong *affinity* for halogens, such as chlorine.
    a. repulsion **b.** odor **c.** attraction **d.** use

10. _____

EXERCISE 4 USING DIFFERENT FORMS OF WORDS

Decide which form of the vocabulary word in parentheses best completes the sentence. The form given may be correct. Write your answer on the answer line.

1. Skunks have a _____ for stealing chicken eggs. *(penchant)*

1. _____

2. The very thought of violence was _____ to Alana. *(repugnance)*

2. _____

3. Was there any real _____ between Julius Caesar and Mark Anthony before the Ides of March? *(animosity)*

3. _____

4. Morris is _____ toward any changes in the French Club's bylaws. *(antipathy)*

4. _____

5. At the beginning of the story, no one realizes that Cheryl is Carla's _____ sister. *(estranged)*

5. _____

6. The author felt only _____ for the editor's effort to correct her work. *(contemptible)*

6. _____

7. Fido looked _____ at the dry dog food. *(disdain)*

7. _____

8. Reptiles have an _____ for warm places. *(affinity)*

8. _____

9. Michelle _____ hoped that it would snow before the weekend so that she could go skiing. *(ardent)*

9. _____

10. The Dunn family has become _____ of city life. *(enamored)*

10. _____

© Great Source DO NOT COPY

READING COMPREHENSION

Each numbered sentence in the following passage contains an italicized vocabulary word or related form. After you read the passage, you will complete an exercise.

I HATE LINES!

(1) For as long as I can remember, I have had a great *antipathy* toward waiting in line. In fact, just the thought of having to undergo such an ordeal fills me with disgust. My distaste dates back at least as far as the early days of grade school, when, at the sound of the bell, we would all scramble to form a line and be marched like little marionettes into our classrooms. The teachers were very strict about this drill: no talking, no turning around, no pushing. (2) One teacher, who evidently saw a close *affinity* between first grade and an army training camp, particularly enjoyed this part of the day.

It is a sad fact of life, as everyone knows, that waiting in line is a common experience. (3) I might have expected that by now maturity and wisdom would have helped me to overcome my *repugnance*, but time has only made the lines longer and my patience shorter. I try to console myself with thinking how much worse it could be. In some countries people have to wait in line for hours for a loaf of bread or a bar of soap, only to find that the person just ahead has gotten the last one, or that the price has gone up while they were waiting! (4) On the other hand, the English are said to have a *penchant* for waiting in line, and where two or three are gathered, they will form a *queue*, which is British English for "line." (5) Perhaps if I visited England, I, too, would become *enamored* of lines.

Lines can have unfortunate consequences and even be dangerous. I once lost a friend because of a line. I had been waiting patiently for a quarter of an hour in the lunch line in the cafeteria when one of my classmates cut in front of me without so much as a thank-you. "I knew I could count on you to save me a place," he said. (6) I was so taken by surprise that I said nothing in reply, but the incident was the beginning of an *estrangement* between us. Cutting a line is not always so safe. (7) One rainy night, as a friend and I were waiting to buy tickets to a very popular movie, a brawny man, who evidently thought waiting in line a *contemptible* display of weakness, strode straight up to the box office demanding "two." (8) This behavior aroused the greatest *animosity* in those nearby, and a fight broke out. By the time the police restored order, we had missed a good part of the film.

When is a line not a line? When it is a button—a "hold" button on the telephone. Being put on "hold" when making a telephone call is similar to waiting in a line, but I find it far more irksome. At least in a line it is possible to see progress, however slow, but time on "hold" is spent in a never-never land of suspense and frustration. It is impossible to know how many calls are ahead, or whether the calls will be taken in order. There may not even be any other callers—the person answering the phone may have other reasons for putting people off! My strategy is simply to hang up after one minute and call back later, at my own convenience. (9) I *disdain* to wait for a person who considers my time of such little worth.

(10) If I have written so *ardently* on this subject, it is because there is more to life than awaiting someone else's pleasure. After all, much as I admire the great poet Milton, he was not standing in line when he wrote, "They also serve, who only stand and wait."

© Great Source   DO NOT COPY

READING COMPREHENSION EXERCISE

Each of the following statements corresponds to a numbered sentence in the passage. Each statement contains a blank and is followed by four answer choices. Decide which choice fits best in the blank. The word or phrase that you choose must express roughly the same meaning as the italicized word in the passage. Write the letter of your choice on the answer line.

1. I have long had a great _____ waiting in line.
   a. dislike for **b.** eagerness for **c.** indifference to **d.** interest in

   1. _____

2. One teacher saw a great _____ between first grade and an army training camp.
   a. disagreement **b.** rivalry **c.** similarity **d.** communication

   2. _____

3. Maturity and wisdom should have helped me overcome my _____.
   a. impatience **b.** inclination **c.** dislike **d.** nervousness

   3. _____

4. The English are said to have a(n) _____ for waiting in line.
   a. dislike **b.** inclination **c.** queue **d.** reason

   4. _____

5. If I visited England, I might become _____ lines.
   a. charmed by
   b. annoyed with
   c. improved by
   d. sympathetic toward

   5. _____

6. An incident in a line caused a(n) _____ between us.
   a. friendship **b.** disagreement **c.** fight **d.** alienation

   6. _____

7. The brawny man thought waiting in line a weakness that was _____.
   a. honorable
   b. disagreement
   c. deserving consideration
   d. deserving disrespect

   7. _____

8. His behavior aroused great _____.
   a. fear **b.** hostility **c.** resentment **d.** scorn

   8. _____

9. I _____ to wait for a person who puts my call on "hold."
   a. consent **b.** expect **c.** scorn **d.** cease

   9. _____

10. I have written _____ on the subject of waiting in line.
    a. passionately **b.** dully **c.** with difficulty **d.** amusingly

    10. _____

WRITING ASSIGNMENT

Social events can be very pleasant, but they can also be unpleasant. You are a reporter for your school newspaper. Write a one-paragraph column describing a recent social event, either pleasant or unpleasant, at your school, such as a football game, a dance, or a club meeting. Use at least five words from this lesson and underline each one.

© Great Source DO NOT COPY

READING SKILLS

COM- AND RELATED PREFIXES

The prefix *com-* is added to roots that come from Latin words. *Com-* has several variants, including *con-*, *co-*, *col-*, and *cor-*. Despite differences in spelling, *com-* and its related prefixes have one basic meaning. Like all prefixes they change the meaning of the root to which they are added.

Prefix Meaning	Root Word	Word	Word Definition
together	*premere,* "to press"	compress	to press together
	gregare, "to assemble"	congregate	to come together in a crowd
	esse, "to be"	coexist	to exist together at the same time or place
	laborare, "to work"	collaborate	to work together
	relatio, "relation"	correlate	to put or bring into relation

To determine the meaning of words with the prefix *com-* or its variants, use the following procedure. Remember that the more prefixes and roots you know, the more often you will be able to analyze unfamiliar words.

PROCEDURE

1. *Substitute the prefix and root definitions for the prefix and root.*
2. *Think of a possible definition of the entire word.*
3. *Use the context to help you develop the possible definition.*
4. *Check your definition of the word in the dictionary.*

EXERCISE USING *COM-* AND RELATED PREFIXES

Each sentence in this exercise contains an italicized word beginning with the prefix *com-* or one of its related forms. The root word and its meaning are given in parentheses after the sentence. *Step 1:* Taking the context into consideration, write your own definition of the word. *Step 2:* Write the dictionary definition of the word. Choose the definition that fits the way in which the word is used in the sentence. *Step 3:* Write a sentence of your own in which you use the word correctly.

1. The student council will *convene* tomorrow to discuss the plans for Sophomore Week. (Root word: *venire,* "to come")

   Your Definition _____

   Dictionary Definition _____

   Sentence _____

© Great Source   DO NOT COPY   *Com-* and Related Prefixes   **179**

2. The investigators had to *collate* a large number of documents. (Root word: *conferre*, "to collect")

   Your Definition _____

   Dictionary Definition _____

   Sentence _____

3. Adela sought a salary *commensurate* with her abilities. (Root word: *mensura*, "measure")

   Your Definition _____

   Dictionary Definition _____

   Sentence _____

4. The overseas relief workers had *compassion* for the refugees from the war-torn country. (Root word: *pati*, "to suffer")

   Your Definition _____

   Dictionary Definition _____

   Sentence _____

5. Eduardo's sixteenth birthday *coincided* with his grandparents' fiftieth wedding anniversary. (Root word: *incidere*, "to occur")

   Your Definition _____

   Dictionary Definition _____

   Sentence _____

6. Damon's *coherent* explanation answered our questions. (Root word: *haerere*, "to cling")

   Your Definition _____

   Dictionary Definition _____

   Sentence _____

7. The mayor *concurred* with the town planning board about the need for housing for senior citizens. (Root word: *currere*, "to run")

   Your Definition _____

   Dictionary Definition _____

   Sentence _____

8. We had seldom heard a more *cogent* argument for stricter fire regulations. (Root word: *agere*, "to drive")

   Your Definition _____

   Dictionary Definition _____

   Sentence _____

9. Crowds *converged* on the ticket office long before it opened. (Root word: *vergere*, "to incline")

   Your Definition _____

   Dictionary Definition _____

   Sentence _____

© Great Source   DO NOT COPY

Y̶ou can perceive time in different ways. If you are busy or if you are deeply involved in a mental activity, you may feel that time flies by. If you are bored or if you are waiting for someone who is late, you may feel that time is dragging. Actually, time passes at an unchanging pace, but how you spend time seems to affect the way you view it. In this lesson you will learn words that refer to the experience or passage of time.

WORD LIST

antecedent
ensue
ephemeral
imminent
interim
interminable
perennial
precipitate
provisional
retrospective

DEFINITIONS

After you have studied the definitions and example for each vocabulary word, write the word on the line to the right.

1. **antecedent** (ăn′tĭ-sēd′nt) *noun*   **a.** Someone or something that precedes or goes before.   **b.** *Plural form only.* Ancestors; forebears.   **c.** An event that occurs before another, especially one that influences or causes another.   **d.** The word, phrase, or clause to which a pronoun refers.   *adjective*   Coming or being before in time, place, or order; preceding. (From the Latin *ante-*, meaning "before," and *cedere*, meaning "to go")

   Example   Many elements of modern building design have classical *antecedents*.

1. _____

2. **ensue** (ĕn-sōō′) *intrans. verb*   To follow as a consequence or result. (From the Latin *in-*, meaning "in," and *sequi*, meaning "to follow")

   Example   The floods caused a great deal of suffering, but the famine that *ensued* devastated the country.

2. _____

3. **ephemeral** (ĭ-fĕm′ər-əl) *adjective*   **a.** Lasting for a very brief time; fleeting; transitory.   **b.** Lasting for one day only. (From the Greek *epi-*, meaning "on," and *hēmera*, meaning "day")

   Related Word   ephemerally *adverb*
   Example   Every year the holiday season generates *ephemeral* feelings of good will and neighborliness.

3. _____

4. **imminent** (ĭm′ə-nənt) *adjective*   About to occur; immediate. (From the Latin word *imminere*, meaning "to overhang")

   Related Words   imminence *noun;* imminently *adverb*
   Example   The building was condemned because it is in *imminent* danger of collapsing.

4. _____
   USAGE NOTE: Don't confuse *imminent* with *eminent*, which means "distinguished" or "prominent."

5. **interim** (ĭn′tər-ĭm) *noun* A period of time between two events or periods of time. *adjective* Belonging to or taking place during an interval of time; temporary: *an interim report.* (From the Latin word *interim,* meaning "in the meantime")

   Example The orchestra gave a matinee and an evening concert; in the *interim* the players snatched a quick meal.

6. **interminable** (ĭn-tûr′mə-nə-bəl) *adjective* Lasting or seeming to last forever; tiresomely drawn out. (From the Latin *in-,* meaning "not," and *terminus,* meaning "end")

   Related Word **interminably** *adverb*
   Example I could sense that Uncle Ed was about to begin one of his *interminable* stories about his boyhood on a potato farm.

7. **perennial** (pə-rĕn′ē-əl) *adjective* **a.** Lasting an indefinitely long time; everlasting. **b.** Appearing or recurring again and again. *noun* A plant having a life span of more than two years. (From the Latin *per-,* meaning "throughout," and *annus,* meaning "year")

   Related Word **perennially** *adverb*
   Example This once lush country is now suffering from a *perennial* drought.

8. **precipitate** (prĭ-sĭp′ĭ-tĭt) *adjective* **a.** Acting or done hastily or impulsively, without proper consideration. **b.** Moving with excessive and often foolish speed. **c.** Occurring suddenly. *trans. verb* (prĭ-sĭp′ĭ-tāt′) **a.** To cause to happen, especially suddenly or before the right time. **b.** To cause to separate from a chemical solution or suspension. *intrans. verb* (prĭ-sĭp′ĭ-tĭt) **a.** To condense and fall as rain or snow. **b.** To separate from a chemical solution or suspension. *noun* (prĭ-sĭp′ĭ-tāt′, prĭ-sĭp′ĭ-tĭt) A solid separated from a chemical solution or suspension. (From the Latin *prae-,* meaning "in front," and *caput,* meaning "head")

   Related Words **precipitately** *adverb;* **precipitation** *noun*
   Example The army made a *precipitate* retreat from its exposed position.

9. **provisional** (prə-vĭzh′ə-nəl) *adjective* Provided for the time being; temporary: *a provisional government.* (From the Latin *pro-,* meaning "forward," and *visio,* meaning "seeing")

   Related Words **provision** *noun;* **provisionally** *adverb*
   Example The government drew up *provisional* regulations to meet the emergency.

10. **retrospective** (rĕt′rə-spĕk′tĭv) *adjective* **a.** Looking back on or directed toward the past. **b.** Applying to or influencing the past; retroactive. **c.** Of or relating to an exhibition of an artist's work that is comprehensive and covers a considerable number of years. (From the Latin words *retro,* meaning "back" and *specere,* meaning "to look")

    Related Words **retrospect** *noun;* **retrospectively** *adverb*
    Example Once, in a *retrospective* mood, my father sketched out his family tree.

5. _____

6. _____

7. _____

USAGE NOTE:
Interminable and *perennial* both refer to something's lasting a long time, but *interminable* has a negative tone.

8. _____

ETYMOLOGY NOTE:
Precipitate translates literally as "head in front," or "headlong." The army rushes headlong toward safety, rain falls headlong to the ground, and the precipitate in a chemical solution falls headlong to the bottom.

9. _____

10. _____

© Great Source DO NOT COPY

EXERCISE I WRITING CORRECT WORDS

On the answer line, write the word from the vocabulary list that best fits each definition.

1. Lasting or seeming to last forever

2. Lasting for a very brief time; fleeting

3. Lasting an indefinitely long time

4. A period of time between two events

5. Someone or something that precedes

6. Directed toward the past

7. To follow as a consequence

8. About to occur

9. Acting or done hastily

10. Provided for the time being

1. _____

2. _____

3. _____

4. _____

5. _____

6. _____

7. _____

8. _____

9. _____

10. _____

EXERCISE 2 USING WORDS CORRECTLY

Each of the following questions contains an italicized vocabulary word. Choose the correct answer to the question, and write *Yes* or *No* on the answer line.

1. Do *ephemeral* things last a long time?

2. Is an *interim* the space between objects?

3. Is an *interminable* speech brief?

4. Does a *perennial* plant live more than one season?

5. If something *ensues*, does it follow as a result?

6. Is an *antecedent* a consequence?

7. Is an *imminent* danger long past?

8. Is a *precipitate* action impulsive?

9. Is a *provisional* government permanent?

10. Is a *retrospective* penalty retroactive?

1. _____

2. _____

3. _____

4. _____

5. _____

6. _____

7. _____

8. _____

9. _____

10. _____

EXERCISE 3 IDENTIFYING SYNONYMS AND ANTONYMS

Decide which word or phrase has the meaning that is the same as (a synonym) or opposite to (an antonym) that of the capitalized vocabulary word. Write the letter of your choice on the answer line.

1. PERENNIAL (synonym):
   a. recurring   **b.** annual   **c.** flowering   **d.** terminal

2. INTERMINABLE (antonym):
   a. unending   **b.** short   **c.** untimely   **d.** last

1. _____

2. _____

© Great Source   DO NOT COPY

3. INTERIM (synonym):
   a. future   b. past   c. interval   d. end

   3. _____ DO NOT COPY

4. ANTECEDENT (antonym):
   a. successor   b. forebear   c. word   d. cause

   4. _____

5. EPHEMERAL (synonym):
   a. flowery   b. brief   c. daily   d. new

   5. _____

6. ENSUE (antonym):
   a. last   b. follow   c. threaten   d. precede

   6. _____

7. PROVISIONAL (synonym):
   a. governmental b. temporary   c. advisory   d. forward-looking

   7. _____

8. IMMINENT (antonym):
   a. far-off   b. looming   c. apparent   d. speedy

   8. _____

9. PRECIPITATE (synonym):
   a. snowy   b. early   c. backward   d. hasty

   9. _____

10. RETROSPECTIVE (antonym):
   a. artistic   b. past   c. prospective   d. influential

   10. _____

EXERCISE 4 USING DIFFERENT FORMS OF WORDS

Decide which form of the vocabulary word in parentheses best completes the sentence. The form given may be correct. Write your answer on the answer line.

1. To those defending the Alamo in 1836, Santa Anna's siege went on _____; however, it lasted only thirteen days. (*interminable*)

   1. _____

2. My great-aunt is a terrible snob; she will befriend you only if she approves of your _____. (*antecedent*)

   2. _____

3. Antarctica is a region of _____ frost. (*perennial*)

   3. _____

4. Despite the official warnings, most residents did not realize the _____ of the hurricane. (*imminent*)

   4. _____

5. The poet was especially good at capturing _____ insights and perceptions that accompany moments of deep feeling. (*ephemeral*)

   5. _____

6. The duke challenged the baron to a fight and was wounded in the _____ battle. (*ensue*)

   6. _____

7. We'll rehearse this quartet again tomorrow, but in the _____ we should each practice the third movement on our own. (*interim*)

   7. _____

8. The publication of the letter _____ an investigation into the private lives of several prominent officials. (*precipitate*)

   8. _____

9. The university _____ approved the design for the new library. (*provisional*)

   9. _____

10. In _____ I think that I should have spent more time studying math and French. (*retrospective*)

   10. _____

© Great Source   DO NOT COPY

READING COMPREHENSION

Each numbered sentence in the following passage contains an italicized vocabulary word or related form. After you read the passage, you will complete an exercise.

MARATHON RACING—A MODERN SPORT

The ancient Greeks have left us many legacies, some directly, like the poems of Homer, and others indirectly, like the marathon race. **(1)** The *antecedents* of the modern sport of marathon racing are to be found partly in Greek history and partly in the history of the modern Olympic Games.

The Olympic Games began in Greece before the beginning of recorded history. Their traditional founding has been calculated as 776 B.C. The games were originally a local amateur event that included religious rites as well as athletic competitions. **(2)** The earliest games lasted only a day, in contrast to the seemingly *interminable* planning and promotion of their modern counterparts. **(3)** The prizes were equally *ephemeral,* as well as symbolic: a wreath of olive leaves from a sacred grove, and a palm branch. The victors received more enduring spoils, however, in the form of gifts and privileges bestowed by their native cities.

(4) The *ensuing* one thousand years saw the Olympic Games become increasingly important as a unifying factor in Greek society, which was very fragmented. Athletes from all parts of Greece and its colonies came to compete. Wars were interrupted so that the games could go on. The Greeks even reckoned time by the games, designating as *Olympiads* the four-year intervals between them.

The ancient Olympic Games were abolished by the Roman emperor Theodosius I around A.D. 400. Fifteen centuries then passed before the Olympic idea was revived. **(5)** In the *interim* the unity of the ancient world was broken up by religious, ethnic, and national strife. The modern Olympic Games were established in 1896 to promote both friendly athletic competition and harmony among nations.

The particular events of the modern Olympics differ from those of the ancient Greek games. **(6)** Foot races, an early and *perennial* component, are important to both. However, the most famous foot race, the marathon, is a modern innovation. **(7)** It was inspired by the same *retrospective* reverence for Greek civilization that led to the revival of the Olympic Games themselves.

The marathon is, to some degree, a sentimental re-enactment of a legendary event. During the Persian wars of the fifth century B.C., the Athenian army won a decisive victory at Marathon, a plain about twenty miles northeast of Athens. Pheidippides, a Greek soldier, ran back to the city with the news. **(8)** According to the legend, although he was in *imminent* danger of collapsing from exhaustion, he managed to deliver his message to the anxious citizens. The first marathon race, run in the 1896 Olympics, was, appropriately, won by a Greek.

Marathon racing did not long remain just an Olympic event. In 1897 an annual marathon was established in Boston, Massachusetts, and although it remained a small amateur affair for many years, it was the most prestigious event of its kind. **(9)** Recent developments, however, have *precipitated* changes in non-Olympic marathons. One is the increased popularity of marathon races, which now number over a hundred. Some races have over ten thousand entrants, both men and women. **(10)** Another change is the *provision* of prize money for the winners. This has resulted in the professionalization of a once-amateur sport. Little did Pheidippides realize, as he ran those twenty-odd miles from Marathon to Athens, what legacy he would leave to posterity.

READING COMPREHENSION EXERCISE

Each of the following statements corresponds to a numbered sentence in the passage. Each statement contains a blank and is followed by four answer choices. Decide which choice fits best in the blank. The word or phrase that you choose must express roughly the same meaning as the italicized word in the passage. Write the letter of your choice on the answer line.

1. The _____ of the marathon race are found in the history of the Olympic Games.   1. _____
   a. rules   **b.** problems   **c.** origins   **d.** legacies

2. The planning and promotion of the modern Olympic Games seems _____.

   a. endless   **b.** professional   **c.** amateurish   **d.** careful

2. _____

3. The prizes awarded in the Greek Olympic Games were _____.

   a. floral   **b.** leafy   **c.** valuable   **d.** short-lived

3. _____

4. During the _____ one thousand years, the Olympic Games became increasingly important.

   a. previous   **b.** following   **c.** last   **d.** first

4. _____

5. In the _____, the unity of the ancient world was broken up.

   a. time between   **b.** fifteenth century   **c.** end   **d.** Middle Ages

5. _____

6. Foot races were a _____ part of the Greek games.

   a. necessary   **b.** recurring   **c.** traditional   **d.** secondary

6. _____

7. The marathon was inspired by a(n) _____ reverence for Greek civilization.

   a. irrational   **b.** noble   **c.** backward-looking   **d.** old-fashioned

7. _____

8. The messenger was in _____ danger of collapsing.

   a. no   **b.** serious   **c.** little   **d.** immediate

8. _____

9. Recent developments have _____ changes in non-Olympic marathons.

   a. caused   **b.** necessitated   **c.** followed   **d.** ensured

9. _____

10. Another change is the _____ of prize money.

   a. giving   **b.** scarcity   **c.** rejection   **d.** appeal

10. _____

PRACTICE WITH ANALOGIES

See page 79 for some strategies to use with analogies.

Directions On the answer line, write the vocabulary word or a form of it that completes each analogy.

1. EXTRAVAGANT : RESTRAINT :: _____ : moderation *(Lesson 26)*

1. _____

2. POMPOUS : BEHAVIOR :: _____ : scheme *(Lesson 26)*

2. _____

3. BOAST : CLAIM :: _____ : statement *(Lesson 26)*

3. _____

4. MISER : THRIFTY :: spendthrift : _____ *(Lesson 26)*

4. _____

5. QUENCH : THIRST :: _____ : appetite *(Lesson 26)*

5. _____

6. HARMONY : COMPATIBILITY :: _____ : hatred *(Lesson 27)*

6. _____

7. LAUDABLE : PRAISE :: _____ : disrespect *(Lesson 27)*

7. _____

8. PENCHANT : INCLINATION :: _____ : dislike *(Lesson 27)*

8. _____

9. IMMORTAL : DIE :: _____ : last *(Lesson 28)*

9. _____

10. ANCESTOR : FAMILY :: _____ : event *(Lesson 28)*

10. _____

11. PERPETUAL : STOP :: _____ : end *(Lesson 28)*

11. _____

12. DELIBERATE : PURPOSEFUL :: _____ : hasty *(Lesson 28)*

12. _____

13. STOPGAP : SOLUTION :: _____ : government *(Lesson 28)*

13. _____

14. PROSPECTIVE : FORWARD :: _____ : backward *(Lesson 28)*

14. _____

© Great Source DO NOT COPY

The will to dominate—over the animal kingdom, over the forces of nature, or even over other human beings—is a basic characteristic of the human race. Depending on how one uses the will to dominate, the trait can be positive or negative. When employed in a positive way—domesticating animals, harnessing the power unleashed in a waterfall to provide cheap energy, instructing others in what is good and virtuous, for example—the will to dominate is perhaps the fundamental well-spring of civilization. Used negatively, this trait can have dire consequences, causing wanton destruction, oppression, and injustice. This lesson introduces words related to dominance and its opposite, submissiveness.

WORD LIST

capitulate
condescend
deference
grovel
lackey
predominate
slavish
subjugation
supercilious
sycophant

DEFINITIONS

After you have studied the definitions and example for each vocabulary word, write the word on the line to the right.

1. **capitulate** (kə-pĭch′ə-lāt′) *intrans. verb*   To surrender under specified conditions; give up all resistance.

   Related Word   **capitulation** *noun*
   Example   After repeated attacks the city *capitulated* to the superior forces of the enemy.

   1. _____

2. **condescend** (kŏn′dĭ-sĕnd′) *intrans. verb*   **a.** To agree to do something one regards as below one's rank or dignity.   **b.** To deal with people in a superior or haughty manner.

   Related Words   **condescending** *adjective;* **condescension** *noun*
   Example   The world-renowned soprano *condescended* to be a judge at our high school talent show.

   2. _____

3. **deference** (dĕf′ər-əns, dĕf′rəns) *noun*   Courteous respect; submission to the opinion, wishes, or decisions of another. (From the Latin *de-*, meaning "away," and *ferre*, meaning "to carry")

   Related Words   **defer** *verb;* **deferential** *adjective*
   Example   During the rehearsal the actors showed *deference* toward the director because they respected her authority and talent.

   3. _____

4. **grovel** (grŏv′əl, grŭv′əl) *intrans. verb*   **a.** To behave in a demeaning or self-abasing manner; kowtow; truckle.   **b.** To lie or crawl on the ground face down as a gesture of submissiveness or abasement. (From the Old Norse *grufa*, meaning "to lie face down")

   Related Word   **groveler** *noun*
   Example   When you meet Tom Tetrazzini, your favorite movie star, you should not *grovel*; rather, act naturally and be polite.

   4. _____

5. **lackey** (lăk′ē) *noun*   **a.** A follower who behaves in the manner of a servant; toady; flunky.   **b.** A liveried manservant; footman. (From the French word *laquais*, meaning "servant")

5. _____
See *sycophant.*

Example   Since Sylvia became the manager of the team, she has behaved like the coach's *lackey,* incapable of making her own decisions.

6. **predominate** (prĭ-dŏm′ə-nāt′) *intrans. verb*   To have greater authority, power, or influence; prevail.

6. _____

Related Words   **predominance** *noun;* **predominant** *adjective;* **predominantly** *adverb*

Example   Because of the seniority rules, senior members *predominate,* and junior members have little effect on policy.

7. **slavish** (slā′vĭsh) *adjective*   Characteristic of a slave; slavelike in manner; servile.

7. _____

Related Words   **slavishly** *adverb;* **slavishness** *noun*

Example   The presumptuous customers expected the salespeople to lavish *slavish* attention on them.

8. **subjugation** (sŭb′jə-gā′shən) *noun*   **a.** The act of bringing under rule or dominion.   **b.** Enslavement. (From the Latin *sub-,* meaning "under," and *jugum,* meaning "yoke")

8. _____

Related Words   **subjugate** *verb;* **subjugator** *noun*

Example   The Greek *subjugation* of the Trojans took ten years.

9. **supercilious** (soo′pər-sĭl′ē-əs) *adjective*   Proudly scornful; disdainful; contemptuous. (From the Latin word *supercilium,* meaning "pride" or "eyebrow")

9. _____

Related Words   **superciliously** *adverb;* **superciliousness** *noun*

Example   When Mrs. Thwaits asked the desk clerk if she could bring her dog to the hotel, he gave her a *supercilious* look that made it quite clear that dogs were not welcome at the Carlton-Savoy.

10. **sycophant** (sĭk′ə-fənt) *noun*   One who seeks favor or advancement through flattering important people; a bootlicker. (From the Greek word *sykophantēs,* meaning "informer")

10. _____
USAGE NOTE: A *lackey* is a follower who obeys orders like a servant. A *sycophant* is a more ambitious follower who serves and flatters for gain.

Example   Although the deposed monarch no longer had any power, his entourage of former cabinet ministers and *sycophants* made him appear every inch a king.

© Great Source   DO NOT COPY

EXERCISE 1 WRITING CORRECT WORDS

On the answer line, write the word from the vocabulary list that best fits
each definition.

1. To agree to do something beneath one's dignity

2. A follower who behaves like a servant; flunky

3. Courteous respect; submission to the opinion, wishes, or decisions of another

4. The act of bringing under rule or dominion

5. To surrender; give up all resistance

6. Characteristic of a slave; servile

7. Proudly scornful; contemptuous

8. One who seeks favor or advancement by flattering important people

9. To behave in a demeaning manner; kowtow; truckle

10. To have greater power of influence; prevail

1. _____

2. _____

3. _____

4. _____

5. _____

6. _____

7. _____

8. _____

9. _____

10. _____

EXERCISE 2 USING WORDS CORRECTLY

Each of the following questions contains an italicized vocabulary word. Choose the
correct answer to the question, and write *Yes* or *No* on the answer line.

1. Is to *capitulate* to resist an onslaught?

2. Is *deference* courteous respect?

3. If someone is a *slavish* follower of fashion, is he or she apt to feel comfortable in
   traditional clothing?

4. Is to *predominate* to topple or falter?

5. Is a *lackey* a leader?

6. If you *grovel,* do you behave in a low, base manner?

7. Is *subjugation* a form of voting for new rulers?

8. Is a *sycophant* a weak servant?

9. Is a *supercilious* person one who is very comical?

10. Is to *condescend* to agree to do something that one thinks is below one's dignity?

1. _____

2. _____

3. _____

4. _____

5. _____

6. _____

7. _____

8. _____

9. _____

10. _____

EXERCISE 3 CHOOSING THE BEST WORD

Decide which vocabulary word or related form best completes the sentence, and write
the letter of your choice on the answer line.

1. "Mother gives me the _____ job of cleaning the bathtub every Saturday,"
   complained Kerry.
   a. supercilious   **b.** condescending   **c.** deferential   **d.** slavish

2. The dictator is supported by a notorious _____, who is a general in the army.
   a. slavish   **b.** sycophant   **c.** predominance   **d.** subjugator

1. _____

2. _____

3. The Trojan War ended when the city of Troy _____ after Greek soldiers hidden in a wooden horse opened the city gates to the Greek army.

   a. condescended **b.** capitulated **c.** predominated **d.** subjugated

   3. _____

4. The snobbish dowager would not _____ to associate with anyone not listed in *The Social Register.*

   a. condescend **b.** grovel **c.** predominate **d.** capitulate

   4. _____

5. Hitler's _____ Poland in 1939 caused England and France to declare war on Germany.

   a. condescension over **c.** deference to
   b. capitulation to **d.** subjugation of

   5. _____

6. Rochelle's constant _____ for approval annoys both her family and her friends.

   a. condescending **b.** predominating **c.** groveling **d.** capitulation

   6. _____

7. Although June wanted to go to the movies, she _____ to her mother's wish that she stay home.

   a. subjugated **b.** deferred **c.** condescended **d.** predominated

   7. _____

8. The petty tyrant came to town on horseback, his _____ following behind carrying his trunks.

   a. grovelers **b.** lackeys **c.** superciliousness **d.** condescension

   8. _____

9. "Because I love black and red, these colors _____ in my new fall clothes," announced the designer.

   a. predominate **b.** capitulate **c.** grovel **d.** defer

   9. _____

10. Van may seem _____, but he is really very modest and humble.

    a. capitulating **b.** predominant **c.** deferential **d.** supercilious

    10. _____

EXERCISE 4 USING DIFFERENT FORMS OF WORDS

Each sentence contains an italicized vocabulary word in a form that does not fit the sentence. On the answer line, write the form of that word that does fit the sentence.

1. In a *condescend* tone of voice, Jeremy's older sister agreed to help him with his homework.

   1. _____

2. A deep curtsy is an example of the *deference* behavior a woman employs to greet the queen of England.

   2. _____

3. Ralph Waldo Emerson wrote that to be *slavish* consistent in everything one does is foolish.

   3. _____

4. Neither wrestler was able to *subjugation* his opponent in the first round.

   4. _____

5. Our early spring garden contains *predominate* daffodils and crocuses.

   5. _____

6. Because of his *supercilious*, Todd did not have many friends.

   6. _____

7. The ill-tempered founder of the firm said that all his corporate officers were just ne'er-do-wells and *sycophant.*

   7. _____

8. What were the principal reasons for the *capitulate* of Germany in World War II?

   8. _____

9. Mona is something of a *grovel*, always begging her teachers to raise her grades.

   9. _____

10. The dictator denounced his opposition as running dogs and *lackey* of imperialism.

    10. _____

© Great Source DO NOT COPY

READING COMPREHENSION

Each numbered sentence in the following passage contains an italicized vocabulary word or related form. After you read the passage, you will complete an exercise.

FEUDAL SOCIETY

In Western Europe during the Middle Ages, feudalism was the most prevalent form of social organization, influencing both the economic and the political structures of that era. (1) The feudal system first arose in the mid-ninth century, *predominated* from the tenth century through the thirteenth, and finally disappeared by the end of the fifteenth. The system was based on the simple principle of give and take. (2) A landowner would grant the use of his land to an individual who, in turn, would show *deference* to the owner and provide services that the owner might require. The landowner was known as the "lord" or "liege," his grant of land as a "fief," and the individual to whom the land was granted as a "vassal."

An elaborate and solemn ceremony established and confirmed the relationship between the liege and his vassal. The liege promised to protect and defend his vassal, and the vassal pledged obedience, called "homage," to the lord. (3) Such a relationship did not make the vassal into a mere *lackey,* forced to do the lord's bidding. (4) He did not *grovel* at the feet of his liege. Rather, he provided military and administrative services in exchange for the fief. (5) Conversely, the lord did not take a *supercilious* attitude toward his underlings. (6) He did not feel that he was *condescending* by establishing fiefdoms for his vassals. Instead, he felt that he provided for common defense and welfare.

(7) Vassals were usually drawn from the ranks of those who had distinguished themselves in battle, but this did not prevent an unscrupulous *sycophant* from seeking favor by whispering a few fine words into the ear of a powerful lord. (8) Should a vain and foolish lord have *capitulated* to such flattery, he might have found that he had vassals less adept at defending his lands than they were at boosting his self-esteem.

(9) Fiefs awarded to faithful vassals most often included land, buildings, equipment, domestic animals, and serfs, who were peasants responsible for carrying out the *slavish* tasks involved in maintaining the fief. Depending upon their size and profitability, fiefs could serve as an opportunity for a vassal to gain considerable influence, sometimes even over other vassals. No matter how powerful, however, the vassal was always under obligation to his lord, and a percentage of the income from every fief belonged to the lord.

The feudal society, then, was very structured, somewhat in the form of a pyramid. At the top of the pyramid were a very few sovereign lords. (10) Their vassals composed a somewhat larger group immediately below, and below them loomed the huge bulk of the majority, the serfs, living in *subjugation* to the rules, and occasionally the whims, of their masters.

READING COMPREHENSION EXERCISE

Each of the following statements corresponds to a numbered sentence in the passage. Each statement contains a blank and is followed by four answer choices. Decide which choice fits best in the blank. The word or phrase that you choose must express roughly the same meaning as the italicized word in the passage. Write the letter of your choice on the answer line.

1. The feudal system _____ in Western Europe from the tenth century through the thirteenth.
   a. grew   **b.** prevailed   **c.** developed   **d.** deteriorated

   1. _____

2. The vassal would show _____ to the landowner.
   a. defiance   **b.** a friendly warmth   **c.** a kingly authority   **d.** due respect

   2. _____

3. The vassal was not a _____ forced to do the lord's bidding.
   a. flunky   **b.** prisoner   **c.** employee   **d.** soldier

   3. _____

4. The vassal did not _____ at the feet of his liege.   4. _____
   a. worship   **b.** sit   **c.** demean himself **d.** wait patiently

5. The lord did not have a _____ attitude toward his people.   5. _____
   a. servile   **b.** disdainful   **c.** respectful   **d.** tyrannical

6. The lord did not feel _____ by establishing fiefdoms.   6. _____
   a. proud of himself
   b. important to the welfare of his people
   c. as though he were acting beneath his dignity
   d. particularly responsible or duty-bound

7. A _____ might seek favor from a strong lord.   7. _____
   a. flatter   **b.** warrior   **c.** servant   **d.** vassal

8. If a lord were to have _____ flattery, he might have found himself with inadequate vassals.   8. _____
   a. shown a need for   **c.** given up resistance to
   b. demanded an expression of   **d.** insisted upon

9. Serfs carried out _____ tasks.   9. _____
   a. boring   **b.** superficial   **c.** simple   **d.** servile

10. Serfs lived in _____ their masters.   10. _____
    a. enslavement to **b.** fear of   **c.** loyal service to **d.** reverence to

WRITING ASSIGNMENT

Imagine that you are a Roman citizen witnessing the invasion of the barbarians in the fifth century. These incursions are going to bring about the collapse of the Roman Empire in the West. (The eastern Roman, or Byzantine, Empire will endure for another thousand years.) Using a fresh, clean papyrus scroll, take out your quill and write to your relatives in the eastern empire to let them know what is happening. Be sure to use at least five words from the lesson and underline each one.

VOCABULARY ENRICHMENT

A glance at the definitions at the beginning of this lesson shows that *supercilious* is derived from *supercilium*, the Latin word meaning "pride" but also "eyebrow." How did this word come to mean two such different things? Originally, the word meant "eyebrow" alone, for it is a compound of *super*, meaning "above," and *cilium*, meaning "eyelid." In time, however, the word acquired the additional sense of using the eyebrows to frown or to show seriousness or to express pride or haughtiness. The last meaning is the one that has persisted. A modern and more colloquial example of this kind of vocabulary transformation is *nosy*, derived from *nose* but referring more properly to one who sticks it where it does not belong.

Activity   A number of English words that we do not associate with parts of the body do in fact derive from words in other languages for parts of the body. *Glossary* comes from the Greek word for *tongue*, and *linguist* from the Latin word for *tongue*. Look up the following five words in a dictionary. Write the part of the body from which each word was originally derived and the language from which it came. Then use it in a sentence explaining what you believe might be the relationship between the English word and the part of the body from which the original word was derived.

1. comet 2. cutlet 3. endorse 4. genuflect 5. harmony

Thick and *thin*, like other pairs of antonyms, are not truly opposites but only two extremes that span a series of infinite gradations. The contrast between thickness and thinness is not absolute, after all, and one must always ask, "Thick compared to what?" or "Thin compared to what?" Objects vary greatly in their density, thickness, and weight. In this lesson you will study words that will help you express the precise degree of density or thinness of many different things.

WORD LIST

attenuate
diaphanous
encumber
evanescent
gossamer
palpable
permeate
pliant
ponderous
viscous

DEFINITIONS

After you have studied the definitions and example for each vocabulary word, write the word on the line to the right.

1. **attenuate** (ə-tĕn'yoo-āt') *trans. verb* **a.** To decrease the density of; rarefy.
b. To make thin in size. **c.** To reduce in force, size, value, or amount; weaken.
d. To reduce the severity or destructiveness of (a disease or germ). *intrans. verb*
To become thin, weak, or less dense. (From the Latin *ad-*, meaning "to," and *tenuis*, meaning "thin")

Related Word attenuation *noun*
Example Radio waves are *attenuated* in certain layers of the atmosphere.

1. _____

2. **diaphanous** (dī-ăf'ə-nəs) *adjective* **a.** So fine or thin in texture as to be transparent or nearly transparent. **b.** Having great fineness and delicacy of form. **c.** Vague or insubstantial. (From the Greek *dia-*, meaning "through," and *phainein*, meaning "to show")

Example The bride wore a veil of *diaphanous* silk.

2. _____
See *gossamer.*

3. **encumber** (ĕn-kŭm'bər) *trans. verb* **a.** To weigh down; burden. **b.** To hinder the action or functions of. **c.** To burden (something) with a legal claim, especially a debt: *encumber an estate.* (From the French word *encombrer*, meaning "to block up")

Related Word encumbrance *noun*
Example While I was shopping, I gave no thought to how I would manage to get home *encumbered* with so many packages.

3. _____

4. **evanescent** (ĕv'ə-nĕs'ənt) *adjective* Vanishing or likely to vanish like a vapor; fleeting. (From the Latin *ex-*, an intensive prefix, and *vanescere*, meaning "to disappear")

Related Words evanesce *verb*; **evanescence** *noun*
Example The actress cherished her moment of *evanescent* fame through long years of obscurity.

4. _____

5. **gossamer** (gŏs′ə-mər) *noun*   **a.** A fine film of cobwebs often seen floating in air or caught on objects.   **b.** A soft, sheer, gauzy fabric.   **c.** Something light, delicate, and of little substance.   *adjective*   Light; filmy; delicate. (From the Old English words *gos*, meaning "goose," and *sumor*, meaning "summer")

   Example   Clouds of pink *gossamer* floated in the crystal blue sky at dawn.

6. **palpable** (păl′pə-bəl) *adjective*   **a.** Capable of being felt or touched.   **b.** Easily perceived by any of the senses or by the mind; obvious; noticeable. (From the Latin word *palpare*, meaning "to touch")

   Related Words   **palpability** *noun;* **palpably** *adverb*
   Example   Osric cried, "A very *palpable* hit" when Hamlet's sword touched Laertes.

7. **permeate** (pûr′mē-āt′) *trans. verb*   **a.** To spread or flow throughout; pervade.   **b.** To pass through the openings or spaces in: *a liquid that can permeate a membrane.* (From the Latin *per-*, meaning "through," and *meare*, meaning "to pass")

   Related Words   **permeability** *noun;* **permeable** *adjective*
   Example   The fragrance of lilacs *permeated* the garden.

8. **pliant** (plī′ənt) *adjective*   **a.** Easily bent or flexed without breaking; supple.   **b.** Easily altered to fit conditions; adaptable.   **c.** Yielding readily to influence. (From the Latin word *plicare*, meaning "to fold")

   Example   These *pliant* willow twigs are excellent for weaving baskets.

9. **ponderous** (pŏn′dər-əs) *adjective*   **a.** Having great weight.   **b.** Graceless or clumsy because of weight.   **c.** Dull and plodding: *a ponderous speech.* (From the Latin word *pondus*, meaning "weight")

   Related Words   **ponderously** *adverb;* **ponderousness** *noun*
   Example   A *ponderous* mass of rock was balanced precariously above us on the mountain trail.

10. **viscous** (vĭs′kəs) *adjective*   **a.** Resembling glue in consistency and stickiness.   **b.** Having a relatively high resistance to flow. (From the Latin word *viscus*, meaning "mistletoe")

    Related Word   **viscosity** *noun*
    Example   Because the gelatin did not set properly, the salad had congealed into a shapeless, *viscous* mass studded with lumps of chicken and broccoli.

5. _____
USAGE NOTE: Both *gossamer* and *diaphanous* describe delicate things. *Diaphanous* stresses transparency and *gossamer*, lightness.

6. _____

7. _____

8. _____

9. _____
USAGE NOTE: Another related word, *ponder* ("to weigh mentally") has none of the negative connotations of *ponderous*.

10. _____

© Great Source   DO NOT COPY

EXERCISE I COMPLETING DEFINITIONS

On the answer line, write the word from the vocabulary list that best completes
each definition.

1. To decrease the density of something is to _____ it.

2. Something so fine in texture as to be transparent is _____.

3. _____ is a fine film of cobwebs.

4. _____ twigs are easily bent.

5. A fluid that spreads throughout something is said to _____ it.

6. Something _____ vanishes like a vapor.

7. A _____ substance resembles glue.

8. An object that has great weight is _____.

9. Something that can be felt or touched is _____.

10. A burden that weighs you down is said to _____ you.

1. _____

2. _____

3. _____

4. _____

5. _____

6. _____

7. _____

8. _____

9. _____

10. _____

EXERCISE 2 USING WORDS CORRECTLY

Decide whether the italicized vocabulary word has been used correctly in the sentence.
On the answer line, write *Correct* for correct use and *Incorrect* for incorrect use.

1. Because the sausages were not *palpable*, Naomi fed them to the dog.

2. The elephants marched in the parade with *ponderous* steps.

3. The spies *permeated* to the inner recesses of the embassy.

4. The meadow was alive with insects that had wings of *gossamer*.

5. The new treatment greatly *attenuates* the effects of the disease.

6. This *evanescent* soft drink tickles my nose.

7. Mr. Hochstein found it impossible to enjoy the fair, *encumbered* as he was with the
picnic basket, two babies, and the dog.

8. A *diaphanous* curtain permitted a tantalizing view of the room beyond.

9. This animal is *viscous* and should be locked up.

10. Some praise Ms. Leslie's *pliant* nature, but I consider her spineless.

1. _____

2. _____

3. _____

4. _____

5. _____

6. _____

7. _____

8. _____

9. _____

10. _____

EXERCISE 3 CHOOSING THE BEST WORD

Decide which vocabulary word or related form best expresses the meaning of the
italicized word or phrase in the sentence. On the answer line, write the letter of the
correct choice.

1. This brown, *gluelike* substance is a very important seasoning in authentic Chinese
cooking.
   a. diaphanous   b. pliant   c. viscous   d. ponderous

2. From time to time, Charles has a *fleeting* idea that startles him with its brilliance
and profundity.
   a. diaphanous   b. evanescent   c. palpable   d. ponderous

1. _____

2. _____

3. The cane had to be soaked in water to make it *flexible* before it could be woven into chair seats.
   a. viscous   **b.** attenuated   **c.** palpable   **d.** pliant

   3. _____

4. The atmosphere of mistrust and suspicion was so strong as to be almost *capable of being felt.*
   a. palpable   **b.** permeable   **c.** diaphanous   **d.** ponderous

   4. _____

5. Many an evening Dr. Anton has fallen asleep over some *dull* volume of ancient medical lore.
   a. ponderous   **b.** encumbering   **c.** attenuated   **d.** viscous

   5. _____

6. The painter has achieved a truly *fine and delicate* effect in representing sunlight shining on a misty lake.
   a. evanescent   **b.** diaphanous   **c.** palpable   **d.** pliant

   6. _____

7. The actress had a proud, regal bearing and wore the heavy brocade costume as if it were *a soft, sheer, gauzy fabric.*
   a. permeable   **b.** evanescent   **c.** viscous   **d.** gossamer

   7. _____

8. Water cannot *pass through* this vinyl cloth, which makes it ideal for raincoats.
   a. encumber   **b.** attenuate   **c.** permeate   **d.** evanesce

   8. _____

9. Over the centuries the ambitions of the middle class caused the *weakening* of the power and privileges of the aristocracy.
   a. encumbrance   **b.** attenuation   **c.** permeating   **d.** evanescence

   9. _____

10. The property was very attractive and quite cheap, but it was *burdened* with a mortgage and unpaid taxes.
    a. ponderous   **b.** palpable   **c.** encumbered   **d.** permeated

    10. _____

EXERCISE 4 USING DIFFERENT FORMS OF WORDS

Decide which form of the vocabulary word in parentheses best completes the sentence. The form given may be correct. Write your answer on the answer line.

1. That yarn he was spinning about sailing around the world was _____ untrue. *(palpable)*

   1. _____

2. Glass is really not a solid but a liquid with a very high _____. *(viscous)*

   2. _____

3. The mature trees were damaged in the storm, but the more _____ saplings survived intact. *(pliant)*

   3. _____

4. I enjoy one-day hikes the most because then I am least _____ with gear. *(encumber)*

   4. _____

5. Ronda experimented with different techniques for capturing the _____ quality of the morning mist in photographs. *(evanescent)*

   5. _____

6. Lisa made sure that the stain _____ the wood thoroughly before she varnished the table. *(permeate)*

   6. _____

7. Both artists liked to draw angels; one gave them powerful birdlike wings, and the other, wings of _____. *(gossamer)*

   7. _____

8. It is hard to believe that someone who moves so _____ and awkwardly was once trained in classical ballet. *(ponderous)*

   8. _____

9. While Napoleon was in power, _____ dresses were the height of fashion, and many women became ill from the cold. *(diaphanous)*

   9. _____

10. This cloth is made from glass fibers _____ to the thickness of a fine silk thread. *(attenuate)*

    10. _____

© Great Source   DO NOT COPY

READING COMPREHENSION

Each numbered sentence in the following passage contains an italicized vocabulary word. After you read the passage, you will complete an exercise.

SPIDER LORE: FACT AND FICTION

Few things in nature are wholly good or wholly bad. The spider, for example, is something that many people both admire and fear. They marvel at its skill in making webs, but they try to avoid getting too close lest they suffer a poisonous bite. **(1)** There are many *ponderous* scientific books that describe spiders in overwhelming detail. Popular lore, however, is concerned with their more observable traits.

(2) The spider's most noticeable and admirable trait is its ability to spin thread and weave beautiful, *diaphanous* webs. **(3)** All spiders produce silk, a fibrous, liquid protein that hardens as it is spun out and *attenuated* to a fine thread. There are different kinds of silk. One kind is used for the cases that protect the spider's eggs. **(4)** Other kinds, including a *viscous* one for trapping prey, are used for webs. **(5)** These delicate structures look *evanescent* and fragile, but the silk is quite strong. In fact, the silk of one kind of spider is the strongest natural fiber known.

(6) Spiders build webs everywhere: on trees, on houses, and even on *pliant* blades of grass. **(7)** The *gossamer* that festoons lawns and meadows was the inspiration for the classical myth about the origins of the spider. Arachne, a weaver of great skill, challenged Athena, the goddess of handicrafts, to a weaving competition. Athena was outraged when she saw that the girl's work was as good as her own, so she changed Arachne into a spider. The spider, called *arachne* in Greek, kept Arachne's skill as well as her name.

While people admire the spider's webs, they also fear its venom. **(8)** Most spiders, however, are not poisonous, and their scarcely *palpable* bite is too weak to penetrate human skin. But some spiders are poisonous, and a very few are dangerously so. The venom of the black widow spider is well known. Although fatal to her prey, and sometimes to her mate, it rarely poses serious danger to human beings. Many poisonous spiders do not produce enough venom to cause serious harm to a creature as large as a human being. A bee or wasp sting is often more painful and more dangerous.

(9) A species of European wolf spider, the female of which goes about *encumbered* with a swarm of young, was once credited with a poisonous bite. The Italians called it the tarantula. Their cure for its bite, which was thought to be fatal, was the *tarantella,* a whirling dance of great liveliness, even frenzy. The tarantella became very popular simply as a dance, and it was accompanied by its characteristic music.

Spinner, weaver, poisoner, rival of the gods—for such a small animal, the spider has loomed large in the imagination of human beings. **(10)** Whatever weighty scientific volumes might say, most people will continue to be of two minds about spiders, and their uncertainty will continue to *permeate* folklore.

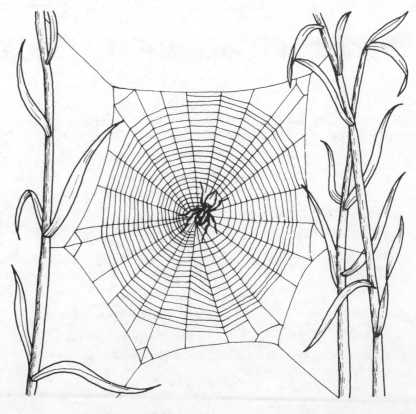

Each of the following statements corresponds to a numbered sentence in the passage. Each statement contains a blank and is followed by four answer choices. Decide which choice fits best in the blank. The word or phrase that you choose must express roughly the same meaning as the italicized word in the passage. Write the letter of your choice on the answer line.

1. There are many _____ scientific books that describe spiders in great detail.
   a. thoughtful   b. dull   c. popular   d. old

1. _____

2. Spiders weave beautiful, _____ webs.
   a. delicate   b. monotonous   c. mythological   d. circular

2. _____

3. A spider's silk is _____ to a fine thread.
   a. spun out   b. reduced in thickness   c. similar   d. hardened

3. _____

4. A _____ kind of silk is used for trapping prey.
   a. thin   b. liquid   c. fibrous   d. sticky

4. _____

5. The delicate webs look _____ and fragile.
   a. long-lasting   b. wet   c. likely to vanish   d. transparent

5. _____

6. Spiders build webs even on _____ blades of grass.
   a. green   b. flexible   c. dewy   d. fresh

6. _____

7. The _____ that festoons lawns inspired a myth.
   a. fine film of cobwebs   b. dew   c. grass   d. spider

7. _____

8. Most spiders have a bite that _____.
   a. resists treatment   b. is poisonous   c. can hardly be felt   d. is harmless

8. _____

9. The female of the wolf spider goes about _____ young.
   a. infested with   b. accompanied by   c. free of   d. burdened with

9. _____

10. People's uncertainty about spiders will continue to _____ folklore.
    a. enrich   b. preserve   c. pervade   d. confuse

10. _____

PRACTICE WITH ANALOGIES

Directions On the answer line, write the letter of the phrase that best completes the analogy.

See page 79 for some strategies to use with analogies.

1. CONDESCENDING : RESPECT :: (A) depraved : purity
   (B) sympathetic : compassion   (C) renowned : celebrity
   (D) merciful : forgiveness   (E) theatrical : emotion

1. _____

2. LACKEY : SERVILE :: (A) pacifist : argumentative   (B) apprentice : skill
   (C) soldier : bravery   (D) egoist : conceited   (E) athlete : victory

2. _____

3. CONQUEROR : SUBJUGATES :: (A) president : elects   (B) guard : protects
   (C) idol : worships   (D) advertiser : buys   (E) judge : votes

3. _____

4. DIAPHANOUS : LIGHT :: (A) porous : liquid   (B) melodious : sound
   (C) raucous : sound   (D) obnoxious : smell   (E) meticulous : detail

4. _____

5. PLIANT : BEND :: (A) valuable : steal   (B) hefty : lift
   (C) elastic : stretch   (D) fluid : melt   (E) slippery : grasp

5. _____

6. VISCOUS : FLOW :: (A) brittle : break   (B) extinct : die
   (C) buoyant : float   (D) perpetual : last   (E) parallel : meet

6. _____

© Great Source DO NOT COPY

READING SKILLS

FIVE ADJECTIVE SUFFIXES

A **suffix** is a group of letters added to the end of a root. (A root is the part of a word containing its basic meaning; a root may even be a complete word.) A suffix has the function of changing the part of speech of the word or root. The suffixes *-ive, -al, -ial, -ish*, and *-less* change nouns and verbs into adjectives. The five suffixes and their adjective meanings are given below. Each suffix and definition is followed by (1) a root or a word containing the root, (2) the adjective that can be formed by adding the suffix, and (3) the definition of the adjective. Notice that adding a suffix may necessitate a spelling change.

Suffix Meaning	Root Word	Adjective	Adjective Definition
1. *-ive:* performing or tending toward an action	create	creative	having the ability to create
2. *-al:* of, relating to, characterized by	autumn	autumnal	like or relating to autumn
3. *-ial:* of, relating to, characterized by	controversy	controversial	characterized by controversy
4. *-ish:* characteristic of, of, somewhat	freak	freakish	characteristic of a freak; unusual
5. *-less:* without	cease	ceaseless	without stopping

To determine the meaning of unfamiliar words ending with these and other suffixes, use the same procedure that you use for analyzing words with prefixes. Remember that context clues may also help you to arrive at a possible definition. Be sure to verify the meaning by looking the word up in the dictionary.

EXERCISE USING FIVE ADJECTIVE SUFFIXES

Each sentence contains an italicized adjective ending with the suffix *-ive, -al, -ial, -ish*, or *-less. Step 1:* Taking the context into consideration, write your own definition of the word. *Step 2:* Write the dictionary definition of the word. Choose the definition that best fits the way the word is used in the sentence. *Step 3:* Write a sentence of your own in which you use the word correctly.

1. Zach said that any further attempts to start the motorboat would be *pointless*.

   Your Definition _____

   Dictionary Definition _____

   Sentence _____

2. Respected by nearly everyone, Mrs. Sandoval is one of the most *influential* people in the community.

Your Definition _____

Dictionary Definition _____

Sentence _____

3. Lauren says that her little brother has a *mulish* disposition.

Your Definition _____

Dictionary Definition _____

Sentence _____

4. As far as a hundred miles inland, the river remains *tidal*.

Your Definition _____

Dictionary Definition _____

Sentence _____

5. Evan spoke of the *reflective* mood of the sonnet.

Your Definition _____

Dictionary Definition _____

Sentence _____

6. Lucky was a charming but utterly *witless* animal.

Your Definition _____

Dictionary Definition _____

Sentence _____

7. As we toured the campus, we were impressed by the *palatial* size of the library.

Your Definition _____

Dictionary Definition _____

Sentence _____

8. The college team's level of play was *amateurish* when compared with that of professional athletes.

Your Definition _____

Dictionary Definition _____

Sentence _____

9. In that school the performing arts are an *integral* part of the curriculum.

Your Definition _____

Dictionary Definition _____

Sentence _____

10. Joanne may not be *demonstrative*, but she is very fond of her grandparents.

Your Definition _____

Dictionary Definition _____

Sentence _____

© Great Source   DO NOT COPY

LESSON I	LESSON I	LESSON I	LESSON I	LESSON I
acronym	affix	coinage	colloquial	malapropism
onomatopoeia	palindrome	portmanteau word	simile	spoonerism

LESSON I	LESSON I	LESSON I	LESSON I	LESSON I

LESSON 2	LESSON 2	LESSON 2	LESSON 2	LESSON 2
diligence	fastidious	foresight	judicious	meticulous
minutiae	prudent	punctilious	selective	systematic

LESSON 2	LESSON 2	LESSON 2	LESSON 2	LESSON 2

LESSON 3	LESSON 3	LESSON 3	LESSON 3	LESSON 3
beguile	civility	decorum	demeanor	foolhardy
glib	ignoble	mores	provincial	unseemly

LESSON 3	LESSON 3	LESSON 3	LESSON 3	LESSON 3

acronym (ăk′rə-nĭm′) *n.* Name formed by combining initial letters of words.

© Great Source

affix (ăf′ĭks′) *n.* A word element that is attached to a base, stem, or root.

© Great Source

coinage (koi′nĭj) *n.* The invention of new words.

© Great Source

colloquial (kə-lō′kwē-əl) *adj.* Referring to informal speech or writing.

© Great Source

malapropism (măl′ə-prŏp-ĭz′ əm) *n.* A humorous misuse of a word.

© Great Source

onomatopoeia (ŏn′ə-măt′ə-pē′ə) *n.* Word that imitates what it stands for.

© Great Source

palindrome (păl′ĭn-drōm′) *n.* Word reading the same backward or forward.

© Great Source

portmanteau word (pôrt-măn′tō wûrd) *n.* A word blend.

© Great Source

simile (sĭm′ə-lē) *n.* Comparison of two unlike things, containing *like* or *as*.

© Great Source

spoonerism (spoo′nə-rĭz′ əm) *n.* Accidental, humorous distortion of words.

© Great Source

diligence (dĭl′ə-jəns) *n.* Earnest effort to accomplish a task.

© Great Source

fastidious (fă-stĭd′ē-əs) *adj.* Difficult to satisfy or please.

© Great Source

foresight (fôr′sīt′) *n.* Ability to see and prepare for future events.

© Great Source

judicious (jōō-dĭsh′əs) *adj.* Having or exhibiting sound judgment.

© Great Source

meticulous (mĭ-tĭk′yə-ləs) *adj.* Extremely careful and precise.

© Great Source

minutiae (mĭ-nōō′shē-ē′) *n.* Minor or trivial details.

© Great Source

prudent (prōōd′nt) *adj.* Using caution in handling practical matters.

© Great Source

punctilious (pŭngk-tĭl′ē-əs) *adj.* Attentive to etiquette; exact.

© Great Source

selective (sĭ-lĕk′tĭv) *adj.* Careful in choosing; discriminating.

© Great Source

systematic (sĭs′tə-măt′ĭk) *adj.* Having a system, method, or plan.

© Great Source

beguile (bĭ-gīl′) *tr. v.* To deceive; trick; amuse.

© Great Source

civility (sĭ-vĭl′ĭ-tē) *n.* Politeness; courtesy.

© Great Source

decorum (dĭ-kôr′əm) *n.* Appropriateness of behavior or conduct.

© Great Source

demeanor (dĭ-mē′nər) *n.* The way in which one conducts oneself.

© Great Source

foolhardy (fōōl′här′dē) *adj.* Foolishly bold daring; rash.

© Great Source

glib (glĭb) *adj.* Performed with careless, often thoughtless ease.

© Great Source

ignoble (ĭg-nō′bəl) *adj.* Not having a noble character or purpose.

© Great Source

mores (môr′āz′) *n.* Accepted customs of a social group.

© Great Source

provincial (prə-vĭn′shəl) *adj.* Of areas away from a country's capital.

© Great Source

unseemly (ŭn-sēm′lē) *adj.* Not in good taste; improper.

© Great Source

LESSON 4 abject	LESSON 5 objectionable	LESSON 5 apprehensive	LESSON 5 inevitable	LESSON 6 assail	LESSON 6 invincible
LESSON 4 conjecture	LESSON 4 projectile	LESSON 5 categorical	LESSON 5 precarious	LESSON 6 bulwark	LESSON 6 mettle
LESSON 4 dejected	LESSON 4 reject	LESSON 5 conclusive	LESSON 5 qualm	LESSON 6 citadel	LESSON 6 resilient
LESSON 4 injection	LESSON 4 subjective	LESSON 5 dubious	LESSON 5 unequivocal	LESSON 6 fortitude	LESSON 6 stalwart
LESSON 4 jetty	LESSON 4 trajectory	LESSON 5 indeterminate	LESSON 5 vacillate	LESSON 6 haven	LESSON 6 stamina

Vocabulary Cards

abject (ăb′jĕkt′) *adj.* Lacking all self-respect; contemptible.
© Great Source

conjecture (kən-jĕk′chər) *n.* Opinion formed from incomplete evidence.
© Great Source

dejected (dĭ-jĕk′tĭd) *adj.* Depressed; disheartened.
© Great Source

injection (ĭn-jĕk′shən) *n.* The forcing of something into something else.
© Great Source

jetty (jĕt′ē) *n.* A structure projecting into a body of water; a wharf.
© Great Source

objectionable (əb-jĕk′shə-nə-bəl) *adj.* Arousing disapproval.
© Great Source

projectile (prə-jĕk′təl) *n.* An object that is launched through space.
© Great Source

reject (rĭ-jĕkt′) *tr. v.* To refuse to accept, use, grant, or consider.
© Great Source

subjective (səb-jĕk′tĭv) *adj.* Taking place within an individual's mind.
© Great Source

trajectory (trə-jĕk′tə-rē) *n.* The path made by a moving body.
© Great Source

apprehensive (ăp′rĭ-hĕn′sĭv) *adj.* Anxious or fearful about the future.
© Great Source

categorical (kăt′ĭ-gôr′ĭ-kəl) *adj.* Without exception or qualification.
© Great Source

conclusive (kən-kloo′sĭv) *adj.* Serving to put an end to doubt.
© Great Source

dubious (doo′bē-əs) *adj.* Doubtful; uncertain.
© Great Source

indeterminate (ĭn′dĭ-tûr′mə-nĭt) *adj.* Not capable of being determined.
© Great Source

inevitable (ĭn-ĕv′ĭ-tə-bəl) *adj.* Incapable of being avoided.
© Great Source

precarious (prĭ-kâr′ē-əs) *adj.* Dangerously lacking in stability; risky.
© Great Source

qualm (kwäm) *n.* A sensation of doubt or misgiving; uneasiness.
© Great Source

unequivocal (ŭn′ĭ-kwĭv′ə-kəl) *adj.* Leaving no doubt; perfectly clear.
© Great Source

vacillate (văs′ə-lāt′) *intr. v.* To waver indecisively; hesitate.
© Great Source

assail (ə-sāl′) *tr. v.* To attack; assault.
© Great Source

bulwark (bool′wərk) *n.* A defensive wall; rampart.
© Great Source

citadel (sĭt′ə-dəl) *n.* A fortress in or near a city.
© Great Source

fortitude (fôr′tĭ-tood′) *n.* Courage in the face of hardship.
© Great Source

haven (hā′vən) *n.* A place of rest or refuge; sanctuary.
© Great Source

invincible (ĭn-vĭn′sə-bəl) *adj.* Too strong or great to be defeated.
© Great Source

mettle (mĕt′l) *n.* Spirit; daring; pluck.
© Great Source

resilient (rĭ-zĭl′yənt) *adj.* Recovering strength or spirits quickly.
© Great Source

stalwart (stôl′wərt) *adj.* Physically strong; sturdy; robust.
© Great Source

stamina (stăm′ə-nə) *n.* Endurance; resistance to fatigue or illness.
© Great Source

LESSON 7 accredit	LESSON 7 credulous	LESSON 8 alacrity
LESSON 7 credence	LESSON 7 creed	LESSON 8 incite
LESSON 7 credential	LESSON 7 discredit	LESSON 8 composure
LESSON 7 credibility	LESSON 7 incredible	LESSON 8 indolent
LESSON 7 creditable	LESSON 7 miscreant	LESSON 8 imperturbable

LESSON 8 ennui	LESSON 8 impetuous	LESSON 9 brazen
LESSON 8 inert	LESSON 8 serenity	LESSON 9 complaisant
LESSON 8 pandemonium	LESSON 9 conspicuous	LESSON 9 intrepid
LESSON 9 docile	LESSON 9 reserved	
LESSON 9 flamboyant	LESSON 9 strident	LESSON 9 pacific
LESSON 9 unabashed		

accredit (ə-krĕd'ĭt) tr. v. To recognize as meeting official standards.
© Great Source

credence (krēd'ns) n. Acceptance as true or valid; belief.
© Great Source

credential (krĭ-dĕn'shəl) n. Something entitling a person to credit.
© Great Source

credibility (krĕd'ə-bĭl'ĭ-tē) n. The quality of deserving confidence.
© Great Source

creditable (krĕd'ĭ-tə-bəl) adj. Deserving commendation; praiseworthy.
© Great Source

credulous (krĕj'ə-ləs) adj. Tending to believe too readily.
© Great Source

creed (krēd) n. Any statement that guides a person's actions.
© Great Source

discredit (dĭs-krĕd'ĭt) tr. v. To cast doubt on; destroy belief in.
© Great Source

incredible (ĭn-krĕd'ə-bəl) adj. Too extraordinary to be possible.
© Great Source

miscreant (mĭs'krē-ənt) n. A person who behaves badly or criminally.
© Great Source

alacrity (ə-lăk'rĭ-tē) n. Speed and willingness in responding.
© Great Source

composure (kəm-pō'zhər) n. Control over one's emotions.
© Great Source

ennui (ŏn-wē') n. Listlessness resulting from inactivity; boredom.
© Great Source

imperturbable (ĭm'pər-tûr'bə-bəl) adj. Not easily disturbed or excited.
© Great Source

impetuous (ĭm-pĕch'oo-əs) adj. Tending toward suddenness of action.
© Great Source

incite (ĭn-sīt') tr. v. To provoke to action; rouse.
© Great Source

indolent (ĭn'də-lənt) adj. Reluctant to exert oneself; habitually lazy.
© Great Source

inert (ĭn-ûrt') adj. Having no power to move or act; lifeless.
© Great Source

pandemonium (păn'də-mō'nē-əm) n. Wild uproar or noise; tumult.
© Great Source

serenity (sə-rĕn'ĭ-tē) n. The quality of being untroubled or unruffled.
© Great Source

brazen (brā'zən) adj. Rudely bold; insolent.
© Great Source

complaisant (kəm-plā'sənt) adj. Showing a willingness to please.
© Great Source

conspicuous (kən-spĭk'yoo-əs) adj. Easy to notice; obvious.
© Great Source

docile (dŏs'əl) adj. Easily managed or taught; gentle.
© Great Source

flamboyant (flăm-boi'ənt) adj. Exaggerated in style or manner; showy.
© Great Source

intrepid (ĭn-trĕp'ĭd) adj. Courageous; fearless; bold.
© Great Source

pacific (pə-sĭf'ĭk) adj. Promoting peace; peaceful; serene.
© Great Source

reserved (rĭ-zûrvd') adj. Quiet and restrained in manner.
© Great Source

strident (strīd'nt) adj. Having a shrill, harsh, and grating effect.
© Great Source

unabashed (ŭn'ə-băsht') adj. Not embarrassed or ashamed.
© Great Source

LESSON 10 avert

LESSON 10 diversify

LESSON 10 diversion

LESSON 10 inadvertent

LESSON 10 incontrovertible

LESSON 10 invert

LESSON 10 irreversible

LESSON 10 revert

LESSON 10 versatile

LESSON 10 vertigo

LESSON 11 flagrant

LESSON 11 sequester

LESSON 11 flaunt

LESSON 11 furtive

LESSON 11 ostensible

LESSON 11 salient

LESSON 11 subterfuge

LESSON 11 latent

LESSON 11 surreptitious

LESSON 11 unobtrusive

LESSON 12 didactic

LESSON 12 edify

LESSON 12 elucidate

LESSON 12 erudite

LESSON 12 explicit

LESSON 12 imbue

LESSON 12 indoctrinate

LESSON 12 instill

LESSON 12 pedagogy

LESSON 12 pedantic

avert
(ə-vûrt´) tr. v. To turn away or aside.

© Great Source

diversify
(dĭ-vûr´sə-fī´) tr. v. To give variety to; vary.

© Great Source

diversion
(dĭ-vûr´zhən) n. Something that relaxes or entertains.

© Great Source

inadvertent
(ĭn´əd-vûr´tnt) adj. Accidental; unintentional.

© Great Source

incontrovertible
(ĭn-kŏn´trə-vûr´tə-bəl) adj. Indisputable.

© Great Source

invert
(ĭn-vûrt´) tr. v. To turn inside out or upside down.

© Great Source

irreversible
(ĭr´ĭ-vûr´sə-bəl) adj. Incapable of being reversed.

© Great Source

revert
(rĭ-vûrt´) intr. v. To return to a former condition or belief.

© Great Source

versatile
(vûr´sə-təl) adj. Capable of doing many things competently.

© Great Source

vertigo
(vûr´tĭ-gō´) n. The sensation of dizziness.

© Great Source

flagrant
(flā´grənt) adj. Extremely or deliberately noticeable.

© Great Source

flaunt
(flônt) tr. v. To show off in order to impress others.

© Great Source

furtive
(fûr´tĭv) adj. Done quickly and with stealth; sly.

© Great Source

latent
(lāt´nt) adj. Capable of coming into existence but not active.

© Great Source

ostensible
(ŏ-stĕn´sə-bəl) adj. Seeming; professed.

© Great Source

salient
(sā´lē-ənt) adj. Standing out and attracting attention.

© Great Source

sequester
(sĭ-kwĕs´tər) tr. v. To remove or withdraw from public view.

© Great Source

subterfuge
(sŭb´tər-fyōōj´) adj. Deception by means of a strategy.

© Great Source

surreptitious
(sûr´əp-tĭsh´əs) adj. Done or acting in secret.

© Great Source

unobtrusive
(ŭn´əb-trōō´sĭv) adj. Not readily noticeable.

© Great Source

didactic
(dī-dăk´tĭk) adj. Intended to teach or instruct.

© Great Source

edify
(ĕd´ə-fī´) tr. v. To instruct in order to improve.

© Great Source

elucidate
(ĭ-lōō´sĭ-dāt´) tr. v. To make clear or plain.

© Great Source

erudite
(ĕr´yə-dīt´) adj. Possessing deep and extensive learning.

© Great Source

explicit
(ĭk-splĭs´ĭt) adj. Expressed clearly and precisely.

© Great Source

imbue
(ĭm-byōō´) tr. v. To pervade or permeate as if with a dye.

© Great Source

indoctrinate
(ĭn-dŏk´trə-nāt´) tr. v. To teach a group's beliefs to.

© Great Source

instill
(ĭn-stĭl´) tr. v. To introduce gradually.

© Great Source

pedagogy
(pĕd´ə-gō´jē) n. The art or profession of teaching.

© Great Source

pedantic
(pə-dăn´tĭk) adj. Marked by a concern for minute details.

© Great Source

LESSON 13 concurrent	LESSON 13 courier	LESSON 13 cursory	LESSON 13 discursive	LESSON 31 incur
LESSON 13 incursion	LESSON 13 precursor	LESSON 13 recourse	LESSON 13 recurrent	LESSON 13 succor
LESSON 14 acrimonious	LESSON 14 chastise	LESSON 14 derogatory	LESSON 14 disparage	LESSON 14 harass
LESSON 14 impugn	LESSON 14 innuendo	LESSON 14 invective	LESSON 14 reprove	LESSON 14 vilify
LESSON 15 aegis	LESSON 15 amends	LESSON 15 conciliatory	LESSON 15 conducive	LESSON 15 extricate
LESSON 15 foster	LESSON 15 importune	LESSON 15 mediate	LESSON 15 mitigate	LESSON 15 rectify

concurrent	(kən-kûr′ənt) *adj.* Occuring at the same time. © Great Source
courier	(kŏŏr′ē-ər) *n.* A messenger. © Great Source
cursory	(kûr′sə-rē) *adj.* Hasty; not thorough. © Great Source
discursive	(dĭ-skûr′sĭv) *adj.* Rambling; digressive. © Great Source
incur	(ĭn-kûr′) *tr. v.* To bring something upon oneself. © Great Source
incursion	(ĭn-kûr′zhən) *n.* An attack on enemy territory; a raid. © Great Source
precursor	(prĭ-kûr′sər) *n.* Something that precedes something else. © Great Source
recourse	(rē′kôrs′) *n.* A turning to something or someone for aid. © Great Source
recurrent	(rĭ-kûr′ənt) *adj.* Happening repeatedly. © Great Source
succor	(sŭk′ər) *n.* Help in time of distress. © Great Source
acrimonious	(ăk′rə-mō′nē-əs) *adj.* Bitter in language or tone. © Great Source
chastise	(chăs-tīz′) *tr. v.* To punish for misbehavior or wrongdoing. © Great Source
derogatory	(dĭ-rŏg′ə-tôr′ē) *adj.* Detracting from the character of. © Great Source
disparage	(dĭ-spăr′ĭj) *tr. v.* To speak of as unimportant or inferior. © Great Source
harass	(hə-răs′) *tr. v.* To bother or torment persistently. © Great Source
impugn	(ĭm-pyōōn′) *tr. v.* To criticize or refute by argumentation. © Great Source
innuendo	(ĭn′yōō-ĕn′dō) *n.* A roundabout, often spiteful reference. © Great Source
invective	(ĭn-vĕk′tĭv) *n.* Sharp, insulting words used to attack. © Great Source
reprove	(rĭ-prōōv′) *tr. v.* To scold or correct with kindly intent. © Great Source
vilify	(vĭl′ə-fī′) *tr. v.* To utter slanderous statements against. © Great Source
aegis	(ē′jĭs) *n.* Sponsorship; protection. © Great Source
amends	(ə-mĕndz′) *n.* Compensation for insult, loss, or injury. © Great Source
conciliatory	(kən-sĭl′ē-ə-tôr′ē) *adj.* Tending to win over or soothe. © Great Source
conducive	(kən-dōō′sĭv) *adj.* Tending to cause or to help bring about. © Great Source
extricate	(ĕk′strĭ-kāt′) *tr. v.* To free from entanglement. © Great Source
foster	(fô′stər) *tr. v.* To promote the development or growth of. © Great Source
importune	(ĭm′pôr-tōōn′) *tr. v.* To press with insistent requests. © Great Source
mediate	(mē′dē-āt′) *tr. v.* To help opposing sides come to agreement. © Great Source
mitigate	(mĭt′ĭ-gāt′) *tr. v.* To make less severe or intense. © Great Source
rectify	(rĕk′tə-fī′) *tr. v.* To set right; remedy. © Great Source

LESSON 16	LESSON 16	LESSON 16	LESSON 16	LESSON 16
gradient	gradation	egress	deceased	concede
LESSON 16	**LESSON 16**	**LESSON 16**	**LESSON 16**	**LESSON 16**
unprecedented	transgress	secession	regress	predecessor
LESSON 17	**LESSON 17**	**LESSON 17**	**LESSON 17**	**LESSON 17**
differentiate	deviate	comparable	antithesis	analogous
LESSON 17	**LESSON 17**	**LESSON 17**	**LESSON 17**	**LESSON 17**
tantamount	nuance	homogeneous	heterogeneous	disparity
LESSON 18	**LESSON 18**	**LESSON 18**	**LESSON 18**	**LESSON 18**
hierarchy	hegemony	feudal	despot	autonomy
LESSON 18	**LESSON 18**	**LESSON 18**	**LESSON 18**	**LESSON 18**
usurp	totalitarian	sovereign	regime	prerogative

concede (kən-sēd') *tr. v.* To acknowledge as true, often unwillingly.
© Great Source

deceased (dĭ-sēst') *adj.* No longer living; dead.
© Great Source

egress (ē'grĕs') *n.* A path or means of going out; an exit.
© Great Source

gradation (grā-dā'shən) *n.* A stage in a series of gradual changes.
© Great Source

gradient (grā'dē-ənt) *n.* The degree to which something inclines.
© Great Source

predecessor (prĕd'ĭ-sĕs'ər) *n.* Something coming before another in time.
© Great Source

regress (rĭ-grĕs') *intr. v.* To go back; return to a previous condition.
© Great Source

secession (sĭ-sĕsh'ən) *n.* Formal withdrawal from membership in a union.
© Great Source

transgress (trăns-grĕs') *tr. v.* To go beyond or over (a limit).
© Great Source

unprecedented (ŭn'prĕs'ĭ-dĕn'tĭd) *adj.* Not having occurred before.
© Great Source

analogous (ə-năl'ə-gəs) *adj.* Similar in certain qualities or uses.
© Great Source

antithesis (ăn-tĭth'ĭ-sĭs) *n.* Direct contrast; opposition.
© Great Source

comparable (kŏm'pər-ə-bəl) *adj.* Having like traits; similar.
© Great Source

deviate (dē'vē-āt') *intr. v.* To move away from a specified course.
© Great Source

differentiate (dĭf'ə-rĕn'shē-āt') *tr. v.* To show the differences in.
© Great Source

disparity (dĭ-spăr'ĭ-tē) *n.* Difference in age, rank, or degree.
© Great Source

heterogeneous (hĕt'ər-ə-jē'nē-əs) *adj.* Consisting of dissimilar elements.
© Great Source

homogeneous (hō'mə-jē'nē-əs) *adj.* Consisting of similar elements.
© Great Source

nuance (noo-äns') *n.* A slight difference in meaning, color, or tone.
© Great Source

tantamount (tăn'tə-mount') *adj.* Equivalent in significance or value.
© Great Source

autonomy (ô-tŏn'ə-mē) *n.* Independence; self-government.
© Great Source

despot (dĕs'pət) *n.* A ruler having absolute power or authority.
© Great Source

feudal (fyood'l) *adj.* Typical of the medieval European social system.
© Great Source

hegemony (hĭ-jĕm'ə-nē) *n.* Dominion of one country over another.
© Great Source

hierarchy (hī'ə-rär'kē) *n.* An order of persons classified by rank.
© Great Source

prerogative (prĭ-rŏg'ə-tĭv) *n.* A hereditary or official privilege.
© Great Source

regime (rā-zhēm') *n.* A government in power.
© Great Source

sovereign (sŏv'ər-ĭn) *n.* The chief of state, usually in a monarchy.
© Great Source

totalitarian (tō-tăl'ĭ-târ'ē-ən) *adj.* Of a government with absolute power.
© Great Source

usurp (yoo-sûrp') *tr. v.* To seize and retain without legal authority.
© Great Source

LESSON 19 apathy	LESSON 19 presentiment	LESSON 20 culpable	LESSON 20 misdemeanor	LESSON 21 banter	LESSON 21 hilarity
LESSON 19 assent	LESSON 19 sensational	LESSON 20 exonerate	LESSON 20 purloin	LESSON 21 caricature	LESSON 21 ludicrous
LESSON 19 empathy	LESSON 19 sensibility	LESSON 20 extort	LESSON 20 ruffian	LESSON 21 droll	LESSON 21 mirth
LESSON 19 pathetic	LESSON 19 sententious	LESSON 20 illicit	LESSON 20 unscrupulous	LESSON 21 facetious	LESSON 21 whimsical
LESSON 19 pathology	LESSON 19 sentiment	LESSON 20 incorrigible	LESSON 20 vile	LESSON 21 flippant	LESSON 21 witticism

apathy (ăp'ə-thē) *n.* Lack of feeling or emotion.

© Great Source

assent (ə-sĕnt') *n.* Acceptance of a proposal or statement.

© Great Source

empathy (ĕm'pə-thē) *n.* Understanding of another's feelings or situation.

© Great Source

pathetic (pə-thĕt'ĭk) *adj.* Expressing or arousing pity or tenderness.

© Great Source

pathology (pă-thŏl'ə-jē) *n.* Scientific and medical study of a disease.

© Great Source

presentiment (prĭ-zĕn'tə-mənt) *n.* A sense of something about to occur.

© Great Source

sensational (sĕn-sā'shə-nəl) *adj.* Arousing great interest.

© Great Source

sensibility (sĕn' sə-bĭl'ĭ-tē) *n.* Ability to feel, sense, or perceive.

© Great Source

sententious (sĕn-tĕn'shəs) *adj.* Likely to give advice self-righteously.

© Great Source

sentiment (sĕn'tə-mənt) *n.* A thought or attitude based on feeling.

© Great Source

culpable (kŭl'pə-bəl) *adj.* Responsible for wrong or error.

© Great Source

exonerate (ĭg-zŏn'ə-rāt') *tr. v.* To free from a charge.

© Great Source

extort (ĭk-stôrt') *tr. v.* To obtain by threats or other coercive means.

© Great Source

illicit (ĭ-lĭs'ĭt) *adj.* Not permitted by custom or law; illegal.

© Great Source

incorrigible (ĭn-kôr'ĭ-jə-bəl) *adj.* Incapable of being reformed.

© Great Source

misdemeanor (mĭs' dĭ-mē'nər) *n.* An offense less serious than a felony.

© Great Source

purloin (pər-loin') *tr. v.* To steal.

© Great Source

ruffian (rŭf'ē-ən) *n.* A tough or rowdy person.

© Great Source

unscrupulous (ŭn-skrōō'pyə-ləs) *adj.* Without scruples or principles.

© Great Source

vile (vīl) *adj.* Unpleasant; disgusting.

© Great Source

banter (băn'tər) *n.* Good-humored, playful conversation.

© Great Source

caricature (kăr'ĭ-kə-chŏŏr') *n.* A distorted, comic representation.

© Great Source

droll (drōl) *adj.* Amusingly odd or comical.

© Great Source

facetious (fə-sē'shəs) *adj.* Playfully humorous.

© Great Source

flippant (flĭp'ənt) *adj.* Marked by a disrespectful frivolity.

© Great Source

hilarity (hĭ-lăr'ĭ-tē) *n.* Loud and lively merriment; boisterousness.

© Great Source

ludicrous (lōō'dĭ-krəs) *adj.* Laughable because of an obvious absurdity.

© Great Source

mirth (mûrth) *n.* Gladness or lightheartedness.

© Great Source

whimsical (hwĭm'zĭ-kəl) *adj.* Playful or fanciful.

© Great Source

witticism (wĭt'ĭ-sĭz'əm) *n.* A witty or clever remark or saying.

© Great Source

LESSON 22 adverse

LESSON 22 averse

LESSON 22 emigrate

LESSON 22 figuratively

LESSON 22 immigrate

LESSON 22 ingenious

LESSON 22 ingenuous

LESSON 22 literally

LESSON 22 persecute

LESSON 22 prosecute

LESSON 23 austerity

LESSON 23 depreciate

LESSON 23 equity

LESSON 23 frugal

LESSON 23 indigent

LESSON 23 munificent

LESSON 23 pecuniary

LESSON 23 recession

LESSON 23 remunerate

LESSON 23 solvent

LESSON 24 adroit

LESSON 24 blasé

LESSON 24 cliché

LESSON 24 clientele

LESSON 24 entrepreneur

LESSON 24 forte

LESSON 24 gauche

LESSON 24 naive

LESSON 24 nonchalant

LESSON 24 rendezvous

adverse (ăd-vûrs′) *adj.* Unfavorable to one's interest or welfare.

© Great Source

averse (ə-vûrs′) *adj.* Having a strong feeling of dislike or reluctance.

© Great Source

emigrate (ĕm′ĭ-grāt′) *intr. v.* To leave one's country for another.

© Great Source

figuratively (fĭg′yər-ə-tĭv-lē) *adv.* In a manner marked by metaphor.

© Great Source

immigrate (ĭm′ĭ-grāt′) *intr. v.* To enter and settle in another country.

© Great Source

ingenious (ĭn-jēn′yəs) *adj.* Having creative or inventive skill.

© Great Source

ingenuous (ĭn-jĕn′yōō-əs) *adj.* Having childlike simplicity.

© Great Source

literally (lĭt′ər-ə-lē) *adv.* According to a word's actual meaning.

© Great Source

persecute (pûr′sĭ-kyōōt′) *tr. v.* To ill-treat persistently.

© Great Source

prosecute (prŏs′ĭ-kyōōt′) *tr. v.* To bring a legal action against.

© Great Source

austerity (ô-stĕr′ĭ-tē) *n.* Strict economy.

© Great Source

depreciate (dĭ-prē′shē-āt′) *intr. v.* To decrease in value.

© Great Source

equity (ĕk′wĭ-tē) *n.* Value of a property after subtracting liabilities.

© Great Source

frugal (frōō′gəl) *adj.* Avoiding the unnecessary expenditure of money.

© Great Source

indigent (ĭn′dĭ-jənt) *adj.* Lacking money to provide life's necessities.

© Great Source

munificent (myōō-nĭf′ĭ-sənt) *adj.* Very generous in giving.

© Great Source

pecuniary (pĭ-kyōō′nē-ĕr′ē) *adj.* Having to do with money.

© Great Source

recession (rĭ-sĕsh′ən) *n.* A moderate decline in economic activity.

© Great Source

remunerate (rĭ-myōō′nə-rāt′) *tr. v.* To pay compensation.

© Great Source

solvent (sŏl′vənt) *adj.* Capable of meeting all financial obligations.

© Great Source

adroit (ə-droit′) *adj.* Showing skill in handling difficult situations.

© Great Source

blasé (blä-zā′) *adj.* Very sophisticated; worldly.

© Great Source

cliché (klē-shā′) *n.* A trite or overused expression or idea.

© Great Source

clientele (klī′ən-tĕl′) *n.* A body of customers or patrons.

© Great Source

entrepreneur (ŏn′trə-prə-nûr′) *n.* Person who organizes a business.

© Great Source

forte (fôrt) *n.* Something in which a person excels.

© Great Source

gauche (gōsh) *adj.* Lacking social experiences or grace; awkward.

© Great Source

naive (nä-ēv′) *adj.* Marked by unaffected simplicity.

© Great Source

nonchalant (nŏn′shə-länt′) *adj.* Carefree and casually unconcerned.

© Great Source

rendezvous (rän′dā-vōō) *n.* A prearranged meeting.

© Great Source

LESSON 25 dilatory	LESSON 25 languid	LESSON 25 lethargy	LESSON 25 quiescent	LESSON 25 repose
LESSON 26 sloth	LESSON 25 somnambulate	LESSON 25 somnolence	LESSON 25 soporific	LESSON 25 stupor
LESSON 26 aggrandize	LESSON 26 exorbitance	LESSON 26 grandiose	LESSON 26 hyperbole	LESSON 26 intemperate
LESSON 26 obsess	LESSON 26 opulence	LESSON 26 profligate	LESSON 26 satiate	LESSON 26 superfluous
LESSON 27 affinity	LESSON 27 animosity	LESSON 27 antipathy	LESSON 27 ardent	LESSON 27 contemptible
LESSON 27 disdain	LESSON 27 enamored	LESSON 27 estrange	LESSON 27 penchant	LESSON 27 repugnance

dilatory (dĭl'ə-tôr'ē) *adj.* Characterized by procrastination.
© Great Source

languid (lăng'gwĭd) *adj.* Lazily slow or relaxed.
© Great Source

lethargy (lĕth'ər-jē) *n.* Drowsy or sluggish indifference.
© Great Source

quiescent (kwē-ĕs'ənt) *adj.* In a condition of inactivity or rest.
© Great Source

repose (rĭ-pōz') *n.* The act or condition of resting.
© Great Source

sloth (slôth) *n.* Laziness; indolence.
© Great Source

somnambulate (sŏm-năm'byə-lāt') *intr. v.* To walk while asleep.
© Great Source

somnolence (sŏm'nə-ləns) *n.* Drowsiness; sleepiness.
© Great Source

soporific (sŏp'ə-rĭf'ĭk) *adj.* Causing or tending to cause sleep.
© Great Source

stupor (stoo'pər) *n.* A condition of reduced consciousness; daze.
© Great Source

aggrandize (ə-grăn'dīz') *tr. v.* To make (something) seem greater.
© Great Source

exorbitance (ĭg-zôr'bĭ-təns) *n.* Condition of exceeding proper limits.
© Great Source

grandiose (grăn'dē-ōs') *adj.* Characterized by affected grandeur.
© Great Source

hyperbole (hī-pûr'bə-lē) *n.* An exaggerated statement.
© Great Source

intemperate (ĭn-tĕm'pər-ĭt) *adj.* Not temperate or moderate.
© Great Source

obsess (əb-sĕs') *tr. v.* To preoccupy the mind excessively.
© Great Source

opulence (ŏp'yə-ləns) *n.* The state of displaying great wealth.
© Great Source

profligate (prŏf'lĭ-gĭt) *adj.* Recklessly wasteful or extravagant.
© Great Source

satiate (sā'shē-āt') *tr. v.* To gratify to excess.
© Great Source

superfluous (soo-pûr'floo-əs) *adj.* Beyond what is sufficient; extra.
© Great Source

affinity (ə-fĭn'ĭ-tē) *n.* A natural attraction; liking.
© Great Source

animosity (ăn'ə-mŏs'ĭ-tē) *n.* Active hatred; a hostile attitude.
© Great Source

antipathy (ăn-tĭp'ə-thē) *n.* A strong feeling of dislike or distaste.
© Great Source

ardent (är'dnt) *adj.* Marked by warmth of emotion or desire.
© Great Source

contemptible (kən-tĕmp'tə-bəl) *adj.* Deserving of dislike or disrespect.
© Great Source

disdain (dĭs-dān') *tr. v.* To consider or reject as unworthy.
© Great Source

enamored (ĭ-năm'ərd) *adj.* Inspired with love; charmed; captivated.
© Great Source

estrange (ĭ-strānj') *tr. v.* To destroy the affection of.
© Great Source

penchant (pĕn'chənt) *n.* A definite and habitual liking.
© Great Source

repugnance (rĭ-pŭg'nəns) *n.* A feeling of strong dislike or distaste.
© Great Source

LESSON 28   antecedent

LESSON 28   interminable

LESSON 29   capitulate

LESSON 29   predominate

LESSON 30   attenuate

LESSON 30   palpable

LESSON 28   ensue

LESSON 28   perennial

LESSON 29   condescend

LESSON 29   slavish

LESSON 30   diaphanous

LESSON 30   permeate

LESSON 28   ephemeral

LESSON 28   precipitate

LESSON 29   deference

LESSON 29   subjugation

LESSON 30   encumber

LESSON 30   pliant

LESSON 28   imminent

LESSON 28   provisional

LESSON 29   grovel

LESSON 29   supercilious

LESSON 30   evanescent

LESSON 30   ponderous

LESSON 28   interim

LESSON 28   retrospective

LESSON 29   lackey

LESSON 29   sycophant

LESSON 30   gossamer

LESSON 30   viscous

antecedent
(ăn′tĭ-sēd′nt) *n.*
Someone or
something that
precedes.

© Great Source

ensue
(ĕn-sōō′) *intr. v.* To
follow as a
consequence
or result.

© Great Source

ephemeral
(ĭ-fĕm′ər-əl) *adj.*
Lasting for a
brief time.

© Great Source

imminent
(ĭm′ə-nənt) *adj.* About
to occur; immediate.

© Great Source

interim
(ĭn′tər-ĭm) *n.* A period
of time between
two events.

© Great Source

interminable
(ĭn-tûr′mə-nə-bəl) *adj.*
Seeming to
last forever.

© Great Source

perennial
(pə-rĕn′ē-əl) *adj.*
Lasting an
indefinitely
long time.

© Great Source

precipitate
(prĭ-sĭp′ĭ-tĭt) *adj.*
Acting or done hastily.

© Great Source

provisional
(prə-vĭzh′ə-nəl) *adj.*
Provided for the
time being.

© Great Source

retrospective
(rĕt′rə-spĕk′tĭv) *adj.*
Directed toward
the past.

© Great Source

capitulate
(kə-pĭch′ə-lāt′) *intr. v.*
To surrender.

© Great Source

condescend
(kŏn′dĭ-sĕnd′) *intr. v.*
To agree to an act
below one's rank.

© Great Source

deference
(dĕf′ər-əns) *n.*
Courteous respect.

© Great Source

grovel
(grŏv′əl) *intr. v.*
To behave in a
demeaning manner.

© Great Source

lackey
(lăk′ē) *n.* A follower
who behaves in the
manner of a servant.

© Great Source

predominate
(prĭ-dŏm′ə-nāt′) *intr.*
v. To have greater
authority.

© Great Source

slavish
(slā′vĭsh) *adj.*
Characteristic of
a slave.

© Great Source

subjugation
(sŭb′jə-gā′shən) *n.*
The act of bringing
under rule.

© Great Source

supercilious
(sōō′pər-sĭl′ē-əs) *adj.*
Proudly scornful;
disdainful.

© Great Source

sycophant
(sĭk′ə-fənt) *n.* One
who seeks favor
through flattery.

© Great Source

attenuate
(ə-tĕn′yōō-āt′) *tr. v.* To
decrease the density
of; rarefy.

© Great Source

diaphanous
(dī-ăf′ə-nəs) *adj.* So
fine or thin as to be
transparent.

© Great Source

encumber
(ĕn-kŭm′bər) *tr. v.* To
weigh down; burden.

© Great Source

evanescent
(ĕv′ə-nĕs′ənt) *adj.*
Vanishing like a
vapor; fleeting.

© Great Source

gossamer
(gŏs′ə-mər) *n.* A fine
film of cobwebs.

© Great Source

palpable
(păl′pə-bəl) *adj.*
Capable of being felt
or touched.

© Great Source

permeate
(pûr′mē-āt′) *tr. v.* To
spread or flow
throughout; pervade.

© Great Source

pliant
(plī′ənt) *adj.* Easily
bent or flexed
without breaking.

© Great Source

ponderous
(pŏn′dər-əs) *adj.*
Having great weight.

© Great Source

viscous
(vĭs′kəs) *adj.*
Resembling glue in
consistency and
stickiness.

© Great Source